Studies in the spectator role

Michael Benton's book develops the concept of spectatorship as an answer to the question of how the visual arts can be related to literature. It explores the similarities and differences in our experiences of these two disciplines, and discusses their implications for pedagogy and their applications in cross-curricular work in the classroom.

Part I focuses upon the spectator role by theorising it in relation to literature, painting and ekphrasis – the literary representation of a work of visual art. Part II consists of eight studies of landscape, childhood, war, myth and others, and includes discussion of detailed examples, with pupils' responses as appropriate. The range of authors and artists discussed is highly relevant to the National Curriculum, post-16 and undergraduate courses and includes:

- Shakespeare
- Blake
- Turner
- Wordsworth and Constable
- Wilfred Owen and Paul Nash
- Ted Hughes and Seamus Heaney
- Anthony Gormley, Stanley Spencer and many others.

The book concludes by drawing together the educational advantages of cross-curricular studies. Teachers will find fresh approaches to familiar visual and verbal texts that can produce enthusiastic classroom responses.

Michael Benton is Professor of Education at the University of Southampton. During the 1990s his interest in cross-curricular studies can be seen in *Double Vision* (in association with the Tate Gallery), *Painting with Words* and *Picture Poems*, all published by Hodder and Stoughton.

Studies in the spectator role

Literature, painting and pedagogy

Michael Benton

London and New York

First published 2000
by RoutledgeFalmer
11 New Fetter Lane, London EC4P 4EE

Simultaneously published in the USA and Canada
by Routledge
29 West 35th Street, New York, NY 10001

RoutledgeFalmer is an imprint of the Taylor & Francis Group

© 2000 Michael Benton

Typeset in Goudy by Taylor & Francis Books Ltd
Printed and bound in Great Britain by
St Edmundsbury – St Edmundsbury, Suffolk

British Library Cataloguing in Publication Data
A catalogue record for this book is available from the British Library

Library of Congress Cataloging in Publication Data
Studies in the spectator role: literature, painting and pedagogy/by Michael
Benton.
Includes bibliographical references and index.
1. English literature – Study and teaching – Great Britain.
2. Art – Study and teaching – Great Britain. 3. Art and
literature – Great Britain. 4. Art in education – Great Britain. I. Title.
PR51.G7B46 2000   99–41947
820'.71'241–dc21   CIP

ISBN 0–415–20827–0 (hbk)
ISBN 0–415–20828–9 (pbk)

For Jette

Contents

Illustrations

Figures

Plates

Plates I–VI are engravings from William Hogarth's *Marriage à la Mode*:

Acknowledgements

I am grateful to a number of editors and publishers who have granted me permission to reproduce revised versions of pieces that have had an earlier incarnation in article or book form. In particular, I am indebted to:

- Oxford University Press for 'The Self-Conscious Spectator' and 'Anyone For Ekphrasis?', which appeared originally in *The British Journal of Aesthetics*, 35, 4, October 1995 and 37, 4, October 1997, respectively and now form the substance of Chapters 2 and 3.
- The Centre for Language in Education, University of Southampton for 'The Reader in the Secondary World', a longer version of which appeared as Occasional Paper, no. 47, March 1997 and which now, in edited form, is Chapter 1.
- The Editor, *The Journal of Aesthetic Education*, for 'Visualising narrative' and 'Painting Shakespeare' which originally appeared in the *Journal*, issues 33, 3, Summer 1999 and 32, 3, Fall 1998, respectively, and now form the bulk of Chapters 4 and 9.
- Human Sciences Press Inc. for 'The Image of Childhood', which originally appeared in *Children's Literature in Education*, 27, 1, March 1996 and has been edited to form Chapter 6.
- Open University Press for extracts from Chapter 11, 'William Hogarth: the author as artist and educator', in my *Secondary Worlds. Literature Teaching and the Visual Arts* (1992), now reworked as part of Chapter 5.

I am also indebted to the following galleries and publishers for permission to reproduce paintings, engravings and pictorial material:

- The Tate Gallery, London, for *Angels' Heads* by Sir Joshua Reynolds, *Totes Meer 1940–41* by Paul Nash, *The Shipwreck* and *Snow-Storm* by J.M.W.Turner, *Ophelia* by John Everett Millais, *Lady Macbeth Seizing the Daggers* by Henry Fuseli, and *The Play Scene in 'Hamlet'* by Daniel Maclise.
- The Yale Center for British Art, Paul Mellon Collection, for *The Beggar's Opera* by William Hogarth.
- The National Gallery, London, for *The Graham Children* by William

Hogarth, *The Cornfield* by John Constable and *Holt Bridge on the River Dee* by Richard Wilson.
- The National Portrait Gallery, London, for *Sir Henry Unton*, artist unknown.
- The British Museum, London, for *Marriage à la Mode*, *The First Stage of Cruelty* and *Characters and Caricaturas* all by William Hogarth; and for *Infant Joy* by William Blake.
- The Victoria & Albert Museum, London, for *A Mother Teaching Her Child* by William Mulready.
- The Museum of Fine Arts, Boston, for *Slavers* by J.M.W. Turner.
- The Imperial War Museum, London, for *Battle of Britain* by Paul Nash.
- The Cecil Higgins Art Gallery, Bedford, for *The Good and Evil Angels Struggling for Possession of a Child* by William Blake.
- Unilever Historical Archives, Port Sunlight, for *Cherry Ripe* and *Bubbles* by John Everett Millais, reproduced by kind permission of Elida Faberge Ltd.
- The White Cube Gallery and courtesy of Jay Jopling, London, for *European Field* by Antony Gormley.
- David Inshaw and The Bridgeman Art Library, London, for *The Cricket Game* by David Inshaw.
- The National Trust Photographic Services and A.C. Cooper, for *The Resurrection of the Soldiers* by Stanley Spencer.
- Leonard Baskin and Faber and Faber for *Crow*; and Faber and Faber for the photograph of 'The Windeby Girl'.
- The Silkeborg Museum, Denmark, for two photographs of 'The Tollund Man'.
- The Moesgaard Museum, Denmark and Niels H. Andersen, for the photograph of 'The Grauballe Man'.
- The Cartography Department, Photographic Services, University of Southampton, for Figures 2.1, 2.2, 4.2, 4.3, and 11.2.

In addition, I am grateful to the following writers and publishers for permission to quote from work on which they hold copyright:

- Gillian Clarke and Carcanet Press for 'European Field' from *Five Fields* (1998).
- Extracts from David Dabydeen's *Turner* (1994), reproduced with permission of Curtis Brown Ltd, London on behalf of David Dabydeen. Copyright David Dabydeen 1994.
- Bloodaxe Books Ltd for Pauline Stainer's 'Turner is Lashed to the Mast' from *The Ice-Pilot Speaks* (1994).
- Tate Gallery Publications for extracts from John Wain's 'The Shipwreck' from *With a Poet's Eye*, ed. Pat Adams (1986).
- Faber and Faber Ltd for Ted Hughes's 'A Childish Prank' and other extracts from poems in *Crow* (1970); for extracts from 'Tollund Man' and 'Punishment' by Seamus Heaney, reprinted in *Opened Ground* (1998); and for lines from Keith Douglas's poem 'Landscape With Figures'.

Every effort has been made to contact copyright holders; the publishers will be happy to hear from anyone whose claim has not been properly acknowledged.

Finally, I owe a personal debt of gratitude to the MA students who took my course on 'Literature Teaching and the Visual Arts' in the Research and Graduate School of Education, University of Southampton; and, especially, to Dr Sally Butcher, who has allowed me to draw on her distinguished PhD thesis for examples of pupils' conversations about paintings and poems cited in Chapters 6 and 9, and who provided an unexpected piece of 'field work' for Chapter 3. My thanks, too, to Ms Ros Sutton, formerly of Swanmore School, Hampshire, for the pupil's annotations to Millais's *The Boyhood of Raleigh* in Chapter 2; to Dr Lisa Coles, Itchen College, Southampton, for allowing me to quote from her assignment on 'Teaching Chaucer' in Chapter 4; and to Ms Dannet Parchment, formerly an MA student at the RGSE, University of Southampton, and David Dabydeen, for permission to quote from their 'Interview' in Chapter 8.

I would like to thank Rita Corbidge for help with word-processing several chapters of the book and for her patience with my frequent requests for changes to the text. Finally, my biggest debt is to my wife, Jette Kjeldsen, whose critical reading of the manuscript has saved me from a number of errors and obscurities; any that remain are my own.

Introduction

Figure 0.1   David Inshaw, *The Cricket Game* (1976), private collection, oil on canvas.

It was some minutes after first coming across David Inshaw's painting, *The Cricket Game* (1976) (Figure 0.1), before I realised how I had been neatly positioned by the artist. Initially, my attention was caught by the atmosphere of an evening landscape, the vibrant greens of the rolling Dorset hills, a pale half-moon and lengthening shadows signalling that the sun was dropping out of sight somewhere to the right. Other landscapes lay behind this one: Hardy's Wessex and Samuel Palmer's *Coming from Evening Church* merged in my mind. A cricket match in such an idyllic setting illuminated – as Palmer's procession of villagers is in his painting – by the dying sun and the rising moon, seemed to invest the scene with its own 'Ruralist' sense of the numinous. Cricket, I reflected, must be

David Inshaw's religion. Then I realised how he had drawn me in: my perceptions adjusted from the sublime to the mundane, from these intertextualities of high culture to the banalities of 'Spot the ball'! Where is it? The fast bowler is on … an aggressive field is set … the left-handed batsman has swung and missed. … The keeper takes the ball: that's the moment of the picture. But, if the batsman had connected, the ball may well have skied on the leg side, if silly mid-on's movement is anything to go by; skied, in fact, towards me, the invisible fielder at deep mid-wicket. I checked the figures just to be sure: two umpires, two batsmen, but only *ten* on the fielding side. As a spectator, I had been accommodated as someone to make up the number. What's more, I had been given a pretty big area of the outfield to patrol – from a fielding position that afforded me a central view of the action like that of a wide-angled lens; and from a vantage point just inside the boundary where the ground must rise, as it does under the trees beyond the bowler.

There are features of this onlooking which are familiar to readers of literature: the evocation of landscape at a particular moment in poem or story, the creation of atmosphere through the texture of the language, an implicit or explicit narrative, intertextual references and, as we have just seen exemplified, the construction of the viewer/reader as part of the creative act of making the work of art. It is not surprising, then, that 'spectator theory' is common to both arts as a way of accounting for what viewers and readers experience. But, if the features have similarities, our means of apprehending them are different. The picture that the viewer of a painting sees is a given object. The image that the reader of literature 'sees' has no such objective existence; it has a virtual one since it is invented through the interplay of the text with the reader's mind. So much is obvious. Yet, the acts of viewing and reading are scarcely explained so simply. What viewers and readers experience, how they perceive works of art, how they construct meanings from them, are issues that are not only interesting *per se*, but ones that have profound implications for teaching and learning. Without some knowledge and understanding of the processes of reading and viewing, the ability to teach the arts is severely limited. This is where the theorising of these activities in recent years, primarily through the concept of spectatorship, has proved useful – if contentious.

Part I of this book seeks to clarify the concept of spectatorship in relation to the two arts and, subsequently, to account for the viewer's/reader's experience when faced with a literary text that is itself based on a visual work. Its premise is that the success of comparative and cross-curricular studies in literature and painting is built upon an awareness of how readers' and viewers' responses operate and how they interrelate. Just when is the optimum time to wrestle with these theoretical issues is a matter of individual choice. They have been placed first as a logical preface to the studies that follow and as a way of clarifying the verbal/visual relationship upon which the book is based. However, some readers may wish to skip Part I initially and prefer to begin with the themes of Part II: the federal relationship of these chapters, each of which is free-standing rather than a stage in an argument, encourages this approach. A reading sequence that is more flexible than that which the linear presentation of conventional book format prescribes is both in tune with the concepts of reading and response that are advocated and honours the relationship between theory, history and practice as each affects the other throughout.

Chapter 1 gives a critical appraisal of the reader's spectator–participant role as it has been developed in the two most influential concepts in literary reading in recent decades: the 'spectator theory' of Harding and Britton, and the notion of the 'implied reader' of Iser. It defines and discusses the reader's stance, role and imaginative world. Chapter 2 is a sequel to Chapter 1 and reviews answers to the question of what happens when a viewer looks at a representational painting. It draws upon the vocabulary of visual perception to explore the relationship between the materiality of the surface and the depicted subject (Wollheim 1987). It considers the concept of aesthetic distance as a way of solving the paradox of the spectator's dual attention and concludes that, in conjunction with the literary notion of the 'shifting viewpoint' (Iser 1978), this offers the necessary flexibility to explain the spectator's awareness of the constantly changing, unstable relationship between surface and scene. Doubleness is thus seen as an essential feature of our engagement with both literature and painting, whether it is expressed in terms of the spectator–participant role of the reader/viewer, or as the relationship between the medium and the imagined subject inscribed within the art object. Chapter 3 complicates this matter by considering the phenomenon of ekphrasis – the literary representation of a work of visual art. Spectatorship assumes a different character when the reader can lift his or her eyes from a poem and actually view the object of the poet's attention: another sort of doubleness is evoked. These issues are explored through a detailed analysis of Gillian Clarke's poem about Antony Gormley's installation sculpture, *European Field*.

Part II identifies eight areas where the intimacy of the two arts enables us to read their aesthetic relatedness, to gain a sense of the history and culture of their times (particularly important in understanding pre-twentieth-century arts), and to develop the idea of spectatorship as the fundamental concept in teaching the arts. Each chapter provides information about the topic, a rationale for its inclusion in cross-curricular work, and discussion of one or more detailed examples, with pupils' responses as appropriate. I have allowed the character of each chapter to govern whether the educational emphasis should fall on issues of pedagogy or upon practical classroom activities. The concluding chapter summarises the educational implications and advantages of such cross-curricular work.

Chapter 4 is the first of these studies not only for reasons of chronology but also because understanding narrative is fundamental to the workings of painting and literature and to the processes viewers and readers engage in. As the title indicates, the discussion focuses on the central issue for this book – the triangular relationship between the two arts and the viewer's/reader's response. Primarily through an analysis of the memorial painting of *Sir Henry Unton* (artist unknown, National Portrait Gallery, 1596) and of Shakespeare's contemporary portrait of

Henry V (1599/1600) in the speeches of the choric narrator, the chapter explores how narrative is visualised. How does the painter give graphic form to events in time? Conversely, how does the writer use language to create an illusion of place or scene? The educational lessons are twofold: the self-awareness pupils need of being cast in a particular role by the artist/writer; and the understanding that is demanded of the conventions peculiar to a given historical period. These issues underlie many of the questions teachers are now asking about how to teach older literature: How does one deal with pupils' lack of knowledge of earlier periods? How and when does one give essential historical information? How much of the social and cultural background is important?

Chapter 5 moves into the eighteenth century and considers another aspect of the cross-overs between verbal and visual arts. It focuses upon Hogarth as painter, 'author', educator and social satirist and upon the demand that his pictures make for us to read them. Conversely, in Fielding, the writing is highly visual and owes much to his training in the theatre. Examples are drawn from Hogarth's painting of Gay's *The Beggar's Opera*, from his *Marriage à la Mode*, and from Fielding's *Joseph Andrews* to show both how the pictures enact a sort of 'dumb show' (in Hogarth's own phrase) and how the prose fiction creates a visual sense of slap-stick theatre. The nature of this material lends itself to classroom activities, yet to many it will be unfamiliar. Accordingly, there are details of teaching approaches focusing upon drama and narrative, together with a list of books for further reading.

The images of childhood in literature and painting reflect not only a changing concept (Higonnet 1998) but also changing attitudes to education (Ariès 1962; Coveney 1967). In the history of this image, Blake and Wordsworth are the central figures. Chapter 6 discusses the superordinate image of the Christ child and its relationship to three oppositional pairs of representations in art and literature: the polite/impolite child; the innocent/sinful child; and the authentic/sanitised child. The main issues for this chapter are: how the two arts represent childhood, the principal influences affecting the construction of their images, and whether the verbal and visual arts conceptualise childhood in similar or different ways. An example of pupils talking about one of Blake's poem/paintings from *The Songs of Innocence and Experience* further illuminates these issues.

Landscape has lost its innocence. A generation ago the representation of the English countryside in paint and print was discussed in critical accounts as though it were some born-again Eden or latter-day Arcadia, depending on the predilections of the writer. Since the 1980s the politics of landscape have been one dominant theme (Barrell 1980; Solkin 1982; Mitchell 1994); the relationship between literary pictorialism and landscape painting has been another (Hagstrum 1958/1987; Dixon Hunt 1976/1989; Heffernan 1985). Starting with the neoclassical version of *ut pictura poesis* in the work of James Thomson and Richard Wilson, Chapter 7 shows how attitudes to Nature developed during the nineteenth century in Wordsworth and Constable and how both poet and painter related experiential knowledge of the natural world to education. The chapter argues for the 'education of the eye' and shows how classroom work on visual and verbal representations of landscapes can interrogate the subject by asking questions about the reading viewpoint, the schema upon which the images are constructed, the significance of the details incorporated in the image and the role of the figures in the depicted scenes.

Turner aspired to be a poet as well as a painter (Wilton 1990) and, although his verse output was itself fragmentary and undistinguished, the idea of the 'poetic' invests his whole approach to painting. Chapter 8 discusses the notion of Turner's 'poetic painting' and then examines readings of his pictures found in modern poems by Wain, Stainer and Dabydeen based, respectively, upon three of Turner's great marine paintings, *The Shipwreck*, *Snow-Storm – Steam-Boat off a Harbour's Mouth*, and *Slavers*. The three poems treat their subjects in radically different ways which, among other things, suggest a variety of classroom approaches to writing about Turner. Further comparative work for post-16 students is also listed: Turner's paintings of scenes from Pope and Thomson with his own accompanying verses; and Turner's six pictures of scenes from *Childe Harold* linked to Byron's text.

Chapter 9 discusses three well-known paintings of Shakespearean scenes and relates them to the texts they depict. They are Millais's *Ophelia*, Fuseli's *Lady Macbeth Seizing the Daggers*, and Maclise's *The Play Scene in 'Hamlet'*. They are considered as representative paintings that reflect the main ways artists have treated Shakespeare – as poem, as script and as performance. Millais's *Ophelia* is an example of a painting that depicts an unstaged scene where the artist responds to a poetic description; Fuseli's painting is a visual metaphor that concentrates the evil of the whole play into a single horrifying image; and Maclise's painting is a documentary picture that reflects contemporary stage performance rather than offering an interpretation of Shakespeare. The chapter concludes by showing how cross-curricular work on these examples might be extended and with the analysis of a transcript of a student discussion of Fuseli's painting that indicates how such cross-curricular work adds another dimension to the study of Shakespeare.

Chapter 10 relates paintings by Stanley Spencer and Paul Nash to poetry from the two World Wars. Spencer's paintings in the Sandham Memorial Chapel provide a striking complement to the poetry of the First World War; Nash's painting *Totes Meer, 1940–41*, generated from photographs of a dump for wrecked aircraft, together with Keith Douglas's three-part poem, 'Landscape With Figures' (1943), offer similar correspondences. The role of the spectator–participant has a singularly acute meaning in this context. The poet writing from the trenches or in hospital, the painter remembering the scenes of battle he has lived through, the official war artist recording images from a relatively detached stance – the viewpoint, purpose, and sense of audience are seen as central to interpreting these images of war. The chapter develops two themes: the Christian soldier and the dystopian landscape. Both are taken up in the approaches to classroom work with which the chapter concludes.

Chapter 11 concerns myth. It focuses upon Ted Hughes's *Crow* linked to Leonard Baskin's picture and upon Seamus Heaney's 'bog poems' arising from photographs of exhumed Iron Age bodies in Jutland. Both poets have also written significant expository pieces that help to set these poems in an educational context – Hughes's essays, 'Myth and Education' and 'Crow on the Beach', and Heaney's essay, 'Feeling into Words'. In such myth-making the spectator role has a generalising weight as the poets seek to develop a verbal/visual image of sufficient resonance and flexibility to carry their ideas of the dark and violent forces within human nature. Their poems are discussed separately since their myths are distinct; and the approaches to teaching the two sequences are necessarily dictated by their singular character.

The final chapter takes a broader view of pedagogy. It summarises the main benefits that follow from teaching literature with painting. It identifies four main advantages. First, that cross-curricular study offers an enhanced historical and cultural awareness. Second, that it provides increased language motivation. Poems, especially, when studied in isolation often present a pedagogical problem in that their language is syntactically complex and may be ambiguous. Paintings are generally more immediately invitational. Paired with poems, they both elicit talk more readily and provide a way-in to poetry. Third, comparative study of the relatedness of the two arts leads to a sense of their individual uniqueness. Finally, both the discussion of the themes and the evidence from the classroom support the earlier contention that the self-awareness of the spectator–participant role in both the arts is *the* essential element in learning how to read and how to look.

One of the ironies of present-day English Studies is that while university English has diversified (some would say disintegrated) into a bewildering variety of themes, 'texts' and options that obscure and sometimes reject the traditional canon of literature, school English has been corseted in a National Curriculum that has no qualms about spelling out who it regards as the 'major' and 'high-quality' authors worthy of study (Department for Education 1995: 20). This book takes an independent course, affirming the importance of canonical texts and writers while seeking to widen the remit of teachers and students who study them by exploring the links with the visual arts. Its stance is grounded in the theory of literary and visual response, in which the concept of the spectator is seen as central, since this offers teachers the most coherent position in relation to their work because it focuses upon the live processes of literary and visual experience with which they operate daily.

Given the ever broader church that English Studies encompasses, it is as well to be explicit about what this book does and does not attempt to do. Its field is the cross-disciplinary one of literature and the visual arts. Its purposes are to provide a rationale for the complementary study of these two art forms, with particular reference to painting in Britain and with the National Curriculum requirements to teach pre-twentieth-century literature in mind. Its approach is to demonstrate good practice through the discussion of pedagogical issues and classroom activities as the nature of individual chapters dictates. In most cases, this discussion takes place in the last section of each chapter.

Those attracted to this agenda in the hope of finding a redefinition of

English within Cultural Studies, or the application of post-modernist theory where everything or nothing is a text, or a new slant on Media Studies, or the study of picture books will be disappointed. The first two stances are ones I do not share; the latter are subjects outside my present scope. Furthermore, this book, like the canon it reflects, is formed by exclusions as well as inclusions. Given its subject, readers might have expected Rossetti, one of our major poet/painters, to have been featured; or for greater prominence to have been given to the representation of women in art and literature. However, both the Pre-Raphaelites and the stereotyping imagery of 'old mistresses' (Parker and Pollock 1981) have received copious critical exposure in recent decades and, in the competition for space, had to give way to themes which have not enjoyed such attention. My principal aim has been to balance the need for the range and diversity that cross-curricular study demands with the equally compelling requirement to demonstrate the importance of understanding the spectator role.

Part I

Reading and viewing:

the spectator–participant role

1 The reader in the secondary world

The spectator–participant

Fictional worlds hold an enduring appeal; they entice us to enter by every conceivable means from gentle seduction to blatant shock tactics. Here, chosen pretty much at random, are six beginnings – invitations into new and potentially exciting worlds, starting with the most celebrated of all.

> It is a truth universally acknowledged, that a single man in possession of a good fortune must be in want of a wife.
>
> > (*Pride and Prejudice*)

> 'Now, what I want is, Facts. Teach these boys and girls nothing but Facts. Facts alone are wanted in life.'
>
> > (*Hard Times*)

> With a single drop of ink for a mirror, the Egyptian sorcerer undertakes to reveal to any chance comer far-reaching visions of the past. This is what I undertake to do for you, reader.
>
> > (*Adam Bede*)

> Once upon a time and a very good time it was there was a moocow coming down along the road and this moocow that was coming down along the road met a nicens little boy named baby tuckoo ….
>
> > (*A Portrait of the Artist as a Young Man*)

> If you really want to hear about it, the first thing you'll probably want to know is where I was born, and what my lousy childhood was like, and how my parents were occupied and all before they had me, and all that David Copperfield kind of crap, but I don't feel like going into it.
>
> > (*The Catcher in the Rye*)

> I did not kill my father, but I sometimes felt I had helped him on his way.
>
> > (*The Cement Garden*)

English teachers are used to discussing such beginnings – extended perhaps to photocopies of the opening pages – and to asking students about the sort of stories that are likely to follow. Typical questions that these narrative openings pose for their readers are:

- What sort of voice is addressing me and how am I meant to interpret this invitation into what appears to be a game of make-believe? The issues are of orientation, or reader stance, and of adjusting to texts that are invented fictions not matters of fact.
- Am I likely to enjoy the experience and what sort of reader am I expected to be – a sympathetic listener? A quasi-detective? A fascinated or amused or frightened observer? ... These issues surround the role that the reader is required to play.
- What am I getting into here? What sort of secondary world is on offer? The questions here concern the plausibility of these fictions and the different genres they represent.

For young readers especially, success with the opening of a story is crucial. Practised readers develop a tolerance, a willingness to wait and trust the writer to engage their interest, where the less experienced may become impatient. 'I couldn't get into it' is the common cry of readers baulked and disappointed by Chapter 1. Of course, novelists know this; hence, the variety of tactics they devise to draw us in. Having chosen to start a new fiction, the opening sentences make us an offer that, for a few minutes at least, we cannot refuse. Then, when we cross the threshold, we are aware of both giving ourselves up to the fiction, yet equally conscious of the process of doing so. We are required to be an involved participant and a detached spectator. Just how this doubling operates during reading is the subject of this chapter; it is approached through considering the three issues that the questions above suggest – the reader's stance, role and world.

The reader's stance

Differences in reader stance are easily overlooked, yet they raise fundamental questions. About reading across the school curriculum, we might ask:

- What are the differences between reading novels in English and reading text books in Science?

And, about reading within English:

- What are the differences between how we read fiction and how we read poetry?

And, about reading fictions:

- What are the different invitations we are offered by the six novel openings above?

The very fact of posing such questions indicates that the act of reading is a unique experience each time we engage in it. Clearly, the answers partly concern purpose (pleasure, study, information-gathering) and the context in which the reading occurs. But they are also to do with the stance the reader adopts towards the experience which, in turn, is decided by the interaction between what the reader brings (knowledge, frame of mind, mood …) and what the text signals (through its language, layout, mode of address …) about the way it should be read.

The most influential account of stance is that of Rosenblatt (1978: 22–47). 'Aesthetic reading' is Rosenblatt's phrase to distinguish the stance readers adopt when engaging with literary texts; 'efferent reading' is her corresponding description of the stance readers take towards informational texts. In 'aesthetic reading', the reader's concern is with the feelings and ideas being produced by the act of deciphering; the orientation is to savour what is being lived through at the time, the focus is upon the experience itself *during* the reading event. By contrast, in 'efferent reading', the reader's concern is with what will be carried away from the act; the orientation is utilitarian, the focus is directed towards the relevance of the information to situations that lie *beyond* the reading event. The attention of the reader of literature is thus circumscribed by the present tense, captured by the world of story; that of the reader of a textbook is projected into the future tense, concerned about the usefulness of new information in the world we all share. Yet, having made this distinction, Rosenblatt then proceeds to soften its boundaries. She comments:

> Actually, no hard-and-fast line separates efferent – scientific or expository – reading on the one hand from aesthetic reading on the other. It is more accurate to think of a continuum, a series of gradations between the nonaesthetic and the aesthetic extremes. The reader's stance towards the text – what he focuses his attention on, what his 'mental set' shuts out or permits to enter into the centre of awareness – may vary in a multiplicity of ways between the two poles.
>
> (Rosenblatt 1978: 35)

The idea of a continuum creates as many difficulties as it solves. For Rosenblatt is attempting to conceptualise the reading state in a metaphor that uncomfortably combines the mobility of the continuum with the specificity of particular terms. Conscious of this problem, perhaps, Rosenblatt retreats from the extremes of the efferent–aesthetic continuum and locates most readings as 'hovering' somewhere near the middle (p. 37). Yet the metaphor is useful in disentangling the orientation of a literary reading from that of other readings. We now need to acknowledge another aspect of reader stance – its relationship to our perceptions of everyday life.

Drawing upon Dewey, Rosenblatt stresses that an aesthetic experience is 'simply the stuff of ordinary day-to-day experience defined, heightened, complete' (Rosenblatt 1978: 37). In particular, she argues, the 'play of attention' between the efferent and aesthetic 'is undoubtedly much more characteristic of our daily lives than is usually acknowledged'.

Surprisingly, Rosenblatt makes no explicit mention of D.W. Harding's theory of the psychological processes in the reading of fiction which also stresses the continuity between art and life, especially that between gossip and the novel – or what has been glossed by Meek *et al.* (1977: 73) as the relationship between the lower-case 'storying' we use to shape everyday living and upper-case 'Stories' between the covers of novels. Saki ('The Storyteller'), Mary Norton ('Paul's Tale') and Jan Mark ('Nothing to be Afraid Of') have all written stories which play upon the boundary lines in this relationship. The assumption of continuity behind these stories and Meek's formulation are the same: the status of literary fictions and the stance we adopt towards them are refinements of the narrative imagination that we use daily to make sense of our actual environment and experiences. The corollary is that we read words in much the same way as we read worlds, a phenomenon that Auden celebrates in his sonnet 'Words', a poem that exemplifies what it argues (Auden 1966: 320–1). Such a statement requires an account of the role the reader adopts within literary experiences and of the fictional worlds that are evoked during these experiences. We turn now from issues of stance to those concerned with the reader's persona, in particular, that of the spectator–participant role.

The reader's role

The concept of a 'role-playing reader' incorporates two fundamental ideas: the notion of taking on a persona for the duration of a reading, and the view of this activity as '*participating* in a game of make-believe' (Walton 1990: 190). But, immediately, questions arise. How do we reconcile the reader taking part in a game with the familiar theory of the reader's role (Harding 1937, 1962; Britton 1970, Britton *et al.* 1975; Applebee 1985) as that of a spectator not a player? And, lying behind this question – how is either of these personae constructed? How much by the author via the text, as Henry James suggested when he claimed that the author makes 'his reader very much as he makes his characters' (James 1866: 485)? How much by the real reader's psychological makeup as, for example, the work of Holland (1975) and Bleich (1978) argues? There are questions lying behind these questions too. As the Fish–Iser (1981) debate highlighted, why must we assume that there is such a thing as the given text and that the act of reading involves this interplay of determinate and indeterminate elements? And since, for Fish, nothing is given, and the reader supplies everything, how can Henry James or anyone else speak of 'making the reader' a quasi-character?

It is evident from the above that reader-response criticism has left unresolved (and perhaps unresolvable) issues which centre on the role of the reader as a virtual construct. The range of such constructs from Gibson's 'mock reader' (1980) to Brooke-Rose's 'encoded reader' (1980) scarcely needs rehearsing. They populate the pages of the various overview books of reader-response criticism. Some are obliquely parodied in the half-a-dozen readers that the protagonist in Italo Calvino's novel *If on a Winter's Night a Traveller* (1982) meets in the great library at the end of that book. The seventh reader, one who is struck by the newness rather than the familiarity of re-readings, concludes that 'reading is an operation without object; or that its true object is "itself"' (p. 203). In saying this, he points to the favourable conditions that breed these putative readers: the fact that reading collapses the subject–object division of conventional perception (cf. Wallace Stevens 1965: 90, 'The House Was Quiet and the World Was Calm'). By becoming 'lost in a book' the reader becomes an insider; text and reader no longer face each other as object and subject, so that if one asks the absorbed reader, 'Where were you during your reading?' the significant reply is not 'in an armchair' or 'in bed', but as a description of themselves as 'a ghostly watcher' (Harding 1967: 12) or as someone who is 'invisible and walking around unseen with the things or people in the book ....'(Holland 1975: 65). Perhaps the most powerful extended account of the interiority of fictional experience is that of Georges Poulet (1972, in Tompkins 1980: 41–9); more simply, 14-year-old Claire's description of her reader's role offers a memorable personification that combines the detachment of spectatorship and the dynamism of playing the fictional game.

> It's as if I'm a sort of dark watcher, who is there at the scene, but none of the characters pays any attention to me. I'm like a power, as if everything is happening because I'm there.
>
> (Fox 1979: 32)

If we listen to what Claire and other young readers tell us about the nature of literary experience (there are similar insights in Fry (1985)), their reflections suggest a role more in line with the collaborative activity anticipated by novelists from Sterne (1767) to Fowles (1977) than that which the extremes of post-war criticism have assigned them. On one side, as Freund (1987: 151) has argued, Fish's view that nothing is given leads into a logical cul-de-sac: without 'something' to be interpreted no act of interpretation can occur. On the other, the inclination of the earlier generation of New Critics to ignore the reader reflects the views of neither novelists nor the readers themselves. Those concepts that do suggest a plausible interior role for the reader, and help to elucidate Claire's experience, are ones that draw their character from both the text and the reader. The two principal ones are 'the reader as spectator' (Harding 1962; Britton 1971) and the 'implied reader' (Booth 1961; Iser 1974).

Both are controversial and, in some respects, ill-defined constructs whose imprecision arises from the inevitable diversity of the answers to the questions raised above, especially the degree to which such constructs owe their virtual existence to the text and to the real reader. One source of confusion may be diagnosed in the fact that these apparently singular, unitary terms disguise a dual persona, a split self, partly constructed by and alive within the fiction, partly detached from and observing the fictional events; yet, as Claire suggests, always in control. Another arises from the suspicion of illegitimacy over the birth of the terms. Britton's appropriation of the term 'spectator' from Harding for his own purposes, as Goodrich (1995: 47–60) has recently argued, distorts the idea of its original; and, correspondingly, Iser's extrapolation of 'the implied reader' from Booth's 'implied author', as the latter has pointed out (Booth 1989: 58), means different things at different places in Iser's writing. Both the double role the reader plays and the vocabulary used to convey it require clarification. As will emerge, however, there are sufficient similarities between the constructs of the spectator and the implied reader for the idea of 'the reader as spectator–participant' to be regarded as a concept that encompasses both. In order to establish this, the two constructs are critically examined in turn.

The two articles that summarise Harding's concept of spectatorship are 'The role of the onlooker' (1937) and 'Psychological processes in the reading of fiction' (1962). The former argues for the continuity between the role of the detached onlooker who watches actual events and the spectator at a play or the reader of a novel who is offered representations of events. The latter stresses the creative participation of the reader. Harding says:

> The imaginary spectatorship of fantasy and make-believe play has the special feature of allowing us to look at ourselves, ourselves as participants in the imagined events. … In spite, however, of seeing himself as a participant in the story, the daydreamer or the child engaged in make-believe remains an onlooker, too; in all his waking fantasy he normally fills the dual role of participant and spectator.
>
> (Harding 1962: 136)

In Harding's account, the reader's role comprises a double figure: the spectator aspect entails detached evaluation; the participant aspect involves imaginative sharing. Harding seems to regard these hierarchically: imaginative participation is regarded as 'elementary'. In fact, it is the main source of pleasure in reading and the essential prerequisite for literary interpretation as Squire (1964), among others, has shown. It is important to establish the spectator role as a portmanteau concept that encompasses spectator–participant activities. Harding (1962: 67) and Rosenblatt (1985: 39), though arriving at it via different routes, both envisage this and show that the reader's persona is ill-conceived if spectatorship is restricted to a detached attitude and a predilection for making value judgements; it requires the complement of involved absorption through the willingness to join in the fictional game – a point so obvious that one would apologise for making it were it not for the fact that Harding's spectator theory has been taken over and, to an extent, distorted by Britton. The problem has been compounded since Britton's work has achieved wide currency in the field of literary education. This is not the place for a detailed rebuttal of Britton's controversial model of language use. Enough criticism has already been levelled at its theoretical and linguistic weaknesses (Williams 1977), its ambiguous terminology (Rosenblatt 1985: 38) and its failure to adequately theorise the spectator role (Goodrich 1995) to render further extensive comment superfluous. In Britton's 'What's the use? A schematic account of language functions' (1971), probably the most succinct account of his model that appeared in numerous incarnations in the 1970s, the roles of participant and spectator are separated out and assigned to the actual and fictional worlds, respectively. Even some of Britton's followers (as opposed to his critics) have recognised the confusion that this formulation entails, notably Thomson (1987: 84–5) who tries to clarify the terminology and concludes that the most valuable literary experiences are those in which readers are 'both spectators and participants'. Goodrich is similarly critical and concludes that the reason for Britton's failure to convince is 'a conceptual problem of presuming that the spectator–participant distinction constitutes two mutually exclusive roles' (p. 58). This is the nub of the matter and affirms the essential dualism of spectatorship.

In the same year that Britton published this early formulation of his theory, Iser also set out what, with hindsight, can be seen as his corresponding professional manifesto in his paper 'Indeterminacy and the reader's response in prose fiction' (1971). Not only did it sketch out a historical perspective on indeterminacy to be elaborated in *The Implied Reader* (1974), together with the main concept of a theory of aesthetic response to fiction, later developed in *The Act of Reading* (1978); but it also pointed the way to his more recent work on literary anthropology (Iser 1989 and 1993). The immediate issue is to ask in what relationship his implied reader stands to the spectator–participant persona outlined above. Are they identical twins, siblings with as many differences as filial similarities, or merely distant relations?

Iser's implied reader is a transformation of Wayne Booth's well-known formula of the implied author: 'The author creates … an image of himself and another image of his reader; he makes his reader, as he makes his second self' (Booth 1961: 138). The active participation of this implied reader is described by Iser in *The Act of Reading* where he stresses that 'the implied reader as a concept has his roots firmly planted in the structure of the text; he is a construct and in no way to be identified with any real reader' (Iser 1978: 34). Yet this textual construct can only be construed by a real reader. Hence, the reader's response is anticipated but not defined. 'The real reader is always offered a particular role to play, and it is this role that constitutes the concept of the "implied reader"' (pp. 34–5). Thus, while remaining anchored in the text, Iser contrives a definition of his concept which conjoins 'the reader's role as a textual structure, and the reader's role as a structured act' (p. 35). The details of how this duopoly functions centre on 'the system of perspectives' and the deployment of 'indeterminacy gaps' in the first element, complemented by the reader's mental imagery and the adoption of an interior 'wandering viewpoint' in the second element. Such a bald summary does little justice to the complexity and sophistication of Iser's arguments, but the present concern is not to engage with these often controversial details but to establish the essentially dyadic character of the implied reader within his overall theory. Freund (1987: 147) provides a lucid summary of the criticisms of Iser's theory; as usual with areas of creative activity, where one person accepts paradox, another finds contradiction.

The implied reader's role for Iser is not inscribed in the text as it is for Booth (1989: 58–9), but comes about as a matter of *performance*. This performative role is consistent with Iser's earlier description of the act of reading as 'a game of the imagination' and with his insistence on the interiority of the moving viewpoint that 'travels along *inside* that which it is to apprehend' during the reading of fiction. 'This mode of grasping an object,' says Iser, 'is unique to literature.' (Iser 1978: 108–9), and entails the adoption of a spectator–participant role that continuously fluctuates between engagement and detachment. Iser says:

> Since it is (the reader) who builds the illusions, he oscillates between involvement in and observation of those illusions; he opens himself to the unfamiliar world without being imprisoned in it. Through this process the reader moves into the presence of the fictional world.
>
> (Iser 1974: 286)

Iser, like Walton (1990: 273–4), refers to the concept of fictional worlds, an issue to which we must shortly turn; but not before the relationship between the two personae we have been considering has been resolved.

Earlier the question was posed as to whether the roles of spectator–participant and implied reader could be regarded as twins, siblings or distant relations. The similarities are self-evident: both are virtual constructs, dyadic in character, intended to express the intimacy of text and reader. The difference lies in their origins. The reader as spectator–participant is a 'double figure', derived from the idea of the onlooker at events in the actual world, and conceived from the position of what the reader does to recreate the fiction from the text. The implied reader is a 'double figure', derived from the idea of the 'implied author' in the fictional world, and conceived from the position of how the text has been constructed by its author. The answer to the question, therefore, excludes blood relationships since the parentage of these two personae is different. Yet, if we have to accept them as merely distant relatives, we can also claim, from this examination of their features, that they often look remarkably alike. Either way, the important point about spectatorship is to realise its doubleness and to exploit it in our teaching methods, a matter taken up presently in the discussion of Doris Lessing's story, 'Through the Tunnel'.

The reader's world

In *Actual Minds, Possible Worlds*, Jerome Bruner writes:

> As our readers read, as they begin to construct a virtual text of their own ...
> (the) virtual text becomes a story of its own, its very strangeness only a
> contrast with the reader's sense of the ordinary. The fictional landscape,
> finally, must be given a 'reality' of its own – the ontological step. It is then
> that the reader asks that crucial interpretive question, 'What's it all about?'
> But what 'it' is, of course, is not the actual text – however great its literary
> power – but the text that the reader has constructed under its sway. And
> that is why the actual text needs the subjunctivity that makes it possible for
> a reader to create a world of his own.
>
> (Bruner 1986: 36–7)

It is just this sort of ontological step that, one suspects, makes Walton (1990:
57–8) wary of too much reliance upon the notion of fictional worlds. In particular,
he argues that fictional worlds are not possible worlds on the grounds that they
are 'sometimes impossible and usually incomplete, whereas possible worlds (as
normally construed) are necessarily both possible and complete' (p. 64). Yet he
acknowledges, if somewhat grudgingly, that fictional worlds cannot be ignored
since they 'undeniably play a central role in our thinking about representation'
(p. 58). It is as if it is more by popular demand than theoretical conviction that
Walton even countenances the idea. Indeed, it is fair to say that the notion of a
world in discussions of fictional experience is the single most common idea. It
appears in a variety of guises. For many, such a world is incidentally described as
'fictional', 'story', 'imaginative', 'alternative', and so on – diverse referential
adjectives that indicate a sense of otherness. What is remarkable is the
frequency with which theorists of fiction reading, via particular coinages, make
special reference to this concept. Langer (1953) uses the term 'virtual', whereas
Tolkien (1938) and Auden (1968) adopt 'secondary', also the preferred adjective here and elsewhere (Benton 1992), as the one that most accurately conveys
the feel of literary creation. Eco (1979) and Bruner (1986) refer to 'possible'
worlds; Iser (1981), under fire from Fish, resorts to 'literary'; Fish (1989), at odds
with all the above, sees fiction and everything else as part of a 'rhetorical world'.
Ingarden's (1973) world is 'portrayed', Sartre's (1972) a mere 'presence', and
Bruner's (1986) is 'subjunctive'. The particular usages differ in their degree of
conceptual commitment, but all are variations on the theme that, during
reading, when we are 'lost in a book', we inhabit a mental space between the
individual psychic reality that is biologically determined for each of us and the
actual world that is our common human property; and, in that space, between
the reader's inner self and the words on the page, these other worlds are deemed
to exist. Our delight and creative surprise in this experience is suggested by
Rosenblatt's remark: 'The boundary between the inner and outer worlds breaks
down, and the literary work of art, as so often remarked, leads us into a new
world' (Rosenblatt 1978: 21).

Clearly, the assumption so far is that such other worlds do not possess a
concrete existence open to inspection, but are considered as abstract models or
metaphorical coinages to be thought of either as actual entities or as conceptual

constructions (Pavel 1986: 43–9). Walton is again cautious to the point of scepticism. He points out that we are 'strangely schizophrenic' about the links that obtain between the actual world and fictional ones. He says:

> On the one hand, fictional worlds and their contents seem insulated or isolated in some peculiar way from the real world, separated from it by a logical and metaphysical barrier. That, indeed, is why we call them different *worlds*. ... On the other hand, we seem to be in *psychological* contact with characters, sometimes even intimate with them. We have epistemological access to fictional worlds; we know a great deal about what happens in them.
>
> (Walton 1990: 191)

Despite Walton's view that the idea of fictional worlds is 'a device to paper over our confusion about whether or not (mere) fictions are real', 'the notion of world as an ontological metaphor for fiction remains too appealing to be dismissed' (Pavel 1986: 50). Yet superficial attractiveness can often mislead. What follows argues that the secondary world is more than a sexy metaphor for, as will be shown, it not only accommodates the dual role of the reader; it is also, in its status as a conceptual construction, itself an expression of the game of make-believe that is central to Walton's thesis.

The reader's apprehension of a three-dimensional virtual world has been alluded to frequently in literary accounts (Price 1971: 83; Iser 1978: 116). Lesser's description explicitly incorporates this sense of a three-dimensional hologram with the dual role of the reader. He remarks:

> We expect the storyteller, out of the mere stuff of words, to create a three-dimensional world so life-like or so much in accordance with certain psychological realities that we can deceive ourselves we are living in it. At the same time we want him to make it clear that this world is no more than an illusion – a painted ship upon a painted ocean. We ask, that is, for the privilege of being at once participants in the action and detached spectators of it.
>
> (Lesser 1957: 142–3)

This view of the world in the head as an analogue of the one we normally inhabit, together with our need to be convinced about the 'psychological realities' that must be met if the illusion is to be 'believed', are two of the notions that originally led me to theorise the concept of the secondary world (Benton 1992: 22–36). In summary, this entailed a discussion of four aspects of this concept: its location and nature, its three-dimensional structure, the viewpoint that brings it into existence, and the 'substance' of which it is composed.

Taking these in turn, the location of the secondary world, as indicated above, is conceived as existing in the limbo between the reader's inner self and the words on the page. It is a sort of mental playground, like Winnicott's (1974:

102–3) 'third area', which the reader is aware of making and entering as a condition of the make-believe play through which he or she constructs meaning from text. The text is the regulator. It sets the limits. Beyond the textual limits lie states that are outside fictional experience.

Inside the secondary world, the reader's apprehension of its structure can be conceptualised in terms of the three axes of level, distance and process, which correspond to how we locate ourselves within the three-dimensional structure of the primary world. During reading we can often sense that narrative is operating at different levels through our awareness of the amalgam of conscious and unconscious mechanisms at work: some elements, say, of setting or character, may be explicit and open to conscious inspection; others, perhaps the ghost of some emotion, may be elusive, appearing only fleetingly from the depths of the unconscious; yet others remain unfathomable. The second axis, that of distance, expresses the now familiar spectator–participant role and describes the varying degrees of involvement and detachment that are experienced according to the reader's changing engagement, commitment and attention at different phases of the reading activity. The third dimension provides the time-axis of the secondary world. As Iser (1978: 116) has argued, readers operate through processes of anticipation and retrospection as they progress through a story. This axis allows for the way memory deals with information during the reading process and defines the limits of the secondary world as beginning 'once upon a time' and ending when all 'live happily ever after'.

The third aspect of the concept is also familiar: the insider viewpoint we adopt during our own experiencing of the secondary world (Iser 1978: 109; Walton 1990: 273). The focal point of any act of reading, what is happening at any moment as we recreate the world of the fiction, is both constantly shifting and constantly defined by the point of intersection of the three axes described above. This shifting viewpoint is the existential present (cf. Rosenblatt's aesthetic stance above) of the reader's reading, giving coherence to the secondary world the reader temporarily inhabits when engrossed in a story. Its mobility as well as its insider quality are both illustrated in the examples of interiority given by Claire and others, quoted earlier.

Finally, if the above aspects offer a schema, the phenomenon that lends it the feeling of 'substance' through colour, sound and movement, with all the power and immediacy that absorbed readers customarily experience, is mental imagery. Images are the carriers of information to the brain about the secondary world and correspond to the functions of the five senses in our perception of the primary world. But for the reader in the spectator–participant role, images are a means to an end, not the end in itself. The 'substance' of the secondary world may be conceived of in terms of images but, as Sartre and Iser make clear, it is the manner in which this substance is processed that endows it with coherence and meaning.

Sartre, in particular, is unhappy with the whole notion of images composing a mental world as an adequate description of the act of reading. He concludes that 'there is no imaginary world. We are concerned rather with a matter of mere belief' (Sartre 1972: 195). In terms of strict philosophical distinctions, this line of argument is sustainable (although, even on these grounds, Warnock (1972, 1976) is sceptical). In practice, however, it is impossible to maintain a distinction between what actually happens and our apprehension of what actually happens during the course of reading. Even Sartre is driven to acknowledge that 'in order to describe correctly the phenomenon of reading it must be said that the reader is *in the presence* of a world' (Sartre 1972: 70). If this awareness is conceded how, we might ask, is the reader to perceive this 'presence' if not through the medium of images? Throughout, Sartre adopts a tone of grudging ambivalence, rather stronger than Walton's caution, whenever he discusses the idea of a story world: no sooner has he deprecated the notion than he has to confess that images do *suggest* a world even if they do not embody one. He admits 'each image presents itself as surrounded by an undifferentiated mass which poses as an imaginary world', and he prefers the description 'atmosphere of the world' to anything more precise (p. 195).

Sartre's argument is instructive. He dismisses the term 'imaginary world' as a mere cover phrase in much the same way as Harding (1962) challenges the term 'identification' as an adequate description of the psychological relationship between readers and fictional characters; that is, the term is still legitimately available to us only so long as we limit its meaning and avoid using it as a convenient gloss for several undifferentiated mental processes. This is the delimitation that has been attempted above in describing the secondary world. It may be objected that in characterising aesthetic experiences through elaborating a metaphor the concept is vulnerable to the literal experiences of readers who may well profess no need for such a figurative explanation of their activities, certainly not one that attempts to create a metaphysical topography that teeters on the edge of reification. How, it may be asked, can we know about an invisible, instantaneous process in the absence of empirical evidence that is not anecdotal and, therefore, by definition, self-referential and self-validated? Yet this objection is one that may be levelled at any attempt to theorise that which, like the reading process, is a covert, mental act. In such circumstances, we tend to resort to metaphor. It may not be too wild a claim to say that metaphor is all we have.

What does such a description allow us to conclude about the reader's spectator–participant role in the secondary world? Walton is again helpful. At the end of his account of our psychological participation in the make-believe games of fictional worlds, he takes *Vanity Fair* as an example, and says:

> Let us recognize two distinct work worlds, one in which Becky resides and one in which *Vanity Fair* establishes a fictional world in which Becky resides. There are two distinct games to be played with the novel. The reader alternates between them. (To some extent, perhaps, he plays them simultaneously.) It is fictional in the world of one game that he learns about Becky, her marriage, her affair with Lord Steyne, and responds with pity or disgust or admiration or whatever; it is fictional in the world of the

other game that the reader examines and reflects on a prop that is to be used in games of the first sort. He alternately inhabits Becky's world and observes it from the outside

(Walton 1990: 285)

Walton decides, in his own words, to 'have it both ways'. His description of this dichotomy reflects the schizophrenia of the reader's role, which requires both reading 'of' and reading 'in' the secondary world. It necessitates a stance that has the mobility to be both 'inside' and 'outside', a role that alternately (or simultaneously) 'inhabits' and 'observes', and a world that is experienced both as a fictional entity and as a textual construct. Doubleness is all. For these reasons, the reader as spectator of and participant in a secondary world is the most coherent formulation of what happens when we read literature.

Reading 'Through the Tunnel'

Reader response is thus a double act. The portmanteau phrase in the subtitle of the first section of this chapter underlines a fact that too often gets overlooked in classroom teaching: namely, readers have both an internal, imaginative involvement with the fictional content of a story and an external awareness that the content is ordered and controlled by a writer – that it is 'only a story'. Classroom teaching should develop from this basis and honour both elements, since the interplay between the two is the source of much of the pleasure and value of imaginative works of art (Lamarque and Olsen 1994: 144). How does this interplay translate into practice?

Doris Lessing's 'Through the Tunnel' (1960: 60–9) is a much-taught short story, compelling in its appeal since it operates on several linked levels: narratively, in its build-up of suspense; psychologically, in its representation of an 11-year-old's need to test himself; socially, as a study of an only child's relationship with his widowed mother and with older youths; and symbolically, as a rite of passage. Pedagogically, with such a rich text, it is possible simply to read the story and to allow the words to have their effect. Yet, on reading the opening sentence of this fiction (as with the earlier examples), our stance is defined both by what the text signals and how we fill in the gaps.

> Going to the shore on the first morning of the holiday, the young English boy stopped at a turning of the path and looked down at a wild and rocky bay, and then over to the crowded beach he knew so well from other years.

We are given the time of day, the finite period of a holiday, an indication of warm summer weather, and a protagonist in a familiar, probably foreign setting (in fact, the South of France) where the contrast between the bay and the beach is between the unknown and the known, between looked 'down' and looked 'over', between hard rocks and soft sand. Young readers may bring a range of responses to this sentence: a sense of the freshness and promise of new

experience – both in the brisk pick-up of the narrative and in their own memories of starting a holiday – that are caught in the mobility of the first few words;
a feeling of association with the 'young English boy' and a readiness to look at
the setting through his eyes; and the hint that the story to come will revolve
around this understated shift from the secure routines of a crowded beach
holiday under mother's watchful eye to the potential dangers of independent
exploration.

Assuming the story maintains its hold and this stance is sustained, the reader
is drawn into the spectator–participant game alongside Jerry, the protagonist.
The emphasis on the twin elements of this role will vary as the story develops
but, as some teachers have discovered to their alarm, imaginative participation
in the final, climactic description of Jerry's attempt on the underwater tunnel is
not for the faint-hearted, even having the potential to destabilise the claustro-
phobics in the classroom. Yet, the very power that draws the reader, after Jerry,
into the tunnel can blot out the technique that achieves this imaginative
involvement. How many teachers ask, in respect of this final sequence, these
vital questions?

- How long is Jerry underwater and how does this relate to the time it takes
  to read the passage?
- How does the length of this passage relate to the time given to the rest of
  the holiday?

Paradoxically, we can become so engrossed with the physical immediacy of
the description that we neglect the crucial dimension of time which frames the
events. The answers to these questions reflect how Doris Lessing has orchestrated the reader's response. Jerry is underwater from the point where, having
filled his lungs, he sinks to the sea floor with the stone and begins to count,
until he emerges gasping 'into the open sea' – a period of about two minutes and
forty-five seconds, which is both the time which, the text tells us, is at the limit
of Jerry's endurance and the time it takes to read the passage. Discourse time
and 'real time' are identical, arranged to bring the reader, like Jerry, to the edge.
The answer to the second question is equally revealing: in the printed text, this
final sequence is barely a side and a half of a nine-and-a-half-page story, which,
in turn, covers eight days of what is probably a ten-day holiday. The temporal
signposts throughout are clear markers of the mounting tension. Day 1 is paragraph 1, the exposition of the mother–son relationship, the 'safe beach' and 'the
wild bay'. Day 2 stretches over five pages, where Jerry watches the local boys
diving, discovers the hole under the promontary, counts 160 seconds that the
boys are underwater, buys some goggles and decides to train himself up to swim
through the tunnel. Days, 3, 4, 5 and 6 are accounted for in rapid succession in
three-quarters of a page, logging the advances and setbacks in his self-training,
hurrying us towards the climax. Then, tightening the tension, we read: 'In
another four days, his mother said casually one morning, they must go home.' In
response, it seems, to the desperate pressure this puts on Jerry, Day 7 is finessed

away and the story is propelled towards the climactic Day 8 for its final three pages. Classroom analysis along these lines not only explicates the steady pace of the early part of the narrative, the acceleration towards the attempt on the tunnel, and the agonisingly slow, second-by-second progress of the attempt itself; it also makes pupils aware of their spectator–participant role when they let go of their hold on their actual surroundings and become readers in a secondary world.

The appeal of fiction that was noted at the outset is located in this double role. 'The twin perspectives of imaginative involvement and awareness of artifice are both indispensable in an appropriate response to works of fiction' (Lamarque and Olsen 1994: 157). We operate with fictions in the same way that we do with life, shuttling endlessly and seamlessly between self-absorbed involvement and a self-aware detachment. In the rest of this book, the spectator role is taken to encompass both these complementary perspectives; in the next chapter, the self-awareness of spectatorship is explored in respect of the visual arts.

2   Reading paintings:
The self-conscious spectator

The viewer's role

As we have seen in Chapter 1, spectator theory has been a recurring source of explanation for questions of how we read literature, from the early psychologically oriented work of D.W. Harding (1962) to Kendall Walton's (1990) more recent studies in philosophical aesthetics. This chapter confines itself to the visual and draws upon the work both of theorists such as Gombrich, who approach such questions from the standpoint of the psychology of perception and those like Walton, who regard a work of art as an invitation to an act of make-believe with 'the picture as a prop in a visual game' (Walton 1990: 301).

As in our discussion of literary reading, while the notion of stance, with its transactional position at the junction of where viewer and viewed meet, is again the starting-point for understanding how we make meaning from works of art, its distinctive feature with reference to paintings lies in the physical relationship it indicates – for example, in the distance between the viewer and the painting on a gallery wall and the angle of gaze that the image dictates. The subject–object division and the playful behaviour that are suggested in the idea of 'a picture as a prop in a visual game' soon lead any exploration of visual understanding from questions of stance to ones of role. The position adopted in relation to a picture rapidly becomes indistinguishable from the engagement with that picture. This has led visual theory to concentrate upon the singular phenomenon of the moment of viewing and to play its own linguistic games to explain what happens between viewer and painting. The prop is invariably a preposition.

'Looking at', 'looking in', 'looking into', 'seeing as', 'seeing in', are all familiar phrases in the titles and texts of recent theorists. Prepositions, as they are generically designed to do, situate the viewer somewhere in relation to the object of attention. Moreover, the term 'viewer' does not grant the onlooker a neutral persona: it may be modified by 'implied' or, more notably, transmuted into the 'beholder' (Gombrich 1960: 153) or the 'spectator' (Wollheim 1987: 101). Both terms colour the position, the one with a suggestion of reverence, the other with the sense of looking on at ordinary events. Thus, whatever the preferred vocabulary for viewing paintings, the basic concept of role is rendered elusive and obscured by accretions of meaning from other areas of experience. Despite the variety of terms in current use, this chapter neither insists upon a single epithet nor invents a new coinage of its own: the term 'viewer' is regarded as having the most general and least encumbered meaning (corresponding to 'reader' in literature), whereas 'spectator' is used to indicate a particular role that the viewer takes on. Let us start with the viewer *in situ* before a painting.

Diané Collinson puts herself engagingly into the spectator role and invents a typical thought-track as a way of disentangling the elements that go to make up the aesthetic experience of viewing paintings. She concludes:

> Perhaps aesthetic experience is even better typified by the gaps between 'the ordinary spectator's' phrases; by the wordless moments when the spectator is poised in the act simply of apprehending the painting rather than when remarking on it. Indeed, if we think back to the remark 'Ah, that sunlit field', it is the 'Ah' more than 'that sunlit field' that reveals the sensuous immediacy of the aesthetic moment. For it is not an experience in which we formulate an intellectual judgement to the effect *that* a vision of a sunlit field has been wondrously depicted. Rather, we experience the vision for ourselves; we are admitted to the painter's point of view. It is a distinguishing mark of aesthetic experience that it is one of participating in, or inhabiting, the world of the picture. Most of the comments or remarks indicative of the experience are retrospective in that they are *about* it rather than part *of* it.
>
> (Collinson 1985: 271–4)

This account focuses us upon 'the sensuous immediacy of the aesthetic moment', upon the spectator as an 'insider', lost in a painting (as in a novel) in the sense of becoming absorbed *for a time* in the 'world' that is to be explored. But absorption is a variable quality of attention, not a stable state; the viewer can only recognise it by being self-consciously aware of its opposite – of standing back in relative detachment, maybe to analyse and comment. Just what happens in these moments of viewing is the puzzle. Formulations vary (see Figure 2.1 below), but the essential dualism between an aspect of aesthetic response located in the primary world we all share (the materiality of the painting) complemented by an aspect located in the secondary world of individual imagination (the artistic illusion) is common to all such accounts. The relationship between the two elements remains debatable in respect of their importance, precedence or simultaneity; what is less contentious is that the problem only exists because we are aware of two aspects of our viewing. We are defined, when standing before a painting, as self-conscious spectators.

By describing such perceptual activity as self-conscious I do not imply the modern meaning of being unduly aware of oneself as an object of attention, but rather the original sense of 'having consciousness of one's identity, actions, sensations ... [of being] reflectively aware ... of action, thought, etc.' (Little *et al.* 1933: 1834). The former describes an aspect of social behaviour; the latter constitutes an element of self-knowledge. This reflexive self-consciousness is a useful concept in holding together the variety of descriptions and diverse terms that critics have employed in their attempts to capture what happens when we engage with a work of art, for it focuses both upon the object of contemplation and upon the subjective reaction. The self-conscious look entails a contraplex process. It cannot look outward at a painting without an accompanying sense of the response evoked within; it cannot look inward without the awareness of the object out there as its catalyst.

Armed with this notion of reflexive self-consciousness, my particular purposes are to examine some of the main positions that have been adopted on the inherent dualism of aesthetic response through a scrutiny of their preferred vocabulary and definitions; and to reconsider the concept of 'aesthetic distance' (Kris 1952/1964: 250) as a continuum, to explain how the mind does two things at once during the process of viewing. These considerations lead to a critical appraisal of Wollheim's notion of 'the spectator in the picture' and to a discussion of the viewer's awareness of occupying a pre-fabricated narrative stance as the principal way in which he or she is implicated in this dualistic activity. The implications for the classroom are explored through an examination of John Everett Millais's painting, *The Boyhood of Raleigh*.

(Un)divided attention

In the course of a well-known discussion of whether we can 'attend twice at once', Ryle comments:

> The fact that we speak of undivided attention suggests that the division of attention is a possibility, though some people would describe the division of attention as a rapid to-and-fro switch of attention rather than as a synchronous distribution of it.
>
> (Ryle 1949/1963: 158)

Subsequent debates of this dualism in the visual arts have reflected both descriptions. Indeed, Wollheim (1991: 146n) has acknowledged that he has adopted both positions at different times. For clarity's sake, the three main contributions to the debate – those of Gombrich (1960), Wollheim (1987) and Podro (1991) – can be presented in tabular form (Figure 2.1), together with those of two others – Clark (1960) and Koestler (1964/1975) – whose comments help to illuminate the point in the context of their writings on other issues. All the terminology is direct quotation.

The five concepts vary in their degree of technicality but all are attempts to explain the experience of viewing representational painting within the general framework of the psychology of perception. They focus upon 'the aesthetic moment' – or, maybe, a series of such moments, as will be suggested presently – when the spectator's self-conscious evocation of the painting consists of a double vision of the virtual subject and of the medium in which it is portrayed.

	CONCEPT	MEDIUM	VIRTUAL SUBJECT
CLARK	transformation	salad of brush strokes	illusion
KOESTLER	bisociation	medium	motif
GOMBRICH	guided projection	mosaic of strokes and dabs on the canvas	illusion
WOLLHEIM	twofoldness	marked surface	depicted subject
PODRO	*disegno*	material procedure	represented subject

Figure 2.1   The vocabulary of visual perception.

Articulating the experience of this double vision labours under a double handicap. As Clark comments: 'quite apart from the shortcomings of perception, there is the difficulty of turning visual experience into language' (Clark 1960: 17). Yet, it was his account of his attempts to 'stalk' Velasquez's *Las Meninas* that initiated the renewed debate. He described his experiments in trying to discover how the illusion was effected as follows:

> I would start from as far away as I could, when the illusion was complete, and come gradually nearer, until suddenly what had been a hand, and a ribbon, and a piece of velvet, dissolved into a salad of brushstrokes. I thought I might learn something if I could catch the moment at which this transformation took place, but it proved to be as elusive as the moment between waking and sleeping.

> (Clark 1960: 36–7)

Clark's final remark suggests that in looking for a single moment we may be seeking the wrong solution; what in fact he describes is a transformational process – a series of moments during which the emphases of our perception change. None the less, this has not deterred others from trying to pinpoint this phenomenon.

Koestler's theory of bisociation is one that seeks to account for all creative activity (Koestler 1964/1975: 35). It distinguishes between the single-minded routine skills of everyday thinking, and creative thinking which is described as 'a double-minded, transitory state of unstable equilibrium where the balance of both emotion and thought is disturbed'. When he comes to discuss painting, Koestler's dualism is conveyed through the terms 'medium' and 'motif' (p. 366). He reminds us of the familiar point that 'the impact (of a painting) does not take place on the canvas, but in the artist's mind, and in the beholder's mind'. Because of the 'limitations of the medium' and 'the prejudices of vision' the painter is forced to cheat and the viewer is forced into complicity:

> The way he (the painter) cheats, the tricks he uses, are partly determined by the requirements of the medium itself – he must think 'in terms of' stone, wood, pigment, or gouache – but mainly by the idiosyncrasies of his vision: the codes which govern the matrices of his perception. Whether Manet's impression of *The Races of Longchamp* looks more 'life-like' than Frith's academically meticulous *Derby Day* depends entirely on the beholder's spectacles. An artist can copy in plaster, up to a point, a Roman copy of a Greek bronze head; he cannot 'copy' on canvas a running horse. He can only create an appearance which, seen in a certain light, at a certain distance, in a certain mood, will suddenly acquire a life of its own. It is not a copy, but a metaphor. The horse was not a *model*, but a *motif* for his creation – in the sense in which a landscape painter looks for a romantic or pastoral motif.
>
> (Koestler 1964/1975: 372)

Koestler is not as explicit about the operation of the split-mindedness of medium and motif in painting as he had been earlier when discussing verbal creation. There he affirms that artistic illusion is 'the simultaneous presence and interaction in the mind of two universes, one real, one imaginary'. He conceives of the aesthetic experience as 'depending on that delicate balance arising from the presence of *both* matrices in the mind; on perceiving the hero as Laurence Olivier and Prince Hamlet of Denmark at one and the same time; on the lightning oscillations of attention from one to the other' (p. 306). Where painting is concerned he places less emphasis upon simultaneity and more upon the viewer's awareness of artistic convention and what he refers to at one point as 'the various bisociative, or bi-focal, processes' of looking at paintings (p. 383). Bi-focalism, in fact, is a useful term in that it suggests both a near focus and a more distant one in combination, and the necessary and rapid movement between the two.

Gombrich's concept of 'guided projection' as a means of explaining the viewer's perceptual process takes Clark's 'transformation' further by stressing the virtuality of the image in a way that is consistent with the bi-focalism suggested by Koestler. For Gombrich has continued to maintain that it is literally inconceivable for the viewer to focus at the same time both upon the illusion and the 'strokes and dabs on the canvas' that produce it. If visual perception entails experiencing the virtual presence of the image while the material painting remains on the gallery wall, how can one's attention to both be anything but divided? Simultaneity between the scene seen and the actual surface is a psychological impossibility. Here is how Gombrich, speaking of impressionist painting, describes what happens to the viewer:

> the beholder must mobilize his memory of the visible world and project it into the mosaic of strokes and dabs on the canvas before him. It is here, therefore, that the principle of guided projection reaches its climax. The image, it might be said, has no firm anchorage left on the canvas ... it is only 'conjured up' in our minds. The willing beholder responds to the artist's suggestion because he enjoys the transformation that occurs in front of his eyes. ... The artist gives the beholder increasingly 'more to do', he draws him into the magic circle of creation and allows him to experience something of the thrill of 'making'.
>
> (Gombrich 1960: 169)

There is a lot of action here: mobilisation, projection, transformation, 'more to do', 'making' – the viewer's perceptual activity loosens an image from the canvas and fastens it in imagination. Both *exist* simultaneously in their separate states for the duration of the viewing, but we cannot *attend* to both simultaneously. We switch between the two, yet each needs the other for the aesthetic experience to be sustained. Mobility between the 'conceptual image' and the actual picture is the key: the image requires constant feeding from the canvas; the canvas requires the viewer's continuous effort of attention if it is to be more than an object on a gallery wall.

Gombrich has not helped his argument against simultaneity and for alternating attention by basing his case on the well-known figure–ground reversals (Gombrich 1960: 4–5). It is one thing to switch between the duck and the rabbit in a composite image drawn in pencil and reproduced on the printed page, and quite another to switch between the scene and the surface of a painting in a gallery. Gombrich's main opponent in this argument is Wollheim (1987: 46–7, 360) who insists upon the unitary nature of 'twofoldness' as being fundamental to visual competence: surface and scene are essentially part of the same phenomenon of aesthetic viewing. If it is easy to counter Gombrich's reliance upon figure–ground reversals because they comprise two homogeneous images, rather than the heterogeneity of surface and scene, it is equally unconvincing of Wollheim to wrap up both aspects in a single enclosing concept that ignores both the mobility of imaginative participation and the variability of attention that the viewer customarily exhibits before a work of art. Common experience and Collinson's account suggest that the character of the moment of viewing cannot be so neatly summarised.

Wollheim is explicit that his foundational concept of 'seeing-in' is a 'distinct kind of perception', suggesting that it is biologically grounded and that young children use it in their learning about the world. To 'see-in' is to have a dual aspect yet unitary experience in response to a painting. It is unitary in that the viewer's absorption in the image is inclusive of two features: the viewer sees both the 'depicted subject' and yet also sees the 'marked surface' as evidenced in, say, the brush strokes, the density of the texture, the cracks in the paint, and so on. Wollheim argues that these are

> two aspects of a single experience, they are not two experiences. They are neither two separate simultaneous experiences, which I somehow hold in the mind at once, nor two separate alternating experiences, between which I oscillate.
>
> (Wollheim 1987: 46)

These two aspects of viewing are thus distinguishable yet inseparable and captured in the concept of 'twofoldness'. He calls the two complementary aspects of seeing-in the *recognitional aspect*, where the spectator discerns something *in* the marked surface, and the *configurational aspect*, which indicates the spectator's awareness *of* the marked surface *per se*. Both aspects of this twofoldness operate in the spectator together, and it is this simultaneous awareness of 'a depicted subject' and 'the marked surface' that ensures that the framed scene registers both in depth and as flat.

Even though Wollheim avoids the difficulty of divided attention inherent in Koestler's and Gombrich's accounts, his two-in-one combination produces a synthetic concept without telling us anything about its *modus operandi*. As Martin Kelly (1991: 161) has pointed out, Wollheim does not elaborate on the 'in' that he attaches to 'seeing' other than to say that figures are seen in a marked surface. Prepositions, as suggested at the outset, locate the viewing experience, and may, as here, indicate its salient features, but they say little about it as a dynamic process. For some insights into this we must turn to the last of the five formulations.

In his paper 'Depiction and The Golden Calf', Podro (1991: 163–89) borrows a term from Vasari and develops what he calls 'the *disegno* thesis – the thesis that we follow the formulating as a way of perceiving what is represented' (p. 185). His paper is concerned with a sense of abstraction which he elaborates as:

> the sense in which the painting selects from, connects and reconstructs the subject *in* the medium and procedures of painting; and, because these things are indissolubly connected, it is concerned with the way that the drawing or painting directs itself to the mind of the perceiver, who sees the subject remade within it, sees a new *world* which exists only in painting and can be seen only by the spectator who attends to the *procedures* of painting.
>
> (Podro 1991: 164, my italics)

The key words here are 'in', 'world', and 'procedures', for they take us on from Wollheim's 'seeing-in' to theorise what the 'in' implies. This is formulated in terms of a virtual world that, in turn, is sustained by the way the viewer's attention is undivided in that subject and medium interpenetrate each other in the viewer's awareness of the procedures of painting.

When Podro asks: 'how do we, the spectators, *use* … the interpenetration of the painting's real presence and the projected or imagined world?' he frames his answer by saying that:

> the subject becomes directed to us and we to it by both of us participating in a new kind of world, a world in which the relation between the spectator and the subject is mediated by the art and procedure of painting; it requires a particular kind of attentiveness on our part and reveals the subject as it can be seen only in painting.
>
> (Podro 1991: 173)

Given Podro's premise that it is the spectators who are active and it is they who need to bring 'a particular kind of attentiveness' to bear, it is unclear what is meant by 'the subject becomes directed to us'. When viewing a painting, the initiation of the imagined world must start with the spectator's activity. While it is notionally acceptable for the purposes of elaborating the *disegno* thesis to hypothesise a sense in which the painting is active in creating a world, the self-conscious spectator's experience of where that world is and how it comes into being is most accurately located as being neither wholly within the painting nor wholly in the mind of the onlooker. As was argued in Chapter 1 in respect of literature, it exists in the space between, in what Winnicott has called the 'third area' between the subjective self and the external world of objects (Winnicott 1974: 102–3). Podro's 'new kind of world' is described in terms of the relatedness between the spectator and the art work and thus avoids the need for a psychological explanation. Others have employed the same notion with different emphases. Indeed, as we have seen in Chapter 1, the 'imagined world' is, perhaps, the commonest of all metaphors to describe mental activity and has particular appeal in the area of aesthetic experience. In recent years it has been developed from many standpoints, notably in reading theory (Smith 1971), in psychological enquiry (Bruner 1986) and in philosophical discourse (Pavel 1986). In the arts, Tolkien's coinage of 'a secondary world' (Tolkien 1938/1964) has found a special resonance. As a metaphor for perceptual activity it is a useful indicator of the virtual power that imaginative engagement with a work of art can generate; but, used on its own, it takes us little further in understanding the actual process of that engagement. Podro's *disegno* thesis suggests that the location of such understanding lies in tracing the 'material procedures' available in the art work. In order to explain this process of engagement we need to focus upon the mental procedures inherent in the viewer's response, to observe the shift from viewer to spectator. And to do this, we need to reconsider the concept of aesthetic distance.

We are familiar with the notion of distance from the discussion of the secondary world in relation to literary reading (Chapter 1). How does it operate with painters and viewers? Both undergo phases of relative absorption with and detachment from the depiction. Painters' makings of their secondary worlds entail some periods of intense absorption during which they seem a part of the very world they are creating; at other times their role, physically and mentally, may be to stand back, to put some distance between themselves and the 'world' they are shaping and, consequentially, to become more aware of the materials with which they are working. For the viewers, too, the onlooker role is not constant. Their spectatorship will vary in the intensity of its commitment and attention at different phases of the viewing process. (Clark (1960: 16) hints at this in his account of his customary pattern – impact, scrutiny, recollection and renewal.). The concept of aesthetic distance expresses our sense of relationship with the depiction; it acknowledges that our sense of scene and materiality is in a state of continuous change; and it indicates the horizons beyond which the secondary world ceases to exist. For if involvement becomes obsessive and takes on psychotic characteristics, it leads to hallucination. (Koestler's theory of bisociation gives a plausible account of how the mind protects itself from this extreme). Conversely, if the sense of detachment from the secondary world is taken to the limit, it is but a short distance before painters or viewers become disengaged and the process of depicting or viewing is suspended. At the extreme, the work may be abandoned by the artist, or a painting may be deemed incomprehensible by the viewer.

What does the reconsideration of this notion of distance achieve? Essentially, it acknowledges the mobility of the process of visual response by means of a continuum. The viewer's attention is itself best seen as neither divided nor undivided but as constantly moving, enabling a range of responses to be generated, some simultaneously, some successively, as the eye perceives and the brain constructs. Spectatorship is not a stable state but the adoption of a continuously shifting viewpoint – to re-use the concept developed in relation to literature by Iser (1978) and which, both there in respect of fiction and here with reference to painting, denotes not arbitrary movements but ones regulated by an awareness of the qualities of the object of attention. This, in turn, suggests that there is an Iserian 'implied viewer' constructed within the painting whose stance is pre-determined and whose viewing experience is partly orchestrated by the form and medium of the painting. As he or she is drawn into the secondary world, the self-conscious spectator looks around, as it were, fully aware that the engagement with the painting has both determined and undetermined elements. What the spectator brings to this experience clearly matters, but the basic schema for the viewing process is laid down in the painting. The painting contains its own directions as to how it should be viewed; the self-conscious spectator knows this.

Looking around

Another preposition has now appeared. Adopting the metaphor of the secondary world invites us to speak of the spectator looking *around* this creation (cf. Walton 1992: 103). Looking around describes the spectator's imaginative participation and suggests the pleasures of exploration and discovery that are commonly felt before a painting in those moments that Collinson characterises as 'sensuous immediacy'. Yet such participation is not a licence to roam without restraint. The self-conscious spectator knows the rules governing the process, the main one of which is that looking around can only be conducted from a vantage point predetermined in the painting. In this sense the painter makes the viewer in the course of making the depicted subject: the viewer is pre-positioned not only in self-evident ways that control the angle of gaze and the sense of distance from the depicted subject, but through less obvious means that decide the amount and nature of the work needed to fill out the indeterminacies of the picture's 'incomplete images' (Gombrich 1960: 119).

If we draw on the idea of reflexive self-consciousness again and ask what sort of activities obtain in this viewer–object relationship, the answer can most plausibly be framed in terms of the responses of the viewer constructed in the painting. This 'implied viewer' is what Wollheim appears to be after in his distinction between the 'spectator of the picture' and the 'spectator in the picture' (Wollheim 1987: 102). The external spectator is located in the actual space the painting occupies in the gallery; the internal spectator is located in the virtual space the painting represents. Wollheim's subsequent discussion of Manet's portraits speaks of this interior persona as a 'mobile spectator' and 'the peripatetic spectator in the picture' (p. 161), recalling Iser's concept of 'the wandering viewpoint' that the reader of fiction experiences during absorption in the world of a novel (Iser 1978: 109). When he describes the actual process of viewing, however, Wollheim is considerably more mechanistic than words like 'mobile', 'peripatetic' or 'wandering' suggest. He outlines the process as follows:

> The function of the spectator in the picture is that he allows the spectator of the picture a distinctive access to the content of the picture.
>
> This access is achieved in the following way: First, the external spectator looks at the picture and sees what there is to be seen in it; then adopting the internal spectator as his protagonist, he starts to imagine in that person's perspective the person or event that the picture represents; that is to say, he imagines from the inside the internal spectator seeing, thinking about, responding to, acting upon, what is before him; then the condition in which this leaves him modifies how he sees the picture. The external spectator identifies with the internal spectator, and it is through this identification that he gains fresh access to the picture's content.
>
> (Wollheim 1987: 129)

As a way of describing our engagement with a painting, Wollheim's account has the virtue of capturing that sense of an inside viewpoint within a reflexive, self-conscious experience; but the specificity of the stages – of looking, of adopting a role, of starting to imagine and so on – seems over-prescriptive. Our engagement with paintings is unlikely to be susceptible to such a strictly delimited procedure. While this account may accurately describe Wollheim's own habitual process of viewing (cf. Clark's customary pattern, noted above), it is unlikely that the 'access to the picture's content' that he speaks of is achieved in the same way by everyone else. Moreover, apart from this suspiciously neat sequence of stages, it is not at all clear what Wollheim means by 'identification'. As a word to bring together his two types of spectator, it is as open to criticism as when used to describe the relationship between a reader and a character in fiction, as D.W. Harding (1962) memorably demonstrated. Wollheim seems to suggest that, following the suspension of disbelief, an imaginative role-play takes place that leads to a degree of empathic insight. Whether such an experience can be aptly described as identification is uncertain. Either way, Wollheim develops his spectator theory in words that tacitly acknowledge that disbelief is suspended, as Coleridge states, only 'for the moment' (Coleridge 1817/1949: 17). Wollheim continues:

> once the spectator of the picture accepts the invitation to identify with the spectator in the picture, he loses sight of the marked surface. In the represented space, where he now vicariously stands, there is no marked surface. Accordingly, the task of the artist must be to recall the spectator to a sense of what he has temporarily lost. The spectator must be returned from imagination to perception: twofoldness must be reactivated. Otherwise the distinctive resources of the medium will lie untapped.
>
> (Wollheim 1987: 166)

Absorption is temporary, variable, unstable. Sooner or later the mind becomes more alert to the marked surface and, consequently, less alert to the invented world depicted in it. Moments later, the viewer may become reabsorbed, and so continue to shuttle to and fro, experiencing varying degrees of involvement in and detachment from the represented world and varying degrees of critical or analytical insight into the ways in which the work is constituted.

It follows from the above that the stance of the implied viewer, or Wollheim's 'internal spectator', is predetermined and self-consciously occupied. The self-conscious spectator's position can be defined initially as a narrative viewpoint from which the painting is to be interpreted, since the interpretation is driven by the impulse to 'storying', to 'narrativise' the representation as a way of making meaning. In this respect, Culler's remark about how we make literary meaning can also apply to the viewer's construction of visual meaning. He comments: 'To speak of the meaning of the work is to tell a story of the reading' (Culler 1983: 35). For the viewer, such stories are regulated by the angle of gaze the picture dictates, and then in more subtle and mobile ways by the form and medium of the representation.

The process of implicating the viewer begins with the establishment of this viewpoint, situating the viewer as, say, a play-goer in the stalls who observes the eye-level scenes of Hogarth's *Marriage à la Mode*, or as a voyeur in the street who observes characters through the windows of lighted rooms in Hopper's *Nighthawks* or *Automat*, or, ambiguously, as Suzon's customer in Manet's *A Bar at the Folies-Bergère*. Most paintings designate stance less explicitly than these examples but all pre-define the position from which they are to be viewed: the self-conscious spectator soon becomes aware of how his or her angle on the depiction is being manipulated.

The process of implicating the spectator, when stance becomes role, commonly develops as a growing awareness that one's attention is orchestrated by the lines, the spaces, the disposition of colours, the nature of materials used and so on that constitute the form and medium of the painting. The spectator may be drawn in by the looks, gestures and body language of represented figures or the way the paint has been applied to the canvas. Viewing instructions are inscribed in the form and materials of paintings, literally, wherever we look. Again, to cite well-known examples which are easily brought to mind, the spectator's responses to Turner's dramatic *Rain, Steam and Speed* are mobilised and controlled by the wedge-shaped form and swirling colours, just as surely as they are by the short, thick gashes of paint of a Van Gogh landscape, or by the eye-lines of the depicted figures and the focusing effect of the light in Wright of Derby's *An Experiment With An Air Pump*.

In summary, awareness of stance and role, form and medium are the principal ways in which the self-conscious spectator is implicated in the aesthetic experience. The 'looking around' the secondary world of the painting that then becomes available is both created and controlled by these factors. The interplay between the spectator's sense of the represented subject and the medium in which it is cast is best conveyed by reconsidering the idea of aesthetic distance and, in particular, by invoking the concept of a shifting viewpoint. This concept facilitates not only such 'looking around' but also reflects the spectator's awareness of the continuously changing, unstable relationship between surface and scene.

Mapping responses

Teachers who have invited pupils to map their responses around a copy of a painting, for example, Lowry's *Man Lying on a Wall* (Benton and Benton 1990: 11), are well aware of the variety of ways in which spectators operate: the idiosyncratic, wandering viewpoint of each pupil is easily demonstrated and can act both as a practical way-in to the study of pictures and as a means of giving pupils confidence in the validity of their own interpretations. However, the distinction between the depicted scene and the marked surface is less easily handled. One obvious approach is to exploit the fact that self-conscious spectators in the classroom are generally looking, not at paintings, but at information about paintings in the form of slides, post cards, posters or book illustrations. The class can be asked to look closely at a reproduction and identify what it is made of. The realisation that they are looking at coloured dots not actual brush strokes emphasises the significance of the materiality of the original. Similarly, attention should be drawn to the dimensions of pictures to counter the reductive effect of reproductions which scale everything down to a convenient size. Or again, it may be appropriate to discuss the original location of a picture – a church, a stately home, a public building – to underline that, while multiple images of, say, Velasquez's *Las Meninas* abound, the picture was originally painted for the royal court of Philip IV of Spain and now hangs in a public gallery, The Prado in Madrid.

With the energetic development of educational services offered by art galleries in recent years, there are now plenty of opportunities for gallery visits. Elsewhere, I have listed suggested activities (Benton and Benton 1990, 1995a, 1997). However, even without a visit to the Tate Gallery to see Millais's *The Boyhood of Raleigh*, pupils can gain a sense of the depicted scene as a visual construct. A class of Year Ten GCSE pupils were shown a colour slide of the painting and given a photocopy of it centred on the page. They were asked to study the painting and, individually, to jot down on their photocopy what they noticed about the people, the details of the clothing, facial expressions and postures as well as any details of other objects in the scene. After a few minutes, they were given a second short task to invent three speech/thinks bubbles to capture what each character might be saying or thinking. The activities were enjoyable and the results instructive, and often amusing, in opening up the picture. Julie's annotations are shown in Figure 2.2.

The reasons why Millais's painting was so popular in the nineteenth century and remains one of the best-known images from the period are fairly obvious. It has an embedded story, two boys listening to a sailor's yarn; it is painted brightly and energetically with a sense of optimism; but, above all, it celebrates the triumph of the British Empire, the Victorian's greatest pride. Different students sensed all these things in various ways but the most frequent comments were

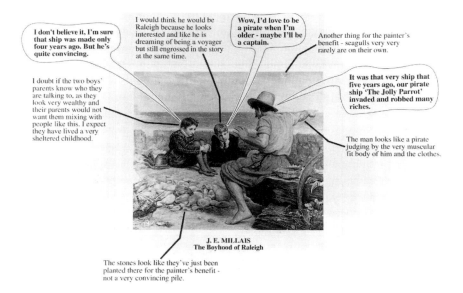

Figure 2.2   Student's notes on John Everett Millais's *The Boyhood of Raleigh* (1870), The Tate Gallery, London, oil on canvas.

about the personalities, dress and social standing of the figures, including a surprising absence of unanimity about which boy was Raleigh. Whatever Millais intended, Julie and some other pupils read a disjuncture between the boys' clothes and their facial expressions; Raleigh on the left can easily be seen as sceptical and bored rather than entranced by the sailor's yarn; certainly his friend, dressed in plain black rather than green velvet, and minus the elaborate hat and buckled shoes, appears to be showing a more intelligent interest. Furthermore, as this pupil's notes above and below the picture show, there is an awareness of how this constructed image has been composed by the painter. Stones and seagulls are commented upon here; other pupils noted the symbolic ship and the exotic bird whose beak can be seen through the spokes of a wheel. Discussion of the reasons for the inclusion of these details and whether the picture was painted on location on the south coast, or in Millais's London studio, or both follows naturally from this approach. It may be helpful, too, to look at Millais's preparatory sketch and his use of his own children as models for Raleigh and his friend. Exploration of these issues – discussion of the implied narrative that the painting embodies and of the positioning of the spectator eavesdropping, as it were, unseen, behind the back of the story-teller – all contribute to that self-conscious awareness of the role in which one is cast when looking at pictures and which is the prime source of visual pleasure and understanding.

3 Reading poems, reading paintings:
anyone for ekphrasis?

Seeing double

Ekphrasis is a rhetorical game played by poets and a spectator sport for the reader who is invited to do what, as we saw in the previous chapter, Ryle said was impossible – to 'attend twice at once' (Ryle 1949: 158). Its history is as old as literature itself but its recognition as 'an invented genre' is relatively recent (Webb 1999).

Playing the game involves writing a poem about a real or imagined work of visual art, usually a painting or a sculpture. The classical paradigm is Hephaestus' description of Achilles' sword in Book 8 of Homer's *Iliad*; the nineteenth-century *locus classicus* is Keats' 'Ode on a Grecian Urn'. Both are examples of what has usefully been termed 'notional ekphrasis' (Hollander 1995: 4), that is, where the poem describes a purely fictional work of art. More recent descendants are virtually all instances of 'actual ekphrasis', where the visual work not only exists but is accessible to the viewer. Of these, Dante Gabriel Rossetti's sonnets on his own pictures are central to the tradition, particularly his celebrated poem 'For "Our Lady of the Rocks" By Leonardo da Vinci', thought to have been written in front of the painting in the National Gallery. The doyen of ekphrastic poems of the twentieth century is Auden's 'Musée des Beaux Arts', where Bruegel's *Landscape with the Fall of Icarus* is the main focus of attention. Among the crowd of contemporary ekphrases, the tenor varies from John Ashbery's intellectual struggle with the notions of portrayal, identity and distortion in his long poem about Parmigianino's *Self-Portrait in a Convex Mirror* (Ashbery 1981: 68–83), to U.A. Fanthorpe's irreverent response to Uccello's *St George and the Dragon* in her poem 'Not My Best Side' (Fanthorpe 1986: 28–9).

Being a spectator involves reading the relationship between two arts, the visual and the verbal, from an unusual and unstable stance. For this sort of spectating means reading poems that, in turn, are reading paintings or sculptures; and, maybe, doing so from a position of knowing the visual work *before* the poem; or, maybe, of coming to it *as a result* of the poem; or, maybe, of reading the visual work through, or alongside, or against the poem's reading of it. This sort of spectator is cast in a different role from that of the ordinary viewer or reader.

We have seen in Chapter 2 that spectatorship in respect of paintings not only entails a sense of the dual attention we give to the depicted scene and the marked surface (Wollheim), but also involves a self-conscious awareness of the changing aesthetic distance that we experience and the shifting viewpoint (Iser) we adopt which, together, offer the necessary flexibility to explain that constant feeling of mobility that spectators customarily have between the represented subject and the materiality of the medium. Similarly, explanations – often entailing personifica-tions – of the role of the literary reader have proliferated in recent years. Chapter 1 considered the two most influential concepts in this area: 'the reader as spectator' (Harding; Britton) and 'the implied reader' (Booth; Iser). Harding's original, if undeveloped, suggestion of the reader as 'spectator–participant' (Harding 1962) was seen as a construct to encompass both, its portmanteau formulation describing a corresponding doubleness in a role that alternately (or simultaneously) 'inhabits' and 'observes' the fiction. The reader of an ekphrasis has another sort of doubleness with which to contend.

The ekphrastic spectator is engaged in a more complex and varied activity than the viewer of a picture or the reader of an 'unattached' poem; for, with an ekphrasis, the poem is always dependent and thus the spectator's role has a disconcerting asymmetry in the sight-lines that connect it with the words on the page and the sculpture or painting to which they refer. The aesthetic response to these 'semi-detached' poems may be construed as either interference or enhancement: the poem may deflect or deepen attention in respect of its visual catalyst. Either way, the problem for aesthetics is how to read an ekphrasis which by definition, uses one medium of representation to represent another. It is a problem that is distinct from other forms of word-painting. The difference between ekphrasis and the literary pictorialism of eighteenth-century pastoral verse (Hagstrum 1958/1987) or the iconicity of, say, George Herbert's 'Easter Wings' or modern 'concrete poetry', is a difference of kind, not merely of degree; for the distinguishing characteristic of an ekphrasis is that it represents in words that which itself is representational. Such a delimitation throws into relief the ambiguous role of the ekphrastic spectator who is asked to cope with the experience of two representations in two different media simultaneously. How do we describe the aesthetic experience of such a role?

As Heffernan (1993: 5–6) and others have shown, one of the principal ways in which poets respond to visual art is through narrative; the corollary is that readers and viewers, faced with this double representation, fall naturally into story-making to resolve this sense of ambiguity and to construct a 'reading' that does justice to both the visual and verbal elements. Interdependence is in the nature of narrative: stories spawn, and are spawned by, other stories. It is unsur-prising that here, as elsewhere, narrative is used to make sense of experience. Yet, as indicated above, this story-making capacity can lead to aesthetic conflict: the potential competition between the reader's 'story' and the poet's 'story' may mean that the poem becomes marginalised. The fact that, when reading an ekphrasis, the reader starts in an unusually well-informed position, maybe with a view of the art work as considered and sophisticated as that of the poet, places a greater risk of rejection upon the poet's interpretation and, consequently, greater demands upon his or her construction of an ekphrasis. Two aspects of narrative assume especial importance in responding to these demands: the poet's awareness of the cultural context in which the ekphrasis tells its story and the spatial dimensions of the art work that it is required to assimilate; and the narrative stance that the writer adopts, and the positioning of the implied reader that follows from it.

The context in which modern ekphrastic poetry operates is itself saturated with narratives of many kinds. As Heffernan points out:

> The ekphrastic poetry of our time ... represents individual works of art within the context of the museum, which of course includes the words that surround the pictures we see, beginning with picture titles. ... From titles we move to curatorial notes on the museum wall, to catalogue entries, to exhibition reviews, to the explanatory notes that invariably accompany reproductions, and to the pages of art history.
>
> (Heffernan 1993: 139)

Public spaces, professional words, and ubiquitous reproductions form the context for modern ekphrases. Contemporary spectator-poets cannot insulate themselves from such features; neither can the ekphrastic spectator's readings of the two arts remain immune from them.

The narrative stances poets adopt within this context 'include addressing the image, making it speak, speaking of it interpretatively, meditating upon the moment of viewing it, and so forth' (Hollander 1995: 4); and we can extrapolate from Hollander's list to identify a range of narrative techniques that spectator-poets employ and a consequent variety of roles in which their implied readers are cast. For example, Gareth Owen's (Adams 1986: 66–7) deployment of fictive time about the depicted woman in J. F. Lewis's painting *The Siesta* and the cast of characters with which he surrounds her defines the ekphrastic spectator as a confidante of his fantasising, voyeuristic narrator who insists on a particular story. By contrast, Michael Longley's (Abse and Abse 1986: 126) playful narrative speculations about Lowry's *Man Lying on a Wall* made in the 'real time' of the viewer interpreting the artist's work invite a role play that is both more light-hearted and more open where there is space to agree or demur. Others explore different aspects of the relationship between spectator, painting and poem: John Wain's poem about Turner's *The Shipwreck* (Adams 1986: 40–3. See Chapter 8, this volume) concerns, amongst other things, the experience of Wollheim's 'twofoldness', playing on the double meaning of 'canvas' as both the artist's material and the ship's sail and asking how the pigments and 'voiceless threads' can make so much noise and violent movement. Charles Causley's poem on Samuel Palmer's painting *Coming From Evening Church* evokes a quite different mood (Adams 1986: 38). Through its touches of quaint diction, its mixing of full and half-rhymes, and its plangent rhythm, it creates a sense of religious harmony to complement one of Palmer's most numinous pictures.

All these ekphrases, as Hollander would say, are poems speaking to silent works of art, doing so with a diversity of voices and with a range of interpretative agendas, but related to the objects of their attention and to each other by their narrative character. The reader/viewer is one and the same person, seeing double in the role of ekphrastic spectator. As was noted at the outset, literary studies speak of the reader in the spectator–participant role, art studies speak of the spectator as a reader of images. The ekphrastic spectator is one who contemplates a painting or sculpture through the eyes of a poet, aware both that the visual work so represented remains, essentially, a poetic fiction, and that the visual work as presented in the gallery remains a representation; the potential either for a clash of 'readings' or for enhanced insight into the art work is ever present.

European Field: a poem reads a sculpture

The ramifications of this unstable position can be explored through a consideration of two contemporary works: Gillian Clarke's ekphrasis in response to Antony Gormley's installation *European Field* (Figure 3.1).

Antony Gormley's sculpture has been installed in various European galleries during the 1990s. It consists of approximately 35,000 figurines, each one of Lilliputian scale and of similar proportion but, as a result of expressing the concept in the means of production, each with its own idiosyncratic character.

Figure 3.1   Antony Gormley, *European Field* (1995), The Tate Gallery, Liverpool, c. 35,000 clay figures, each 8–26 cm tall.

The sculpture is both a collection of individual figures and a representation of community. The representation is reflected in the making, for the figures are created by a group of people who work together (Gormley 1995: 143). *European Field* thus breaks with the convention of the single artist producing a permanent work of art. It is communal art with a single director where the (re)presentation will differ according to the location. There is an element of self-conscious performance about an artistic process that is communally made, sensitive to the spaces in which the work is to be temporarily installed, and so evidently aware of planting a field of gazes that sets up a powerful two-way relationship between the viewer and the viewed.

Three aspects of *European Field* immediately challenge the viewer: its elemental materiality where clay and flesh are synonymous (Gormley 1995: 130); the ambiguity of the diminutive size of the figurines and the vast scale of the whole work; and the consequent multiplicity of eyes – or, more precisely, eye-sockets – that gaze upwards as if in supplication to draw the viewer in and, because of the skeletal emptiness of their cavities, simultaneously to stare the viewer out, turning his or her attention inwards. *Field*, in John Hutchinson's memorable phrase, is 'a landscape of gazes' (Hutchinson 1995: 94). Moreover, the mood in which the viewer responds to this landscape may be one of amusement or solemn contemplation; or, quite probably, a mixture of the two. Gormley himself has observed viewers' responses:

> While some people get annoyed and they perhaps want to kick [the figures] but don't, other people lie down on the floor with their chin on their hands and gaze out across the *Field*, engaging with its intimacy.
>
> (Gormley 1995: 17)

He is conscious of the aesthetic response that his sculpture invites and explicit about involving the viewer in this landscape. In his interview with Gombrich, he twice speaks of this relationship as 'a confrontation' (Gormley 1995: 12, 16) and each time glosses it with the idea not of alienation but of imaginative engagement. He remarks that he thinks of his work as 'a kind of intimate architecture that is inviting an empathetic inhabitation of the imagination of the viewer' (Gormley 1995: 17).

Given the challenge of the work and this communicative impetus behind it, the response of a poet as we read it in her ekphrasis is of singular interest. Which of the various stances mentioned earlier will the spectator-poet adopt? How will she interpret the intelligibility of the gaze with which she is confronted? And how will we, as ekphrastic spectators with knowledge of both the visual work and the poem, respond to the poet's 'reading' of the sculpture?

Gillian Clarke saw the installation in Cardiff. In 1996 she wrote the following poem.

European Field – *an installation by Antony Gormley*

Thirty-five thousand faces in a field
the colour of clay and flesh and blood
crammed between clean white walls of a gallery.
Thirty-five thousand on tip-toe
craning their necks
breathing like a field of corn.

Thirty-five thousand voices asking
why, why, why
like wind in the grasses
of graveyards and old battlefields.
Seventy-thousand ears listening
to no answer.

We have paid to see them.
We did not expect to be stared at,
or that they would move in to live with us,
taking root in the field of our minds,
whispering all night
'we are you, you, you.'

Thirty-five thousand figures
crumbling in my head
to bones and dust and ashes
under a field of flowering grasses.

(Clarke 1998: 48)

Nowhere in Antony Gormley's remarks about the installation is there mention of the two world wars that have savaged Europe this century. Yet he does call his sculpture, *European Field*, a title with unmistakable resonances and implicit directions as to how the work might be read; it influences the singular narrative that is evoked. Gillian Clarke takes up the materiality and location of the figures in the opening sections of her poem. Clay is both the warm, terra-cotta red of a hospitable crowd – it stresses the continuity between earth and humanity; and it is also a cold landscape of skulls staring inquisitively, the huddled masses with their insistent voices, filling the spaces between the clinical walls of the gallery. No twentieth-century poet can ignore the symbolism of thousands of clay figures described with this title. Two intertextual ghosts are awakened in the poem – Owen's 'Futility' (Hibberd 1973: 98) and McCrae's 'In Flanders Fields' (Gardner 1964: 49). The first, like these figures, poses a question – 'Was it for this the clay grew tall?' The second, as these figures testify, shows that the dead remain alive in the communal memory – 'We shall not sleep, though poppies grow / In Flanders fields.' The colour and texture of clay opens the poem with the explicit connection with living flesh and blood, which the figures represent; by the end, the representation has invaded the poet's consciousness and the clay figures continue their terrible narrative, disintegrating into the earth from which they came. In between, the imagery of the field runs like a thread through the poem: it supplies the metaphor for the two symbolic places in which the thoughts and feelings of the poem are located – the gallery in the first two verses, the spectator-poet's mind in the latter two. From being thousands of faces in a field, the figures become a field of grasses through which the voices of the dead speak to us. Here is ekphrasis in the classical sense that Hagstrum defined, the poem literally 'speaking out' for the sculpture (Hagstrum 1958: 18). More pertinently, it is an ekphrasis that demonstrates those aspects of narrative discussed above that characterise the aesthetic response of poets as represented in their poetic fictions: the narrative stance that the writer adopts to elicit a meaning from the response and to tell the story of her reading; and the influence of the narrative context of the gallery in which the encounter with the art work takes place.

And what of the aesthetic mood which permeates these aspects of narrative? One feeling dominates Gillian Clarke's poem: pressure. The insistent numbers recurring five times, the balanced repetitions of 'why, why, why' and 'you, you, you' with their tone of accusation, the claustrophobic pressure of the two confined spaces and, above all, the experience of being transfixed by the sightless gaze of seventy thousand eye sockets when 'we did not expect to be stared at' – all increase the sense that these figures have a claim on those who view them. The spectator-poet, it seems, has been taken over by an army of occupation that has moved in quite unexpectedly to inhabit her mental space, disturb her sleep, and lodge in the mind as an image that will not be denied. Perhaps it is the shock of this invasion that accounts for the tone of the poem's narrative closure. The poem resists the obvious symbolism of the poppies which, none the less, lies behind the text; instead, it leaves us with the interior landscape of mind coloured with the elegiac imagery of death and disintegration beneath the 'field of flowering grasses'.

If this is how the spectator-poet reads the visual work, where does this leave the ekphrastic spectator who, let us assume, comes to both sculpture and poem as new experiences? There is, of course, overlap between the two spectators: my reading of Gillian Clarke's reading of Gormley's installation cannot be separated neatly from my response to the sculpture on its own. The issue for ekphrasis lies precisely here: what are the implications of its dependency upon another work of art? If it cannot be read without reference to the representation that it is interpreting, how, if at all, is this different from any other object of the poet's attention? And, if ekphrasis is deemed to be a special category, how is the reader to handle the duality of responding to two linked works of art?

The basis for answering all such questions is the acknowledgement, justified in previous chapters, that spectatorship is not a stable state but a variable one, characterised by readings and re-readings, by moments of intense absorption and others of more detached assessment or reflection. When one becomes 'lost' in the words and world of the poem, the 35,000 'faces', 'voices', and 'figures', as they successively appear, sustain the experience of the subject as a poetic fiction. In this sense, ekphrasis is self-referential as all poems are. Yet, whenever the ekphrastic spectator looks up from the words on the page, holding this poetic fiction in mind, *there* is the visual work, in this case, looking directly back, sometimes in reality, usually – as here – as a reproduction. Either way, the unique quality of actual ekphrasis is this proximity, the immediacy of the referent. So that, in the course of reading and reflecting upon an ekphrasis, there is a process of cross-checking with the details of the visual work and with the 'reading' of it that we have already made or are currently making. This process is integral to our feeling for and evaluation of the ekphrasis. It puts a premium both upon its plausibility and upon our sense of creative surprise at finding a poetic response which adds to and illuminates our own. It is a process that makes readers more aware of their own creative potential.

From Lessing (1766/1930: 54–55) to Krieger (1992: 5), comparative accounts of painting and poetry have characterised the two arts in terms of what the latter calls the opposition of 'space versus time'. So here, the spatial and temporal dimensions implicit in the sculpture and the poem are especially suggestive of the impact that these art objects make when considered together. The spaces the figures occupy are 'filled up', variable in the framing they provide, and temporary; an installation, by definition, negates the old idea of art as capturing a frozen moment. Both the materiality and the subject matter, as Gormley's own remarks testify, aim at a more generalised statement about humanity, community and history. In the reading of Gillian Clarke's poem given above, history is temporally foreshortened to the twentieth century. Spatially, however, its implications are expanded. The poem sharpens the focus of the image, exploring the details of its fiction, making them personal, constructing them into a poetic confrontation to complement that of the visual work. It is through the operation of this narrative impulse to generate in words a virtual space in which the story of the spectator-poet's reading can be told that ekphrasis makes its dyadic aesthetic appeal.

Poem and sculpture together thus become more than they are apart; each illuminates the other. The verbal may start in a dependent relationship but, as Gillian Clarke shows, ekphrastic poems can rise above their status as mere amanuenses. Not all poems achieve this but, by avoiding the twin traps to which rhetoric in the service of ekphrasis is vulnerable – the demeaning, myopic scrutiny of visual detail and, at the other extreme, the patronising, distanced appraisal that treats the visual as merely a utilitarian catalyst for its own verbal agenda – ekphrasis can deepen our reading of the art to which it refers while, simultaneously, making its own statement and establishing its own autonomy. The creation of a narrative that responds to and transforms the actual spatial elements of the visual work into the virtual space of the verbal one is fundamental in achieving this end.

Speaking out

As was indicated at the end of Chapter 2, looking at a photograph of a painting or sculpture is not the same as looking at the original. The differences are particularly marked with three-dimensional art, and dramatically so with an installation such as *Field*. It is worth asking, therefore, how viewers – young ones especially – react in the gallery. Simon (aged 10) and Sophie (aged 12) saw *Field for the British Isles* at the Hayward Gallery, London. They responded physically in the second way Gormley mentioned above – by getting down to floor level. They also chatted about the sculpture; here are some of their comments:

Simon: It's weird. How many are there?

Sophie: They're not all the same. It'd be boring if they were.

Simon: Look, there's patterns in the clay, different colours.

Sophie: That's to show ... different countries.

Simon: There's fat ones, thin ones, little ones, ... they're a clay people. A lot of helpless, little people.

Sophie: It's like they're trapped in here in a big cold world, waiting to see what happens next.

They're all looking at us, not at each other, a whole army looking at us. What do you think they want?

They've only got eyes. It'd be different if they had mouths or ears – they'd just look, well, like this; (*Draws two simple circles, one with a smiling mouth, the other with a down-turned mouth*) but eyes are dominant. You can do everything with eyes: you can see ... you can show everything, you communicate with your eyes. They look sad.

Simon: They're people of clay, like we're made of earth ... they're all squashed in.

Sophie: They're like us, a whole community but different individuals as well.

Even these few incidental exchanges show that they are open and responsive to both the physical features of *Field* and to its aesthetic impact. In particular, they sense that these 'helpless little people' are our representatives, 'trapped in here in a big cold world' who, by the power of their gaze, compel the spectator to participate in visual terms. They exhibit what Gormley himself has described:

With *Field*, the space is entirely occupied by the work and the work then seems to make us its subject; ... I hope that this work makes the viewers experience its subject; the experience of looking.

(Gormley 1994: 61–2)

Elsewhere, I have outlined how classroom exploration of photographs of Gormley's sculpture and Gillian Clarke's poem can be developed (Benton and Benton 1997: 70–2). In addition to mapping responses to the picture and the poem around copies of the texts, clearly there is scope for pupils to make their own 'gorms' and to write their own poems about them. Here, as throughout this book, cross-curricular work in Art and English is a natural development, the advantages of which are summarised and discussed in Chapter 12. However, the peculiar intimacy of the two arts when reading or writing ekphrastic poems with pupils does confer particular benefits. As indicated earlier, pupils can learn much from experiencing the sheer diversity of poems reading paintings. To take a few examples from the most recent anthology, *Picture Poems* (Benton and Benton 1997), the variety of narrative stances and voices includes:

- stories told as third-person accounts, as in Heather Harvey's 'Narcissus' – a sonnet in response to Dali's painting;
- first-person reflections of the poet, as in Moniza Alvi's 'Swinging', after Kandinsky's painting;
- the thought-track of the sitter in Sylvia Kantaris's 'Growing Pains' about a Whistler picture;
- the interior monologue of the viewer in Gregory Harrison's poem 'Child with a Dove' about Picasso's picture;
- and various dialogues, either between depicted figures in different paintings, as in Anna Adams's poem 'Prince Baltasar Carlos in Silver and Miss Cicely Alexander', linking pictures by Velasquez and Whistler; or between painter and sitter, as in U.A. Fanthorpe's 'Woman Ironing', after Degas; or as one half of a desperate and hilarious dialogue on a mobile phone in Gareth Owen's 'Icarus by Mobile' – a contemporary response to one of the most popular paintings with poets, Bruegel's *Landscape with the Fall of Icarus*.

By talking and writing about these poems and pictures, by comparing their own responses with those of the poets, and by writing their own ekphrases, pupils can develop often surprisingly sophisticated insights into how these two art forms create their effects.

Part II
Words and images

4 Visualising narrative:
Henry Unton and *Henry V*

Past and present

'The past', when we are teaching literature – as L.P. Hartley claimed within fiction itself – 'is a foreign country: they do things differently there' (Hartley 1958: 7). The difficulties of engaging with pre-twentieth-century arts lie not merely in the imaginative demands they make upon us to become time travellers, but also in understanding – once the journey has refocused our attention in the earlier century – the aesthetic conventions that control the art works that we find there. We look at the paintings of earlier periods through eyes conditioned by Impressionism and the cross-currents of twentieth-century art, unable to see them as contemporaries did. We read texts containing Christian and classical references of which our knowledge is, at best, hazy and where the means of representing the world is often unfamiliar. When we backtrack much before 1900, we look at the arts, not just across a metre or two of gallery space, not merely troubled by the occasional sense of alienation from an unknown allusion, but across a psychological and interpretative chasm. In our response to them, there is, in short, an 'aesthetic gap'.

Narrative is a useful means of bridging this gap for several reasons:

- its pervasiveness allows period conventions to be explored in both art forms at the same point in literary and art history;
- it offers insights into the representation of time and place, both fundamental aspects of how the two arts communicate;
- it enables us to examine the use of visual elements in verbal art, and literary elements in visual art and, through comparative study, make each more accessible.

This chapter sets out to establish how painting and literature draw upon each other in creating their effects and how the spectator is positioned in relation to the art work; then, through a consideration of two particular examples from Elizabethan England, to illustrate the importance of understanding the conventional principles governing our responses to the visual and verbal arts; and, finally, to indicate the pedagogical advantages of cross-curricular study in helping us to come to terms with the aesthetic gap that exists between twenty-first-century students and pre-twentieth-century arts.

Positioning the spectator

The title, 'Visualising narrative', is intended to indicate the triangular relationship between the two arts and the spectator's response to them. It signals the painter's problem of how to give graphic form to events in time; the writer's problem of how to deploy language to create an illusion of place or scene; and the spectator's problem of how to engage imaginatively with visual and verbal narratives and scenes often far distant in place and time, especially those governed by conventions from much earlier centuries.

As a way of further defining and illustrating these three dimensions, let us hear briefly from a painter, a writer and a spectator: three extracts from three classic texts – one visual, two verbal – which show the intimacy of the arts in action . First, is William Hogarth who attempted to overcome the limitations of the single canvas through his anecdotal series paintings. A full discussion of *Marriage à la Mode* is given in Chapter 5. For the moment we concentrate upon the climax of the series, 'The Death of the Earl' (Plate 5, p. 81), where the spectator is positioned, as it were, in the centre of the stalls and given a tableaux, conceived in theatrical terms, that needs to be 'read' to be understood. We are required to read both the *temporal context* of the scene in the flow of events in Hogarth's six-act drama and this *visual text* representing a fatal sword thrust that, narratively speaking, must have occurred moments earlier. Because we are aware of looking at a dramatic action (whether or not we are conscious of its climactic significance in the sequence of six paintings), we tend to overlook the fact that nothing in the picture literally moves. As Nelson Goodman says of another narrative painting, when a painter 'tells a story and tells it so compellingly … we tend to forget … that no part of the picture precedes any other in time, and that what is *explicitly* shown is not actions taking place but a momentary state' (Goodman 1981: 101, my italics). *Implicitly*, of course, the events of Hogarth's narrative are told in the picture, inviting us to infer their order of occurrence. So here, we may deduce that, after a visit to a masquerade (signified by the masks and witch's hat on the floor), a fashionable lady and her lover have retired to a rented room for the night; and that her husband, having surprised the lovers, has challenged his rival to a duel. The dramatic moment represented is just after the deadly thrust that kills the husband since we can see the lover making his escape through the window. The commotion has roused the proprietor of the house who enters the room with the constable to find the lady on her knees pleading for forgiveness from her dying husband as both he and his sword fall to the floor. All this is the inferred past until this moment of 'freeze frame'. The implied future lies in our speculations about the fate of the lady and her lover. (The final picture will resolve these when we learn of her suicide and his being hanged for murder). But, for the depicted present, the effect is of arrested movement. The emphasis remains the painterly one of stillness and permanence: the figures are constructed as characters in a visual play, presented to us as if on a proscenium stage set, complete with its exits and entrances, its props and lighting, only to find themselves de-animated into fixed positions and gestures.

Conversely, to move from a literary artist to a painterly novelist, in Henry James's *The Ambassadors* the reader is given a description, derived from the imagery of painting, that needs to be visualised to be understood. Strether's day out in the countryside some eighty minutes by train from Paris is represented to us in Book Eleven, Part Two as a deliberate act of visual recall. His memory of a painting by Lambinet in its 'oblong gilt frame' functions as a palimpsest for the rural scene that he observes, enters, walks about in and falls asleep in. 'He really continued in the picture – that being for himself his situation – all the rest of this rambling day', James tells us (James 1903/1994: 346). Then, to prepare us for the shift from Strether's internal reverie to the arrival of Chad and Madame de Vionnet, James says of 'the spell of the picture – that it was essentially more than anything else a scene and a stage, that the very air of the play was in the rustle of the willows and the tone of the sky' (pp. 346–7). It is in this scene, as Strether leans against the post of a small wooden pavilion overlooking the river, that words depict an Impressionist painting. Here is Strether by the river:

> What he saw was exactly the right thing – a boat advancing round the bend and containing a man who held the paddles and a lady, at the stern, with a pink parasol. It was suddenly as if these figures, or something like them, had been wanted in the picture, had been wanted more or less all day, and had now drifted into sight, with the slow current, on purpose to fill up the measure. They came down slowly, floating down, evidently directed to the landing-place near their spectator and presenting themselves to him not less clearly as the two persons for whom his hostess was already preparing a meal.
>
> (James 1903/1994: pp. 348–9)

As so often in James, the narrative viewpoint he offers us is that of the internal spectator – in this case, the spectator constructed to observe a scene 'as if' it were an Impressionist painting; and yet the river and the narrative flow on, animating the scene through the temporal movement that words create. The effect here is of a still, silent painting coming alive. The emphasis is upon transience; no sooner have the figures completed the picture than they 'drift' out of it, deconstructing it before the spectator's eyes, 'presenting' themselves to him as people.

The spectator is 10-year-old Jane Eyre who, at the beginning of Charlotte Brontë's novel, takes refuge from the appalling Reeds in a window seat in the breakfast room with an illustrated book, Bewick's *History of British Birds*. Words and pictures combine with an unexpected power: the pictures make their immediate impact, the words generate an imaginative engagement. Jane remarks that, though the pictures were the initial attraction, she could not ignore 'certain introductory pages'. Names from the Arctic are listed like an incantation before she quotes some of the text and comments on the connection between word and image.

> Nor could I pass unnoticed the suggestion of the bleak shores of Lapland, Siberia, Spitzbergen, Nova Zembla, Iceland, Greenland, with 'the vast sweep of the Arctic Zone, and those forlorn regions of dreary space – that reservoir of frost and snow, where firm fields of ice, the accumulation of centuries of winters, glazed in Alpine heights above heights, surround the pole, and concentre the mutiplied rigours of extreme cold.' Of these death-white realms I formed an idea of my own: shadowy, like all the half-comprehended notions that float dim through children's brains, but strangely impressive. The words in these introductory pages connected themselves with the succeeding vignettes, and gave significance to the rock standing up alone in a sea of billow and spray; to the broken boat stranded on a desolate coast; to the cold and ghastly moon glancing through bars of cloud at a wreck just sinking.
>
> (Brontë 1847/1953: 10)

And, shortly after, she remarks that 'Each picture told a story' at least as interesting as the fairy tales, ballads and novels that Bessie narrated on winter evenings. This (albeit fictional) spectator is drawing upon two sources of information – the given images and her own mental imagery – in her effort to engage with a text about distant lands. The effect here is described in terms of ideation – words evoking concepts that are 'shadowy', 'half-comprehended', and 'strangely impressive'; pictures endowed with a 'significance' that amounts to a symbolism for the desolation of these 'death-white realms'. The emphasis is upon the complementarity of literary pictorialism and pictorial narration.

Three 'snapshots' of verbal and visual narratives which, from different perspectives, show the interplay between two art forms and, more particularly, how each senses the limitations of its medium and attempts to push these back by exploiting the narrative conventions of its 'sister art'. So much for the ramifications of my main title: each example shows, in its own way, how the spectator is drawn into visual/verbal representations of time and place. Yet, this triangulation of the spectator's role also reminds us that, along with this sense of being drawn in, there is a complementary sense of being a 'construct' of the artist (cf. Henry James's remark, quoted in Chapter 1, about the author making 'his reader very much as he makes his characters … '). To explore the theme of visualising narrative further, we need to shift attention from the role in which the spectator is cast to the conventional principles that control the art works themselves. An examination of the painting *Sir Henry Unton* (1596–1600) by an unknown artist and of the choric narrator in Shakespeare's *Henry V* (c. 1600) will show how comparative study of two works from the last five years of the sixteenth century can help to elucidate the conventions peculiar to the art forms of this period and, in doing so, will suggest ways of approaching the problem identified at the outset – that of bridging the aesthetic gap.

A tale of two Henrys

There is a time slip to be registered immediately. While both works are histories – the painting telling the story of one man's life of nearly forty years, the play dramatising a period of national politics and battlefield triumph over six years – the former is a contemporary biography while the latter chronicles events from 180 years earlier. The painting is a pictorial record of the life of the Elizabethan soldier and diplomat, Sir Henry Unton, who lived from 1557 to 1596; Shakespeare's *Henry V* covers events that took place between 1414 and 1420. Yet, along with the differences there are similarities. The unknown artist of the Unton panel was commissioned by the subject's widow to depict the main incidents and locations in her late husband's career; the Chorus in *Henry V* is given the job of painting in words the shifts in time and place that plot the course of events before, during and after Agincourt. Both works, too, are celebrations, motivated by a sense of pride in achievement and the common need, whether at a personal or national level, to endow particular narratives with significance. What can be learned from the 'constructedness' of these works about the conventional principles underlying the ways in which these narratives are visualised?

First, the picture (Figure 4.1). The annotated diagram accompanying the picture (Figure 4.2) is offered not only to aid the interpretation of detail in this small black-and-white reproduction but also to clarify the singular route the eye is invited to take in following this narrative.

Perhaps the first question the painting poses is: Why are we asked to read this history backwards? Looking from left to right, in conventional fashion, is to observe an exaggerated 'present' and a miniaturised 'past': the church with its funeral service and the tomb are relatively large-scale representations of local scenes of recent memory; by contrast, the right side of the panel shows a clutter of tiny pictures, ranging from Oxfordshire to several Continental countries, spanning most of Unton's life from birth to his final illness and death in France. In visualising this narrative, the artist has represented the events of this life history as funnelling back retrospectively from an expansive present to a tiny past: the further back in time and, especially, the further away in distance, the smaller these events appear in memory and thence in art. Visits to France, Italy and the Netherlands particularly are given little space. But this principle of naive representation, based on a diminishing mnemonic scale, appears to be offset by another – that of biographical symbolism, which dictates that the most important aspects of a life should take precedence. Hence, it is not surprising that the largest detail on the left side of the panel dealing with Unton's death is the church; while on the right side dealing with his life, it is Wadley House with its 'doll's house' view of the rooms on four levels. Moreover, there is a further aspect of narrative to be noticed on this side of the picture. My

Figure 4.1 Artist unknown, *Sir Henry Unton*, (c. 1596–1600), oil on wooden panel.

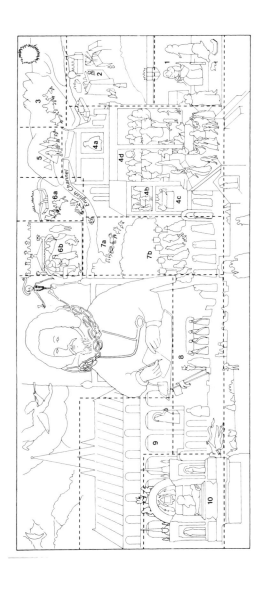

1 Henry Unton as a baby, held by his mother, Lady Anne Seymour

2 As a student at Oriel College, Oxford

3 Henry on his European Tour with his tutor. Here, having crossed the Alps, he is in Italy near Padua

4 Wadley House, near Faringdon, Oxfordshire. This cut-away, 'doll's house' view of the family seat shows Henry in four main scenes, viz:-

    a) seated in his study
    b) music-making with his friends
    c) engaged in theological discussion (although it is uncertain whether he is depicted here)
    d) seated at a banquet while being entertained with a masque

5 Sir Henry as a soldier at the siege of Nijmegen in the Netherlands

6 a) Sir Henry as ambassador to France
   b) Sir Henry, fallen sick in France, is bled by a doctor. He recovered but, on a later visit, died in France

7 a) His body is transported across the Channel to Dover and back to Wadley House
   b) Villagers and peasants from the estate mourn his passing

8 The funeral procession to Faringdon Church

9 The funeral service and sermon

10 Sir Henry's tomb with his armour-clad figure

Figure 4.2   Annotated diagram of Sir Henry Unton.

annotated diagram divides the picture into ten lexias (Barthes's term seems especially appropriate in this context, where the details of the picture yield different meanings according to which of the narrative principles is involved (Barthes 1974: 13)). In the sequence, number four, Wadley House, is the only one arbitrarily placed. The reason for this is that, clearly, there were many comings and goings from Wadley House during Unton's life. Hence, the miniature scenes within number four have a different narrative significance from those that surround it. Those within the house are *typical*, emblems of repeated activities of varying duration and recurrence; those depicted in an arc around the house are *particular*, records of actual, finite periods of time spent elsewhere as a student, on tour, or on official duties, after which Unton returned home. Between life and death is the portrait of the man himself, dominating the whole picture and introducing a third and superordinate principle of timelessness since its very presence in the flow of events 'stills' the history and invites us to interpret Sir Henry at his optimum as an important, cultured man of affairs, steady of eye and sound in judgement. This image is the most finished and carefully executed part of the panel; it raises the status of its subject by the composure of its 'formal portraiture'. I adopt this term not only to contrast this element of the panel with the naive, busy prolixity of the rest of the picture but also to draw attention to the second question that the picture poses: Are we meant to view this portrait as an incidental insertion into a biographical narrative, or to view the scenes from Unton's life as an elaborate background to a portrait? The question is sharpened by the balanced inclusion of two antithetical details: the skeleton perched above Unton's left shoulder holding out the hour-glass, symbolising the 'Vanitas' theme as it turns away from the narrative transcience of worldly accomplishments towards the inevitability of death; and the pen and paper with which Unton the diplomat is supposedly working on affairs of state, conversely symbolising the ability of man's achievements to last beyond the grave and leave their mark upon posterity. The whole picture thus hangs tantalisingly between portraiture and narrative. It is constructed on the basis of multiple perspectives which, in turn, are a reflection of an aesthetic epistemology that is made up of these three competing principles.

   In coining these terms to describe the narrative principles that appear to control the Unton panel – 'mnemonic scale', 'biographical symbolism' and 'formal portraiture' – I am conscious of reacting against Lew Andrews's interesting analysis of continuous narration in Renaissance paintings (Andrews 1994: 84–94). Its unsuitability for the present task is instructive. He discusses the Genettian distinction between story and discourse that has been central to narratology in recent years and questions the usefulness of its transfer from literary to visual art, arguing that a more appropriate means of understanding narration in paintings is to consider the distinction between 'surface' and 'depth'. (This is not Wollheim's notion of 'twofoldness' – the interplay between the materiality of the picture and the depicted scene, discussed in Chapter 2; rather, it is a description of the relationships between people and events that exist *within* the picture space). Setting aside the 'double-time ordering' of literary narratives, he advocates a 'more specifically visual' approach that 'instead of distinguishing one temporal progression from another, think(s) more in terms of an interplay or exchange between two and three dimensions, between the two-dimensional design and the illusion it creates' (p. 85). While this approach suits the comparatively sophisticated art of the Italian Renaissance, and while its surface/depth distinction is suggestive of different ways of giving graphic representation to events in a variety of times and places, it does not elucidate the diversity of visual registers that confront the spectator of the Unton panel. To explain these we need to turn to the conventions of the Elizabethan memorial picture. In a seminal article, after noting the reading process 'from right to left' and 'on occasion … up and down', Roy Strong points out that the mix of portraiture and narrative incident in the structure of the Unton panel derives from two sources: Christian iconography which, in medieval art, represents the figure of Christ, or the Virgin, or a saint surrounded by miraculous events from their lives; and secular iconography which illustrates, say, the Seven Ages of Man or 'the effects of various planetary influences upon mankind' (Strong 1965: 54). Strong's remarks go some way towards answering the second question raised above about the relationship between the portrait and the surrounding scenes; yet an inherent tension remains between reading the image as having, in Strong's terms, a 'dominating central figure' and reading its narrative from right to left and sometimes up and down. Whatever we make of this unusual memorial picture, it is clearly governed by conventions of visual narrative that, as my three principles argue, draw upon several, sometimes competing, modes of representation. It is governed, as Andrew Stott comments, by

> a representational system (which) is familiar for emphasizing the social status of certain people over others in terms of their size, depicting episodes metonymically (a book and a cap designates a university education), and condensing together the map, the seasons, day and night, the living, and the dead.
>
> (Stott 1997: 1)

While it is helpful to be reminded of this conventional description of Elizabethan painting, what the above analysis suggests is the necessity of problematising what Stott takes to be familiar. This is essential, for both aesthetic and pedagogic reasons, if we are to understand the representational systems of earlier periods as being anything more than a collection of surface features. This account of the Unton memorial picture indicates that beneath such features there is a deep structure, based on narrative principles, that supports its representational system. An individual's rank and status, geographical locations, the passing of time – all find their corollary in the word-painting of Shakespeare's Chorus in *Henry V*. What happens when these narrative principles are applied to this contemporary verbal text?

As has been frequently noted, the mood and substance of the choruses in

Henry V are unique in Elizabethan drama (Walter 1954: 5n). How are we to read them? In one sense, the Chorus acts as a poetic frame for the play, with a Prologue in epic tone and an Epilogue in the form of a valedictory sonnet. In between, he is dramatised narrator, continuity man, patriot and eulogist of the monarch, polite apologist for the limitations of the theatre and, especially before Agincourt, mouthpiece for some of Shakespeare's finest poetry. Yet, if one lays his six speeches alongside each other, thinking of them as six panels, they provide a strikingly vivid depiction of King Henry V, which documents six years of his reign with an editorial licence that exaggerates some aspects at the expense of others upon principles analogous to those of the Unton memorial picture. While these speeches, like the historical panorama they describe, 'cannot in their huge and proper life / Be here presented', six juxtaposed extracts can provide a composite image of the temporal and spatial dimensions of the play (see Figure 4.3).

Part of the Chorus's job is to render the mnemonic scale of this historical pageant fit for theatrical presentation. His speeches select and order the events of history into a manageable narrative where the fictive present of Agincourt looms large and where Henry's actual travels and activities during these six years are severely edited and foreshortened. (No mention is made, for example, of Henry's second campaign to France in August, 1417 (Walter 1954: 136n).) In breaking the proscenium boundary and addressing the audience directly, the Chorus is explicit about the imaginative collaboration needed: the spectators must understand that space and time have been miniaturised, reduced to the scale of the 'wooden O', condensed into the time span of 'an hour-glass'. Yet, while the Globe's visual representation of events shrinks place and time, the verbal imagination expands the play's horizons both in shifting locations and in evoking the atmosphere and detail of the 'still image'. Thus, the 'playhouse' can be 'transported' to Southampton and France; and the sights and sounds of the night before Agincourt can be elaborated with a painterly symbolism in which 'the cripple, tardy-gaited night' is a 'foul and ugly witch', the English soldiers appear under 'the gazing moon / So many horrid ghosts', and the King visits and cheers his troops with 'a largesse universal like the sun'. Here, as in the top corners of the Unton panel, life and death are signalled in the archetypal symbols of the sun and the moon.

Similarly, the biographical symbolism of this representation of Henry V dictates that the Chorus makes no mention of Prince Hal; no unsavoury revelations from the King's past are allowed to subvert his present as England's 'conquering Caesar'. Indeed, the only reference the Chorus makes to events outside the charmed circle of heroic success with which he encompasses Henry's achievements is the safe, sad acknowledgement in the Epilogue that they were all thrown away by his son, 'Which oft our stage hath shown'. In representing the life of Henry V as a staged narrative, Shakespeare's selective use of historical data was calculated to fulfil two complementary purposes, both related to the epic form of the story: first, to establish the fluidity of action, place and time which, though at odds with the neoclassic unities espoused by contemporaries

Prologue
Act 1
London

    ... can this cockpit hold
The vasty fields of France? or may we cram
Within this wooden O the very casques
That did afright the air at Agincourt?...
For 'tis your thoughts that now must deck our kings,
Carry them here and there, jumping o'er times,
Turning the accomplishment of many years
Into an hour-glass...   (lines 11-14; 28-31)

Act 2
To Soton

    Linger your patience on; and we'll digest
Th'abuse of distance; force a play.
The sum is paid; the traitors are agreed;
The king is set for London; and the scene
Is now transported, gentles, to Southampton:
There is the playhouse now, there you must sit;
And thence to France shall we convey you safe,
And bring you back, charming the narrow seas
To give you gentle pass;...   (lines 31-39)

Act 3
To Harfleur

    Thus with imagin'd wing our swift scene flies
In motion of no less celerity
Than that of thought. Suppose that you have seen ...
      (lines 1-3)

Act 4
Before
Agincourt

    Now entertain conjecture of a time
When creeping murmur and the poring dark
Fills the wide vessel of the universe...
And so our scene must to the battle fly;
Where, O for pity! we shall much disgrace
With four or five most vile and ragged foils,
Right ill-dispos'd in brawl ridiculous,
The name of Agincourt. Yet sit and see;
Minding true things by what their mock'ries be.
      (lines 1-3; 48-53)

Act 5
Five years
pass between
Agincourt
& Treaty
of Troyes
in Act 5

    Vouchsafe to those that have not read the story,
That I may prompt them: and of such as have,
I humbly pray them to admit th' excuse
Of time, of numbers, and due course of things,
Which cannot in their huge and proper life
Be here presented. Now we bear the king
Toward Calais....   (lines 1-7)

Epilogue

    Thus far, with rough and all-unable pen,
Our bending author hath pursued the story;
In little room confining mighty men,
Mangling by starts the full course of their glory.
Small time, but in that small most greatly liv'd
This star of England ...   (lines 1-6)

Figure 4.3 Six extracts from the Chorus's speech in Shakespeare's *Henry V.*

such as Ben Jonson and Sir Philip Sidney, was necessary to the grand scale of
the narrative (Frye 1980: 335); and, second, to substantiate the moral values of
the ideal king as the epic hero. In both, the role of the Chorus is central.

Portraiture is, perhaps, the most obvious of the choric functions in representing the King. Shakespeare gives us a composite portrait for posterity made
up of the 'warlike Harry' who assumes 'the port of Mars' (Prologue); the rigorous
and just monarch who deals summarily with corruption and treason (Act II);
the determined leader who cannot be bought off (Act III); the 'royal captain'

whose rapport with his troops gives them courage for the fight (Act IV); and the conquering hero who avoids triumphalism, 'Being free from vainness and self-glorious pride', and attributes his victory to God (Act V). It is from these elements that the portrait of 'this star of England' (Epilogue) is created. Here, as with the Unton portrait, the balance of qualities speaks out from the depiction: the demands of public leadership are tempered by the common touch; dignity and importance are free from pompousness and egotism; personal achievement is represented as gaining its value from public works on behalf of the nation in the service of God. Just as our image of Sir Henry Unton derives from his formal portrait situated within a narrative framework, so our picture of Henry V is created from the carefully selected flow of events that Shakespeare's Chorus depicts. Both panel and play visualise 'the accomplishment of many years' as significant narrative. Equally, both exemplify its transient nature through a shared symbol: while in the play text it refers to the time the performance takes and in the painting to the span of a man's life, in both portraits the hourglass has a prominent place.

Mind the gap

So far we have concentrated upon the sophisticated ways in which visual and verbal texts themselves contain instructions as to how they are to be read, in particular, in respect of the positioning of the spectator and the pervasive power of artistic conventions. The pedagogical challenges of such sophistication are self-evident: we ignore the aesthetic gap at our peril! Our assumptions of *what learners already know* and, more especially, of *how learners regard* the visual/verbal texts we put before them, are nowhere more liable to mislead us than when dealing with pre-twentieth-century literature and painting. The 'what' and the 'how' are, in fact, the two main dimensions of difficulty and, over the years, it has been common for academics to throw up despairing hands at their students' lack of knowledge of both the content and the conventions of the arts of earlier centuries. Thus, twenty-five years ago, Delaney wrote in the less gender-conscious idiom of the time:

> From a traditional point of view the modern student is handicapped. He does not fear hell, observe nature closely, go to church or to prostitutes, listen to people die or be born, die of love or consumption or the pox, venerate old men – the experiences from which much of our poetry is made. What was experience has become scholarship.
>
> (Delaney 1972: 318–19)

This is one measure of the gap. More recently, Lawrence Lipking has empha-sised the other – the difficulties modern readers encounter in coming to terms with the conventional means of expression demanded, in this case, by eigh-teenth-century poetry. He says: 'To put it bluntly: the vast majority of modern readers are blind to eighteenth-century poetry. We do not see poems well; we do not make the pictures in our minds that the poets direct and excite us to make' (Lipking 1983: 5). He goes on to acknowledge that while complacent ways of reading may partly explain the difficulty, the power of artistic conventions is also a significant factor (p. 10). Most teachers will recognise (perhaps in themselves as well as in their students) a sense of alienation from past ways of representing past worlds. We need to find the means of assimilating these past worlds into our own, to familiarise ourselves with their nature and conventions without reducing the attraction of their strangeness, a process that Chatman (1978) describes as 'naturalising' the past. How does the literature or art teacher help students in this naturalising process?

While there are no instant solutions, the substance and arguments of this chapter suggest that three points are worth consideration in trying to bridge the aesthetic gap: first, to exploit narrative in all its forms as our best ally; second, to develop cross-curricular work on narrative in the visual and verbal arts; and, third, to find explicit ways of teaching the representational conventions, especially those of the arts in earlier centuries. A brief word, by way of conclusion, about each.

Narrative, as has often been said, is our common human property, a 'primary act of mind' (Hardy 1975: 4). Its universality, crossing languages, cultures and historical periods gives it a unique status as a shared phenomenon of human experience. The study of narrative texts, therefore, entails telling the story of our readings (Culler 1983: 35), as we have seen in the earlier examples. In doing so, we discovered that the sites upon which narrative builds have an architectural inclusiveness. In summary, they demand commentary on the historical context, on the contemporary conventions of modes of representation, on the structural principles upon which a story is erected, on the ways in which the spectator is positioned, and on the means by which different narrative media shape and convey a sense of space and time. The study of narrative offers a rich pedagogical agenda.

This agenda holds particular benefits in the comparative study of literature and painting. In Chapter 9, I will argue the merits of the case for studying paintings that are illustrative of scenes or themes from Shakespeare. In Chapter 3, I theorised the complementary phenomenon – ekphrastic poems written in response to works of visual art – and indicated how cross-curricular work on the two arts can be developed in the classroom, a topic more fully explored in the final chapter. The common denominator in each instance is the feature I have attempted to capture under the present chapter title and to explicate through successive examples – the imperative in the study of both painting and literature to visualise narrative, whether the demand is to interpret a pictorial fiction that is 'given' by an artist, or the fictive picture in the mind's eye that we create from a writer's words. In other words, visualising narrative is a dialogic notion intended to express not only what painters and poets do, but also how viewers and readers respond in return. As suggested at the outset, the failure to 'see', the inability to narrate a meaning, is particularly acute with the arts of earlier centuries, a factor that leads me to a final point of practical pedagogy.

It can be made most succinctly by quoting from the recent account of a young student teacher faced, for the first time, with teaching Chaucer's *The Franklin's Tale* to a lively, able class of 17-year-olds. She commented that dealing with background information about art, architecture, social history, living conditions and the like could be tackled fairly easily and effectively from pictorial and documentary sources. Similarly, placing this story within the narrative conventions of *The Canterbury Tales* was fairly straightforward, given the framework Chaucer himself outlines in the *Prologue*. However, she went on:

> what was difficult was the depth of religious ignorance which prevailed in my classroom … the concept of the Holy Trinity and the story of Adam and Eve were wholly alien concepts to many of my (relatively bright) class. I dealt with this lack of knowledge as I did with the similar ignorance of the Graeco-Roman deities and the medieval use of rhetoric – each subject had a lesson on background devoted to it, together with a detailed handout, and was then dealt with in any further necessary detail as it arose.
>
> (Coles 1997: 5)

The issue here concerns the need for explicit knowledge in aesthetic education. The arts are 'open', accessible areas of study in ways that, say, mathematics and foreign languages are not, where ignorance of the basic knowledge of number and vocabulary renders these subjects, literally, as 'closed books'. Compared with such subjects, students bring a wealth of implicit verbal and visual literacy to bear upon literature and painting. Yet, it is an illusion to believe that the untutored response and native wit can take students very far in understanding and appreciating the arts of their own, let alone those of an earlier, century. The pedagogical challenge is to teach the necessary knowledge of a given period and its representational conventions with sufficient explicitness for them to be useful, but without making the experience into an arid, decontextualised exercise. The trick, as the student-teacher's remarks suggest, is to integrate information about *then* with the living experience of reading *now*, acknowledging with Norman Bryson that 'the "then" is only known as it arises within the "now"' (Bryson 1991: 72). To return to the two Henrys, Angela Cox's short booklet places the Unton picture in its historical setting and offers an excellent starting point for classroom work (Cox 1982). With this introduction, students can be asked to tell the story of Unton's life, using Figures 4.1 and 4.2 above, recreating the narrative in much the same way as with a wordless picture book. They can tell the story of Henry V from the six speeches of the Chorus, regarded as six memorial panels. Finally, as the two Henrys are now not far apart, a combined visit to the National Portrait Gallery and the new Globe Theatre can evoke the feel of the period and its people with an immediacy that brings the past to life. Whatever particular methodology is adopted, students need information about such matters as the history, conventions, materiality, means of production and so on that helped to shape the pre-twentieth-century works of art they are studying; but they need it in forms of pedagogy that start from the validity of their twenty-first-century perceptions and responses. We cannot expect them to see clearly and navigate confidently in this foreign country of the past without giving them up-to-date guide books, maps and ways of seeing to enable them to do so.

5   Theatrical fictions:
Hogarth, Gay and Fielding

Animating the image

In his novel, *English Music* (1992), Peter Ackroyd has his young hero, Timothy Harcombe, experience a succession of dreams in which he encounters writers, artists and characters from earlier centuries. One of the figures he meets is William Hogarth who conducts Timothy on a walk round London's streets and, together, they inhabit and observe the world of Hogarth's pictures recreated in Ackroyd's prose. The artist is constantly didactic, explaining to Timothy the general principles that sustain his work.

After a harrowing walk along Gin Lane, Ackroyd has Hogarth say to Timothy: 'Only when you view my works do you understand the reality that is mirrored within them' (Ackroyd 1992: 261). The continuity of history, the deep structure of inherited features of body and mind manifest in the arts, that constitute 'English music' are Ackroyd's themes, but it is his technique that is especially suggestive. For, by creating a vivid, verbal image of eighteenth-century London from Hogarth's pictures and animating the artist to give both his readers and his main character a guided tour round this 'living gallery', Ackroyd not only makes Hogarth our contemporary, but he can also have his fictional artist point out, as he does in this remark, the limitations of the very medium of which he is made – words – in comparison with the insights offered by the 'actual' paintings and engravings in which, as he says, he has attempted to mirror reality. Ackroyd thus plays a complex ekphrastic game of make-believe, representing in fiction what Hogarth has already represented in pictures and giving his novel its narrative movement by means of a theatrical, almost cinematic, animation. In doing so, Ackroyd suggests the theme of this chapter. Through a discussion of narrative and theatrical techniques principally in selected works by Hogarth, Gay and Fielding, I want to show how spectatorship involves the arts in mirroring both the society in which they exist and one another; and, further, how study of the relationships between the arts can enrich classroom teaching.

The idea of painting, theatre and fiction 'mirroring society' implies multiple reflections. Spectatorship is fundamental in two complementary senses: Hogarth, Gay and Fielding are, above all, acute observers of their society; but, while onlooking and recording and thus interpreting the social scene are fundamental to the comic and satiric eye they all share, their respective arts also show a second order of mirroring: their intertextuality crosses the boundaries of genre. Indeed, the innovative character of these arts – anecdotal series painting, ballad opera and the novel – is intimately bound up with their interdependence. Enabling students to experience these close relationships is invaluable both in making the mid-eighteenth century period come alive and in understanding how these arts create their effects. The popular theatre of the day is the best starting point.

The theatrical mirror

On Friday, 16th February 1728, Henry Fielding (then aged 21) saw the premiere of his first play, *Love in Several Masques*, performed at the Theatre Royal, Drury Lane. It ran for just four nights. Even in a period when to reach double figures was an achievement, this was not a propitious start for a career as a dramatist that was to last for a decade. Yet, as we shall see presently, Fielding's theatrical training was to serve him well when he later turned his attention to the novel.

One of the reasons for this modest beginning was the competition. A few streets away, at John Rich's theatre in Lincoln's Inn Fields, John Gay's *The Beggar's Opera* had opened on 29th January and had begun its astonishing run of sixty-three consecutive nights. The success of what Swift called Gay's 'Newgate pastoral' is legendary: it delighted the public, angered the politicians (especially the Prime Minister – Sir Robert Walpole) and made stars of the players, especially of Lavinia Fenton who played Polly Peachum; and, as some contemporary wit put it, 'it made Gay rich and Rich gay'.

For a season, Gay's 'ballad opera', with its new words set to old tunes, displaced Italian-language opera, a form which had been popular with the wealthy for a decade or more, and had been boosted after Handel's arrival in London in 1711. For the members of the Scriblerus Club (including Swift, Pope and Gay) whose aim was to ridicule 'all the false tastes in learning', Italian opera was a prime example of imported decadence, a betrayal of English culture and an attack upon Nature. In his Introduction, Gay has the Beggar apologise for not making his opera 'throughout unnatural, like those in vogue'. False values in art were one butt for Gay's satire; hypocrisy in public affairs and political life was another. The topical references and identifiable people added spice and satirical point. Many in the audience no doubt linked the central character, Macheath, to the notorious highwayman Jonathan Wild, who had been executed in 1725 and was later to become the subject of a mock biography by Fielding. They might well see, too, in the central relationship in *The Beggar's Opera* – that between Macheath and his 'two wives' – Polly Peachum and Lucy Lockit – a reference to Walpole's long-standing affair with his mistress Maria Skerrett, whom he married on his wife's death in 1737, and which is sharply caught in Macheath's song in Act 2:

How happy could I be with either,
Were t'other dear charmer away!

(*The Beggar's Opera*, Act 2, Scene 8)

But, as Jenny Uglow has pointed out, Gay played it safe by attacking the general culture of politics and the Court, and leaving the audience to make whatever connections they fancied. She comments:

> You could, for example, see Walpole as Macheath, the dashing high-wayman preying on innocent travellers, and then squandering the profits in gambling; or as Peachum, ... weighing the gains from his gang of thieves against the rewards from betraying them; or as Lockit, the lumbering Newgate gaoler who extorts fees for the very chains he puts on.
>
> (Uglow 1997: 134)

The central theme of the opera is given in the Beggar's celebrated words in his final speech:

> Through the whole piece you may observe such a similitude of manners in high and low life, that it is difficult to determine whether (in the fashionable vices) the fine gentlemen imitate the gentlemen of the road, or the gentlemen of the road the fine gentlemen.
>
> (Act 3, Scene 16)

Why dwell on these well-documented details? Not only because Gay's ballad opera eclipsed Fielding's debut as a playwright, but because of its effect upon a member of the audience who warmed to this theme, shared the Scriblerians' attitudes on taste, and was moved to make a quick pencil sketch of the key scene in which Polly and Lucy plead for Macheath's life: this, of course, was William Hogarth. In a little over a year, Hogarth produced six oil-painted versions of the climactic scene (Act 3, Scene 2): this, the fifth, is dated 1729 and was commissioned by John Rich, probably to hang in the theatre (see Figure 5.1).

It is generally regarded as the best, combining the expressiveness of earlier versions within a balanced composition and a sharp satirical eye that is not content just to *record* Gay's stage scene; it *transforms* it by painting a theatrical narrative that consciously explores the relationship between art and life: in fact, it is an example of the traditional 'mirroring' – a study of the nature of reality based upon the old metaphor of life as a stage. For what Hogarth is doing is giving substance to his declared aims:

> to compose pictures on canvas similar to representations on the stage. ...
> I have endeavoured to treat my subject as a dramatic writer: my picture is

Figure 5.1   William Hogarth, *The Beggar's Opera* (1729), Yale Center for British Art, Paul Mellon Collection, oil on canvas.

my stage, and men and women my players, who by means of certain actions and gestures are to exhibit 'a dumb show'.

(Hogarth in Nichols (ed.) 1833: 8–9)

Here, then, the scene is Newgate Prison with Lucy and Polly pleading with their fathers to save Macheath from the gallows at Tyburn while, at the back, a group of minor actors prepare for Scene 12, 'The Dance of Prisoners in Chains'. So much for the theatrical record; but there is much more happening. Notice that Hogarth has pointedly placed some spectators, either side of the actors, on the stage, something that the play's popularity led to in practice at some performances (Uglow 1997: 134). He thus gives visual form to the dramatic concept that the audience themselves were being satirised by Gay and were implicitly part of the action. To signal the point, he hangs over the stage the inscription: *Velute in speculum* ('Even as in a mirror'). Second, Hogarth took delight in portraying well-known people in the audience, so his painting encompasses a double drama: that of celebrated actors and actresses playing fictional roles, and that of recognisable notables among the spectators responding to actors as real people.

Thus, on the far right of the painting, Hogarth shows the Duke of Bolton staring fixedly at Lavinia Fenton playing Polly, his mistress in real life, while

Lavinia/Polly is shown with her back to her stage lover and her gestures and gaze ambiguously linked to the figure of her real lover. In case we miss the idea, Hogarth has the statue of the satyr on that side of the stage pointing downwards towards the Duke of Bolton with its index finger. In these two ways, as well as through the circumscribed space and sense of enclosure in the setting, the psychological interplay between the figures, the delight in detail, the theatrical lighting and the eye-level position of the implied viewer, *The Beggar's Opera* anticipates the character and style of the moral cycles to come.

Gay's *The Beggar's Opera* was significant in the artistic development of both Hogarth and Fielding. It provided the paradigm for the artist's subsequent 'pictur'd morals' (as Garrick called them); and it showed the young Henry Fielding how to write burlesques with that two-faced intention characteristic of Augustan satire: first, the adoption of a mock-heroic mode that subverted contemporary artistic forms by contrast with their revered classical models; and second, the exploitation of this mode to attack the vices of the society and politics of the day.

Fielding's *Tom Thumb* (1730; enlarged 1731) does both. The main thrust of this play was a Scriblerian one against the cultural values of the time; indeed, Fielding's title page refers to himself as 'Scriblerus Secundus', the author who provided the text with a high-flown preface and mock academic notes modelled on those of Pope's *Dunciad* (1728). Just as these annotations poke fun at contemporary criticism, so the play itself sends up the heroic and pseudo-classic tragedies. The characterisation, stilted diction and absurd similes are all contained within a farcical plot that culminates in six murders and a suicide within eight lines and has the hero eaten by a cow! The general absurdity of applying a tragic treatment to a theme as trivial as a nursery rhyme signifies its affinity with the mock-heroic masterpiece of the period, Pope's *The Rape of the Lock* (1715).

As for the political and social satire, Fielding's recent biographer Battestin (1989: 88) suggests audiences and critics may have been too eager to see in Tom Thumb the Great (usually played by a tiny – often child – actress, swaggering about the stage in hero's attire), an ironic figure of the great man himself, Prime Minister Sir Robert Walpole. None the less, while the political jokes were mostly good-humoured enough to cause no offence, the political allusions to Walpole and the Court are there. At this early stage, at least, Fielding emulates Gay and resists making his satire too specific.

In *Tom Thumb*, Fielding gives post-Restoration tragedy a hero–muse commensurate with its stature. In the spirit of the Scriblerians, contemporary pretensions in the arts were cut down to size and the affectations of public life were exposed by the arts of belittlement. It is easy to underestimate the significance of Fielding's theatrical career, which was ended so abruptly by the censorship of Walpole's Licensing Act in 1737. He wrote more plays and in a greater variety of comic modes than any other playwright of his era. In ten years he produced eight regular five-act comedies and eighteen 'irregular' plays – ballad operas, burlesques, parodies and farces – of varying lengths (Battestin

1989: 231–2). His political attacks on the Whig government became increasingly strong so that Walpole finally silenced him. In doing so, Walpole unwittingly did English fiction a good turn: within three years, Fielding had turned his hand to *Joseph Andrews*.

While Fielding was becoming the country's most successful playwright, Hogarth was achieving similar status in the visual arts. He painted many portraits and conversation pieces but his reputation rested mainly on his two anecdotal series, *A Harlot's Progress* (1732) and *A Rake's Progress* (1735). In these, he developed the technique of theatrical narrative outlined in his declared aims quoted above and built on the compositional and psychological elements he had shown in *The Beggar's Opera*. To plot 'Hogarth's progress' through these series is beyond the scope of this chapter; but the shift from the single image from Gay's play to the complexity of Hogarth's invented visual drama can be discussed to show both how his anecdotal series demand a more sophisticated response in the spectator role and how theatrical representation is the common link between his pictures and Fielding's fiction.

The comic mirror: Hogarth and Fielding

How does this decade of experience in theatrical narrative show itself in the mature work of Hogarth and Fielding in the 1740s? And how does it help to formulate their shared idea of comic satire?

To answer these questions, I will concentrate on two texts: Fielding's *Joseph Andrews* (1742/ 1910) and Hogarth's *Marriage à la Mode* (1745). Their work is linked explicitly by their creators – in Fielding's celebrated *Preface* to his novel, and in Hogarth's engraving *Characters and Caricaturas* (1743) the subscription ticket for the engravings of this series. Both are commented upon below but, first, how does Fielding's stage comedy translate into the novel?

Joseph Andrews started life as a send-up of Richardson's *Pamela* (1740) with Fielding making his protagonist the brother of Richardson's heroine. Fielding's novel soon outgrew its initial parodying of Richardson but in the early chapters, particularly in the presentation of Joseph – the young, handsome, innocent abroad in the fleshpots of London – the satirical catalyst is readily apparent. Having travelled to London with another innocent, Parson Adams, Joseph is immediately lusted after by both Lady Booby and her chambermaid, Mrs Slipslop. A sense of theatre is everywhere in the writing. Consider this sequence of extracts from Book I, Chapter vi, after Lady Booby has made her first advances, where the bewildered Joseph next finds himself the object of Slipslop's passion!

The chapter begins with Joseph's letter to his sister Pamela, in which he alludes to Lady Booby's behaviour in these terms:

> *Dear Pamela, don't tell anybody; but she ordered me to sit down by her bedside, when she was naked in bed; and she held my hand, and talked exactly as a lady*

does to her sweetheart in a stage-play, which I have seen in Covent Garden, while she wanted him to be no better than he should be. (p. 12)

For Joseph, life is imitating art; through the metaphor Fielding prepares the way for the theatricality in both visual and verbal humour of what follows. The narrator 'plays the audience', as it were, by directly engaging the reader in his story-telling. First, we are given a Hogarthian portrait of Slipslop, then some stage dialogue, and finally some witty mock-heroic. Here is the grotesque Slipslop who, the narrator tells us with studied understatement, was not 'remarkably handsome':

> As soon as Joseph had sealed and directed this letter he walked downstairs, where he met Mrs Slipslop, with whom we shall take this opportunity to bring the reader a little better acquainted. She was a maiden gentlewoman of about forty-five years of age who, having made a small slip in her youth, had continued a good maid ever since. She was not at this time remarkably handsome; being very short, and rather too corpulent in body, and some-what red, with the addition of pimples in the face. Her nose was likewise rather too large, and her eyes too little; nor did she resemble a cow so much in her breath as in two brown globes which she carried before her; one of her legs was also a little shorter than the other, which occasioned her to limp as she walked. This fair creature had long cast the eyes of affection on Joseph, in which she had not met with quite so good success as she prob-ably wished. (pp. 12–13)

Fielding then shifts to dialogue as Slipslop entices Joseph to her room, plies him with wine and suggests he should be her 'toy boy'. There is stage farce in the situation, the timing of the exchanges and the 'Slipslopisms', in which the lowly Slipslop tries to emulate the language of her superiors. Her verbal errors look back to Shakespeare's Mistress Quickly and forward to Sheridan's Mrs Malaprop in *The Rivals* (1775). Look out, especially, for 'sophisticates' (= suffices), 'result' (= insult), and 'ironing' (= irony). Slipslop speaks:

> 'Sure nothing can be a more simple *contract* in a woman than to place her affections on a boy. If I had ever thought it would have been my fate, I should have wished to die a thousand deaths rather than live to see that day. If we like a man, the lightest hint *sophisticates*. Whereas a boy *proposes* upon us to break through all the *regulations* of modesty, before we can make any *oppression* upon him.' Joseph, who did not understand a word she said, answered, 'Yes, madam.' – 'Yes, madam!' replied Mrs Slipslop with some warmth. 'Do you intend to *result* my passion? Is it not enough, ungrateful as you are, to make no return to all the favours I have done you; but you must treat me with *ironing*? Barbarous monster! How have I deserved that my passion should be *resulted* and treated with *ironing*?' 'Madam,' answered Joseph, 'I don't understand your hard words; but I am certain you have no

occasion to call me ungrateful, for, so far from intending you any wrong, I have always loved you as well as if you had been my own mother.' 'How, sirrah!' says Mrs Slipslop in a rage; 'your own mother? Do you *assinuate* that I am old enough to be your mother?' (pp. 13–14)

As Slipslop slips and slides on these verbal banana-skins, her attempt at seduction is subverted by her language. Middle-aged outrage soon subsides. Within a few lines, passion reasserts itself over wounded pride, and Fielding switches the register of his comic satire into another mode: the mock epic. Listen to the change up into the 'lofty' vocabulary and rhythms of the epic simile and the change back down again as the incident comes to an end with the bathetic ringing of the servants' bell. Slipslop ends her entreaty, then the narrator comments:

> 'Yes, Joseph, my eyes whether I would or no, must have declared a passion I cannot conquer. – Oh! Joseph!'
> As when a hungry tigress, who long has traversed the woods in fruitless search, sees within the reach of her claws a lamb, she prepares to leap on her prey; or as a voracious pike, of immense size, surveys through the liquid element a roach or gudgeon, which cannot escape her jaws, opens them wide to swallow the little fish; so did Mrs Slipslop prepare to lay her violent amorous hands on the poor Joseph, when luckily her mistress's bell rung, and delivered the intended martyr from her clutches. (p. 14)

Here are beauty and the beast reversed! The animal imagery already introduced in the earlier description of Slipslop's bovine breasts is here inflated to encompass the whole predator ('the hungry tigress' and 'the voracious pike'). It is mock epic, certainly, in its precious phrasing ('liquid element' for water), its extended Miltonic simile ('as … as … so …'), and its consciously rhetorical word order ('sees within the reach of her claws a lamb'). Yet, it is also exactly the sort of comic language that Fielding had learned how to use during his writing for the stage and had exploited so effectively in *Tom Thumb*. The portrait, the dialogue and the mock heroic set-piece are all exaggerated beyond life size (beyond 'nature' to use Fielding's word). They are larger than life in the way that theatrical convention demands. The reader is placed in a spectator role, as a member of an audience watching a scene (cf. Hogarth), yet simultaneously, is also watching Fielding's dramatic skills deployed so overtly and self-consciously. Fielding achieves a sort of Brechtian alienation: the reader is never allowed to forget the artifice; yet the reader's imaginative participation is enlisted by the 'indeterminacy gaps' (Iser 1978: 170–9) in the text. There is nothing as dramatic as the gaps Sterne leaves for us in *Tristram Shandy* – the blank page for the reader to draw Widow Wadman, or the 'chasm of ten pages' for the reader to write. But the spectator–participant role of the reader of fiction (as discussed in Chapter 1) is subtly exploited by Fielding, and nowhere more so than in the second seduction scene with Lady Booby.

Joseph, rather more wary now but just as innocent, is soon ensnared by Lady Booby's mixture of accusation and suggestiveness. She takes his hand and suggests that kisses are a mere 'hors d'oeuvre' to the banquet she has in mind; Joseph recoils, calling loudly on his virtue. Instead of describing Joseph's horror at the height of this crisis, Fielding stops the narrative and invites the reader in:

> You have heard, reader, poets talk of the statue of Surprise; you have heard likewise, or else you have heard very little, how Surprise made one of the sons of Croesus speak, though he was dumb. You have seen the faces, in the eighteen-penny gallery, when, through the trap-door, to soft or no music, Mr. Bridgewater, Mr. William Mills, or some other ghostly appearance, hath ascended, with a face all pale with powder, and a shirt all bloody with ribbons; – but from none of these, nor from Phidias or Praxiteles, if they should return to life – no, not from the inimitable pencil of my friend Hogarth, could you receive such an idea of surprise as would have entered in at your eyes had they beheld the Lady Booby when those last words issued out from the lips of Joseph.
>
> 'Your virtue!' said the lady, recovering after a silence of two minutes; 'I shall never survive it!' (p. 20)

The reader as spectator now has to turn actor. Reader-response criticism has taught us among other things how texts manipulate readers in their spectator– participant role. As Iser comments: 'The nondescription of Lady Booby's surprise, and the insistence on its inconceivability, create a gap in the text. The narrative breaks off, so that the reader has room to enter it' (Iser 1974: 38). The two putative readers of Fielding's Preface, the 'mere English reader' and the 'classical reader' are both catered for: the first may associate the scene with the melodramatic effects of contemporary acting or Hogarth's prints; the second with classical precedents. Yet all analogies are deemed inadequate and it is thus down to the reader to animate the scene; to take over the whole production, as it were, and elevate it from the paucity of the verbal into the richness of the visual imagination.

Fielding is constantly playing off the visual and verbal against each other in a brand of humour that he translated directly from the stage. It takes many forms from the farce-type exits and entrances that occur between these two seduction attempts as Lady Booby has Slipslop waddling to and fro as she changes her mind three times over the dismissal of Joseph, to the constant slapstick of char- acters falling over, spilling things, messing up their clothes, falling off horses, getting into the wrong beds, and the like. Parson Adams is the main vehicle for this humour. Fielding's extravagant prose is frequently used to create a humorous mental image by slowing the pace of an otherwise rapid series of events. This is perhaps most obvious in the scene where Adams becomes involved in a pub brawl (Book 2, Chapter V). Provoked by the innkeeper's threats to the injured Joseph, Adams punches the innkeeper on the nose and the innkeeper punches him back:

Adams dealt him so sound a compliment over his face with his fist, that the blood immediately gushed out of his nose in a stream. The host being unwilling to be outdone on courtesy, especially by a person of Adams's figure, returned the favour with so much gratitude, that the Parson's nostrils likewise began to look a little redder than usual. (pp. 85–6)

Adams then flattens the innkeeper whose wife flings a pan of pig's blood in his face, just as Slipslop enters to pummel the woman into submission, tear out her hair, and claim victory. This is the stuff of pantomime – a theatrical genre with which Fielding was very familiar and in which John Rich was the acknowledged master. The whole scene is written in this elaborate, inflated language so that the effect is one of slow-motion. The pace, timing and technique are straight from that sort of comic stage-fighting in which violence can be taken as humour because no-one is going to get seriously hurt.

With *Joseph Andrews*, we have been able only to take a few snapshots; with *Marriage à la Mode*, we can read the whole story. (A fuller discussion of the series can be found in my *Secondary Worlds* (Benton 1992: 142–7). There is a long tradition of commentary on Hogarth's pictures, beginning with that sanctioned by the artist during his lifetime (Paulson 1975b: 201), which draws upon the evidence in the pictures for the names of many of the characters. For clarity's sake, the prints which follow are of the engravings of the series which, due to the copper-plate production process, are laterally the reverse of the paintings. Readings of these parallel sequences are significantly affected by the medium in which the pictures are viewed (Paulson 1975b: 40–3; Uglow 1997: xvi). The paintings tend towards balancing the figures through colour and through merging forms, thus understating the story-line; the engravings tend to lead the eye through an easier viewing sequence where figures are causally related from left to right as in a written text. The paintings make the viewer pause to explore colour, line and mass, whereas the engravings make the viewer move forward to interpret the plot.

The summary account of the pictures that follows concentrates on the plot-line and makes no attempt to elucidate the multiplicity of details examined elsewhere (Cowley 1983). As with any complex text, *Marriage à la Mode* is open to fresh observations; there is no single, authoritative explanation (Egerton 1997: 12). 'Every picture,' as Jenny Uglow has remarked, 'may *suggest* a story but it is the viewer who *tells* the tale, frames the narrative and fills the gaps' (Uglow 1997: xv).

The narrative begins with the concluding negotiations for an arranged marriage (Plate I). The father of the bride-to-be, the merchant in the centre, scrutinises the settlement while the bridegroom's father, Earl Squanderfield, receives a redeemed mortgage and cash as a dowry and points proudly to his family tree. The betrothed couple sit together in the background: the Viscount more interested in his own reflection in the mirror than in his intended; the merchant's daughter more interested in the attentions of the young lawyer, Silvertongue, than in her future husband. The seeds of dramatic conflict are sown: the intrigue and ultimate

Plate I   William Hogarth, 'The Marriage Contract', *Marriage à la Mode* (1745), The British Museum, London, engraving.

downfall of the main characters derive from both the dictates of commercially minded parents and the inherent weaknesses of the bride and groom. Hogarth signifies not only the groom's vanity but also his already degenerate life style, witnessed by the large patch on his neck indicating VD.

Plate II shows the young marrieds in their own rooms early one afternoon. Breakfast is still on the table and lights are still smouldering in the chandelier. The husband wears his hat, and his broken, undrawn sword lies at his feet. A small dog sniffs inquisitively at a woman's cap in his coat pocket. We are to infer that the husband has been out on the town and has recently returned exhausted. His wife, meanwhile, has apparently been at an all-night card party held in the further room; she stretches with sensual robustness as she casts a knowing sidelong glance at her husband. The steward, carrying a sheaf of unpaid bills and only one receipt, has been dismissed and leaves with an ambiguous gesture of disgust at his employers and mock benediction towards the implied viewers. The marriage is at the point of disintegration; the scene prepares us for the separate lives of the couple in the next two pictures.

In Plate III, the young nobleman is now seen in the laboratory of a quack doctor. With him is a sad young girl, a child prostitute dressed in adult finery – perhaps the owner of the mob-cap in his pocket in the previous picture. The

Plate II   William Hogarth, 'The Breakfast Scene', *Marriage à la Mode* (1745), The British Museum, London, engraving.

Plate III   William Hogarth, 'The Visit to the Quack Doctor', *Marriage à la Mode* (1745), The British Museum, London, engraving.

subject of the scene is syphilis. With a show of bravado in his grin and the bran-
dishing of his stick, the Viscount suggests he does not take this 'nobleman's
disease' too seriously, as he holds out a box of ineffectual pills. (In fact, there
were several euphemisms for syphilis: the French called it 'the English disease';
the English returned the compliment by referring to 'Maladie Alamode'!) Either
this complaint or the raised cane, or both, produces a look of momentary
annoyance on the face of the tall woman, thought to be an ex-procuress, who
acts as the quack doctor's assistant.

There has been a considerable passage of time between the events depicted
in Plate IV and the preceding ones. The old Earl has died (his coronets are
above the mirror and the bed), and the young Countess is now a mother (a
child's comforter hangs from the back of her chair). The Countess is at her
toilette, having her hair done, while Silvertongue reclines on a sofa in the easy
manner of a frequent and privileged visitor; he points to a picture of a
masquerade on a screen and, ticket in hand, invites the Countess to accompany
him to one. Behind the lovers is a mock-heroic altar, reminiscent of Belinda's
dressing-table in Pope's *The Rape of the Lock*, surmounted by drapery arranged
ironically like a bridal veil around the mirror. In front of them the black boy
gleefully points to the horns of Actaeon, sharing the joke of incipient cuckoldry

Plate IV   William Hogarth, 'The Countess's Levée' *Marriage à la Mode* (1745), The
British Museum, London, engraving.

directly with the implied viewer. The gathering is being entertained by an Italian castrato, whose performance is being received with everything from ecstasy and delight to indifference and sleep by his audience.

After the masquerade (signified by the masks and witch's hat on the floor), the Countess and Silvertongue spend the night at a Covent Garden bagnio. Meanwhile, her husband has learnt of the assignation (perhaps through the hairdresser in the previous scene) and, surprising the lovers, has challenged Silvertongue to a duel. The dramatic moment represented in Plate V is just after the fatal sword thrust that kills the nobleman, because Silvertongue has had time to make his escape out of the window. The commotion has roused the proprietor of the house, who enters the room with a constable to find the Countess on her knees pleading for forgiveness from her dying husband as both he and his sword fall to the floor.

The Countess has now returned to the sparsely furnished home of her father on the Thames waterfront near Old London Bridge. In Plate VI, the plot is resumed at the point when she has just received news of the hanging of Silvertongue at Tyburn for murder. (His 'Last Dying Speech' lies at his mistress's feet.) The Countess has committed suicide by taking poison just as her father was about to have lunch. The apothecary berates the half-witted servant,

Plate V   William Hogarth, 'The Death of the Earl', *Marriage à la Mode* (1745), The British Museum, London, engraving.

Plate VI   William Hogarth, 'The Death of the Countess', *Marriage à la Mode* (1745),
        The British Museum, London, engraving.

presumably for conspiring to buy the poison; the physician leaves in the background, unable to revive the Countess; and, seeing that his investment in the
marriage contract in Plate I has not paid off, the merchant cuts his losses by
retrieving the ring from his daughter's finger before rigor mortis sets in. The
only sign of real sorrow comes from the old nurse who lifts up the crippled child
with its heavy leg-iron and tell-tale patch on her neck to kiss its mother. In the
confusion, the house dog eats its master's lunch.

   The theatrical construction of this plot is like a Molière play: it moves from
exposition (Scene 1) where all the principal characters are introduced, through
intrigue (Scenes 2, 3 and 4) as the infidelities develop, to crisis (Scene 5) with a
violent murder, and finally to denouement (Scene 6) with a suicide and the
reminder of the monetary contract upon which this fashionable marriage had
been based. If the early scenes are the stuff of social comedy, the outcome is
bleakly tragic. Each of the first four scenes has a different kind of humour
(Uglow 1997: 381). The marriage contract, presented as a comedy of manners,
establishes the class differences between the merchant and the aristocrat
through their body language. With the breakfast scene we are watching a psychological comedy, reading its import in the faces, postures and gestures of the three
main figures. The third scene at the quack doctor's surgery is black humour – as

desperate as it is amusing. The Countess's levée brings the satirical humour to its height, combining the mockery of fashionable culture (especially the taste for foreign music) with that of the infidelities of fashionable marriage. Thereafter, the satire dips towards tragedy, with a touch of melodrama about 'The Death of the Earl' and an atmosphere of sombre elegy about 'The Death of the Countess'. Yet, such is Hogarth's mordant wit that, even here, he cannot resist the inclusion of humorous details such as the crude composite picture on the back wall in Plate V, and the dog eating the lunch in Plate VI.

The story-telling potential of the six pictures operates in two complementary ways: within each image and in the gaps between the images. The dominant movement of the narrative from left to right, from past to future and from cause to effect is created both by the main events of the plot as we have deduced them from the subjects of the six pictures and by the particular anecdote depicted individually in each scene. The story is robust, the actors strong. Each picture has its own 'before' and 'after', its open windows, angled doors, gesturing arms, characters coming or going – all of which invite our collaboration, ask us to fill in the gaps, and prompt us to think about cause and consequence.

The time-scale of the narrative is subtly organised. The light in Plate I (together with the date of 4 June on the steward's receipt in Plate II) suggests the marriage contract was made in late spring or early summer; the duel (Plate V) occurs on a night wintry enough to need a large fire; and the final picture (Plate VI) shows another day warm enough for the windows to be wide open onto the river. One seasonal cycle is clearly insufficient; just how many years elapse depends upon the viewer's own estimate of the age of the child in the last scene. Story-time and discourse-time are cleverly handled: the first impression is of a discourse comprising a rapid sequence of events, culminating in the tragic deaths of the protagonists; once the 'indeterminacy gaps' between and, to a lesser extent, within the scenes are filled in by the viewer, the more extensive chronology of the story becomes apparent. Locations are equally significant. The setting of the narrative shows a downward progress in a different manner from that of Hogarth's earlier series. We begin in the Earl's grand mansion in West London and end in the bare Thames-side house of the merchant in East London; the incidents in between take place at different locations in central London.

The ways in which time and place are organised leave the viewer of the series much to do. Connections are inexplicit, the emphasis in each scene is upon the dramatic moment, and the gaps in time and place are often large ones to bridge. All this puts a heavy interpretive demand upon the viewer but, such is Hogarth's skill at enticing the implied viewer to become a reader, the story seems to grow out of the mass of significant details connecting the scenes.

This ambiguous spectator role – viewer and/or reader? – is reminiscent of Fielding's exploitation of the visual/verbal elements in *Joseph Andrews*. Here, on the one hand, we are clearly defined as people watching a play: the implied viewer's position is that of the playgoer in the front row of the stalls, looking at eye-level scenes enacted, as it were, within the proscenium frame. Hogarth exploits this position, as we have noticed, by occasionally having one of his characters make a theatrical connection with the 'audience' by crossing the proscenium boundary. The black boy's gesturing (Plate IV) is the clearest example in this series, but the steward's leave-taking (Plate II) is partly for the onlooker's benefit, and even the recumbent chained dog (Plate I) appears to be casting a knowing eye towards us!

Equally, on the other hand, we are cast as readers. As we saw in Chapter 1, one of the main elements of reading fictional narrative in books is the oscillating process of anticipation and retrospection: predictions, made with an increasing sense of the ending, based on the steadily accumulating knowledge of the story so far. Anticipation of what happens next is the motor that drives the reading. The narrative mode of Hogarth's picture sequence places the emphasis upon the other half of this process, encouraging the reader to take a retrospective, ruminative stance. Predicting about the future of the characters is much less important than piecing together the past and present moments: the reader is drawn to interpret causes rather than to hypothesise about future effects. In this respect, coming to terms with a Hogarthian series offers a useful reading lesson to complement those learned from verbal texts.

In focusing my comments on Hogarth's techniques of theatrical narrative, much has been left unsaid about the social and cultural background, the composition and details of the pictures. (There is no shortage of commentary upon these aspects. See Further Reading, p. 88.) A final issue that signifies the tone and purpose of the series and links both to Fielding's comic satire cannot remain unremarked: that is, Hogarth's metaphors.

The dominant metaphors of *Marriage à la Mode* are disease and money. The former runs through the series, from the old Earl's gout and his son's beauty patch on his neck to hide a sore, which would be venereal (Plate I), through the dissolute, debilitating lives shown in Plate II, to the unsavoury sight of the diseased Viscount and his child mistress, both with their box of pills at the quack doctor's at the heart of the series (Plate III). Diseased relationships infect the fashionable lifestyle of the Countess's levée (Plate IV); adultery and murder follow (Plate V); and the sad progeny of the marriage is depicted in the crippled child with its inherited deformities in the final scene (Plate VI). The diseases of these individuals both extend from the parents to children in time and spread through the social structure.

Monetary dealings – investment, payment, debt, redeeming losses – infect the series almost like a form of disease. Money initiates the narrative in the contract (Plate I) and closes it with the merchant's retrieval of his dead daughter's ring (Plate VI). In between, there are unpaid bills (Plate II) and the suggested squandering of money in pursuit of fashionable pleasures: the Viscount's outlay for pills (Plate III), the Countess's for musicians and the adornments of high life (Plate IV) and Silvertongue's for the masquerade and the hire of the *bagnio* (Plate V) are all one to Hogarth's satirical eye.

Clearly, disease and money have a particular role in deciding the tone of this series, perhaps a rather darker satire than Fielding's. Yet, they also indicate a more general criticism of the society of the times. In doing so, these local meta-phors raise questions about the whole status and orientation of Hogarth's and Fielding's new, experimental art forms in relation to the world they reflect. Both Hogarth and Fielding saw themselves as innovators. Hogarth speaks of 'painting and engraving modern moral subjects, a field not broken up in any country or any age' (Hogarth, quoted in Nichols 1833); Fielding regards himself as 'the founder of a new province of writing' who is initiating 'a species of writing ... hitherto unattempted in our language' (Fielding 1742/1910: xviii).

Clearly, they regarded each other as kindred spirits artistically, as well as valuing a friendship which dated back to the early 1730s and was to continue until Fielding's death in 1754. Fielding's celebrated Preface argues that Hogarth had created a new art form which was both uplifting and yet true to nature, one which lay between the classical depictions of gods and humans in traditional 'history painting' and the comic distortions of 'caricature'. This middle way was the portrayal of 'character' – the ability to show the whole person as a thinking and feeling human being. Fielding said of Hogarth, 'It hath been thought a vast Commendation of a Painter to say his Figures seem to breathe; but surely, it is much greater and nobler Applause that they appear to think' (Fielding 1742/1910: xix). In turn, Hogarth produced a subscription ticket for *Marriage à la Mode* called *Characters and Caricaturas* (1743) (See Figure 5.2).

In Figure 5.2, above a bottom row of three character heads by Raphael and four caricature heads by Leonardo and others, he engraved over a hundred faces intended to show the variety of nature and establish the merits of his position 'between the sublime and the grotesque'. Beneath, he directs the reader/viewer: 'For a Farther Explanation of the Difference Betwixt Character and Caricatura See ye Preface to Joh Andrews.' Both innovators needed to establish their posi-tions in relation to classical precedent and to the prevailing taste of the times. The difficulties of doing so perhaps account for the strained phrases that Fielding used to describe their work, calling Hogarth a 'Comic History-Painter' and labelling his own *Joseph Andrews* as a 'comic epic in prose'. None the less, it is in their notions of narrative and in their shared sense of the serious nature of comedy, one that can educate as well as entertain, that both painter and novelist held a common vision. Hogarth's humble subscription ticket contains a visual clue to this affinity. A close look at this print, concentrating on the expressions of the faces, shows that the majority are solemn or, at best, smiling. Yet, when we home in just below the centre of the picture, we find two heads facing each other, with mouths open and eyes creased with humour, both laughing uproariously: Fielding is on the left, Hogarth on the right – a mirror image, as it were, that reflects both their friendship and their shared artistic enterprise

Drama and narrative

The emphasis on theatrical fictions in this chapter has highlighted a fresh aspect of spectatorship: looking at the acting out of a dramatic sequence of

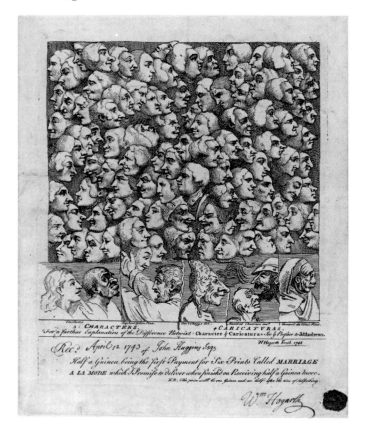

Figure 5.2 William Hogarth, 'Characters and Caricaturas' (1743), The British Museum, London, engraving.

events as a communal, as well as an individual, activity. Teaching approaches may take their cue from this, perhaps along the following lines:

- a sixth form Theatre Studies group works on scenes from Gay's *A Beggar's Opera*, aiming to stage Act 3, Scene 11 as a tableau representing Hogarth's painting. (In the film of *Tom Jones*, Tony Richardson directed a tavern scene in just this way, utilising Scene 3 of Hogarth's *A Rake's Progress*).
- the sequence of extracts from *Joseph Andrews* quoted earlier could be scripted into two or three scenes and acted out under the title of, say, 'The Temptation of Joseph'.
- the plot-lines and characters of *Marriage à la Mode*, *A Harlot's Progress*, and *A Rake's Progress* can be scripted and dramatised as a theatrical response in the long tradition of commentary upon Hogarth's series.

The above suggestions focus upon drama; the following emphasise narrative:

- using shuffled packs of photocopies of the six pictures of either *A Harlot's Progress* or *Marriage à la Mode*, students work out the correct sequence of the story, perhaps adding brief captions to indicate the plot-line and including details of the settings and the time-scale of the events.
- students work on photocopies of one of the anecdotal series and turn it into a comic strip. Gillray, Cruikshank and many other later graphic artists used speech and thinks bubbles as part of their satires (George 1967). What might Hogarth's characters be saying and thinking?
- Hogarth our contemporary. Newspapers and television are full of stories similar to the ones Hogarth tells: teenagers arriving alone in London live out their versions of *A Harlot's Progress*; inherited fortunes or lottery winnings are 'blown' in a few short weeks, mirroring Hogarth's Rake; the arranged marriages and fashionable affairs of *Marriage à la Mode* continue to make the headlines. Students either rework Hogarth's stories 'in modern dress', or take a modern news story and give it the Hogarthian treatment, retelling it as a picture sequence with appropriate captions and commentary.

A related aspect of narrative mentioned in this chapter are the media through which Hogarth's stories are told. Comparison of the paintings and engravings brings out not only the materiality of the images but also the different relationships in which they stand to their respective audiences. These issues are most easily approached through study of *A Rake's Progress*:

- students compare the paintings and engravings of Scene 4, 'Arrested for Debt' and Scene 8, 'Bedlam' and list the differences they notice in the details included in the pictures, the portrayal of the characters, the definition of the images and so on, and discuss Hogarth's purposes in these two versions.

Finally, the impetus of personal and social education behind Hogarth's work can be further explored through his more overtly didactic engravings where many current issues such as alcoholism, the treatment of animals, the living conditions of the poor and homeless are dramatised with his uncompromising visual shock tactics:

- students study engravings of *Gin Lane* and *Beer Street*, *The Four Stages of Cruelty*, and *Industry and Idleness* and discuss the messages they promote and the means of communicating them.

Further reading

The books listed below are the most useful and accessible ones for teachers.
Details of other publications mentioned in this chapter are given in the general
Bibliography at the end of the book.

Bindman, D. *Hogarth*, London: Thames and Hudson, 1981.
Cowley, R.L.S. *Marriage à la Mode: A Review of Hogarth's Narrative Art*,
    Manchester: Manchester University Press, 1983.
Einberg, E. *Hogarth the Painter*, London: The Tate Gallery, 1997.
Egerton, J. *Hogarth's 'Marriage à la Mode'*, London: The National Gallery, 1997.
Paulson, R. *The Art of Hogarth*, London: Phaidon, 1975.
Scull, C. *The Soane Hogarths*, London: Sir John Soane Museum/ Trefoil
    Publications, 1991.
Uglow, J. *Hogarth, A Life and a World*, London: Faber, 1997.

Three useful books relating to the literature discussed in this chapter are:

Battestin, M.C. *Henry Fielding. A Life*, London: Routledge, 1989.
Hampden J. (ed.), *Eighteenth Century Plays*, London, Dent, 1928, which
    includes *A Beggar's Opera, Tom Thumb* and Colman and Garrick's *The
    Clandestine Marriage*, based on Hogarth's *Marriage à la Mode*.
Varey, S. *Joseph Andrews. A Satire of Modern Times*, Boston, Twayne, 1990;

6   The image of childhood:

variations on a Blakean theme

Introduction: the innocent and experienced spectator

Figure 6.1   William Blake, *The Good and Evil Angels Struggling for Possession of a Child* (1793/94), Cecil Higgins Art Gallery, Bedford, watercolour.

William Blake painted *The Good and Evil Angels Struggling for Possession of a Child* (Figure 6.1) in about 1793/94. The good angel, standing in the clouds, sweeps a young child beyond the grasp of the evil angel, shackled at the ankle. The image is full of 'contraries' (to use Blake's word), oppositions which signify the struggle: light and dark figures, freedom and bondage, the sun and the flames. The figures incline inwards, challenging each other; where they overlap, the evil hand is blanched by goodness. It is tempting to read the image, there-fore, as a statement about the human condition: the superiority of good in the eternal spiritual battle. But little is solely as it seems in Blake. The picture is contemporary with his *Songs of Innocence and Experience* which show 'two Contrary States of the Human Soul'; and 'contraries' for Blake generate 'progression'. In his broader philosophical system good and evil need each other. 'Good is passive and obeys Reason; Evil is active springing from Energy' (Blake 1793/1956: 181). No other English artist explores this dualism with Blake's rigour and passion. Blake's 'contraries', reflected in his images of childhood in the 1790s, suggest a framework with which to consider visual and literary representations of the child during the eighteenth and nineteenth centuries. As will become apparent, the oppositions are all variations on the Blakean theme.

The questions I will be addressing are:

- What are the main 'representations' during this 200-year period where Blake stands at the mid-point?
- What are the principal influences affecting the construction of these images?
- Do the verbal and visual arts conceptualise childhood in similar or different ways?

Three mutually influential factors affecting how painters and writers interpreted the child and conveyed childhood experiences will recur. They concern ideology, artistic conventions and money. A word about each.

In her book on nineteenth-century women writers on childhood, Penny Brown remarks upon the 'preconceived, philosophical or literary ideologies and models' that permeate such literature. As will emerge, a similar claim can be made about the painters of childhood. I want to define ideology, then, in the present context, as a set of ideas and presuppositions that feed the need, in the adult artist, 'to believe in and endorse a certain mythology of childhood' (Brown 1993: 8).

Second, we need to pay attention to the conventions of the art forms and cultural practices through which these representations of the child are mediated and expressed. Portraiture or poetry for children, for example, are both subject to the accepted characteristics of their particular medium.

And third, there is money – the commercial appeal of the work to its intended audience. William Hogarth and John Newbery in the 1740s; Dickens and the social realist genre painters a century later – all were conscious of the need to earn a living. Art and economics are rarely apart. In a period which regarded explicit sexual imagery as unacceptable, the art market became increasingly aware of the saleability of the imagery of childhood, both for its sentimental appeal and, in Victorian times, as a covert expression of sexuality.

Indeed, it is only in the 1990s that we have been made aware of what might be called in this context the innocent and experienced spectator. For childhood has become both an unstable concept and a 'hot' issue. In recent years, the care and education of children has been conducted against a background of unprecedented public discussion of child abuse, the treatment of paedophilia, even of child murder. We are nervous and uncertain about childhood, not least because we sense that it is a changing, ill-defined concept. A century ago, physical maturation, social independence and economic power all came several years later than is the case with today's children. But, if childhood *now* is an embattled, attenuated phase of human life, childhood *then* was far from the protected period of innocence that those who advocate a return to Victorian values would have us believe. Visual representations of nineteenth-century childhood were, at best, ambivalent images. For all her technical accomplishment, Kate Greenaway's 'designer children' are invariably bland elements in a larger composition; and, within a year of *Under The Window* (Greenaway 1878) being praised by Austin Dobson for its vision of 'clear-eyed, soft-faced, happy-hearted childhood' (Dobson in Holme 1976: 7), Millais's ambiguous *Cherry Ripe* (1879) (Figure 6.2) had begun its transition from art gallery to advertising image, courtesy of Pears' Soap Company.

At first glance, a cute little girl with big eyes and the hint of a smile; an oversized mob-cap, long wavy hair, clasped hands and dangling feet. In all, a charming if sentimental picture of innocence. But, is she? Kinkaid (1992) and Higonnet (1998) have taught us to interrogate such images; and N. Walter, reviewing the latter book and drawing upon Polhemus (1995) and Reis (1992), has posed the question: Is she angel or sex kitten? (*Guardian* 9 June 1998). Her reading of the image directs us to 'look at the positioning of the girl's hands in their black fingerless gloves, the fingers pressed together into a fleshy line just

Figure 6.2　John Everett Millais, *Cherry Ripe* (1879), Unilever Historical Archives, Port Sunlight, oil on canvas

below the black triangle of her wrists in the very centre of her lap. Don't they look bizarrely, and surely deliberately, like female genitalia?' Perhaps the experienced eye of the Victorian adman saw something in the image that the innocent eye of the art lover had overlooked. Certainly, the saleability of this image is not merely that Millais was here consciously adapting a familiar painting by an earlier master (*Portrait of Penelope Boothby* (1788) by Sir Joshua Reynolds), in the knowledge of its market appeal (Higonnet 1998: 47), but his adaptation raises altogether more uncomfortable issues, challenging us to question what we bring to the image as well as what is embedded within it. Spectatorship is no more innocent than the object of its attention.

I will return to these factors at the end in drawing some tentative conclusions. First, in order to contextualise the images, some remarks about the invention of the idea and about the superordinate image from which all others derive.

In Chapter 2 of his classic if controversial book, *Centuries of Childhood* (1962), Philippe Ariès argues that the 'discovery' of childhood as a discrete phase of existence came about as a result of the developing notion of the *family* as distinct from the community life of the Middle Ages. He has been taken to task for his portrayal of the unfeeling 'brutal parents of the past' by Keith Thomas (1989: 45–57) among others (hence the controversy); but, his account of how the essential 'difference' of children can be diagnosed and recognised in pictorial representation remains valuable and, so far as I am aware, unchallenged. Ariès discusses several strands in this history from the thirteenth century onwards, the three most significant of which are the child portrait, the *putti*, and, above all, the infant Jesus.

Ariès sees 'the new taste for the portrait' in the fifteenth century as an indication that 'children were emerging from the anonymity in which their slender chance of survival had maintained them' (p. 40); but it is not until the seventeenth century that portraits of children on their own appear in the work of Rubens, Van Dyck and Franz Hals. More recently, Simon Schama (1987, especially Chapter 7) has written a fascinating account of the role of children in seventeenth-century Dutch art and culture; and there has long been the belief that the appearance of the mortal child in English art in the work of Hogarth derived, in part, from the pictures of his Dutch predecessors, particularly those of Jan Steen.

As for images of the immortal child, the *putti* (they are usually present in numbers), those winged infants commonly found in Renaissance and baroque art, they feature both as angels in religious painting and as attendants of Cupid, the messengers of profane love in secular works. They prefigure another aspect of the image of childhood – the naked child, a convention that Ariès sees as running from the ornamental, decorative *putti* of the Renaissance, through to modern 'artistic portraits' in the photographer's studio (Ariès 1962: 46).

Unlike the *putti* who might signify sacred or profane love, the infant Jesus is a consistent and pervasive icon, the model (explicitly or covertly) for all the little children in the history of Western art. Either alone, or portrayed with his mother, the image of the Christ-child is imitated, adapted, subverted and exploited in a variety of ways in the eighteenth and nineteenth centuries, as we shall see. But, as Ariès demonstrates, the evolution of the idea of the 'holy childhood' had a long history in medieval and Renaissance art. It took time for Virgin and Child pictures to extend beyond the frontiers of religious iconography but, by the seventeenth century, the lay imagery of childhood had detached itself from its religious origins and the child is increasingly seen as a character in anecdotal genre painting (Ariès 1962: 36).

In their different ways, all three of these images of childhood became adapted and domesticated into the paintings of subsequent centuries.

So far, I have said nothing about literary images. This is because, in literature, childhood is an even more strictly delimited concept than in visual art – which is not to say that children did not appear in pre-eighteenth-century literature; they did. But their appearance in mainstream literature – in Shakespeare and his contemporaries, for example – is merely incidental and usually for the purposes of the amused indulgence of the adult world except when the demands of history (the little princes in *Richard III*) or tragedy (MacDuff's son in *Macbeth*) occasionally require a different role. Or again, in juvenile literature, perusal of, say, the first fifty pages of the Opies' *The Oxford Book of Children's Verse* yields little that, in the editors' own words, is not either 'didactic or divine'; and even those verses that are affectionately addressed to particular young people are invariably either admonitory or attempts by their authors to ingratiate themselves with the parents (Opie and Opie 1973: viii–ix). The mortal child is seen in such verses through a lexical barricade whose key words are 'chastise', 'counsel', 'warn', 'control', 'exhortation', and so on; the immortal child, in the figure of the infant Jesus, is held up as the image of perfection, nowhere more delicately than in Robert Herrick's poem:

A Child's Present

Go pretty child, and bear this flower
Unto thy little Saviour;
And tell him, by that bud now blown,
He is the Rose of Sharon[1] known:
When thou hast said so, stick it there
Upon His bib, or Stomacher:
And tell Him (for good handsel[2] too)
That thou has brought a whistle new
Made of a clean straight oaten reed,
To charm His cries (at time of need):
Tell Him, for coral,[3] thou hast none;

---

1   See Song of Solomon 2:1
2   A gift bringing good luck
3   Polished coral for baby's teething.

> But if thou hadst, He should have one;
> But poor thou art, and known to be
> Even as moneyless, as He.
> Lastly, if thou canst win a kiss
> From those mellifluous[4] lips of His;
> Then never take a second on,[5]
> To spoil the first impression
> > (Opie and Opie 1973: 30)

Herrick's poem suggests that the image of childhood, through its very vulnerability and fragility, provides a powerful vehicle through which to concentrate the tension between sensuality and delicacy, between the sinful and the pure. This tension manifests itself in different ways in representations of childhood during the eighteenth and nineteenth centuries. I will consider these images as three oppositional pairs.

Constructions of childhood

The polite child

Hogarth's *The Graham Children* (1742) (Figure 6.3) was painted just two years before the publication which, Harvey Darton (1982: 1) claims, marks the start of commercial children's literature – John Newbery's *Little Pretty Pocket-Book* in 1744. It is reasonable to assume therefore that, as all involved were then living in London, these children of a wealthy and educated apothecary at Chelsea Hospital might come to know of Newbery's book. *The Graham Children* has been described as 'one of the definitive accounts of eighteenth century childhood' (Bindman 1981: 143). Certainly, the ages, personalities and preoccupations of these children are all differentiated with a conscious psychological precision that is new to English art. Left of centre, the eldest girl subtly reflects the contradictions of adolescence as her self-conscious, motherly demeanour and responsible restraint of the baby in the cart contrast with her tantalising of this youngster with a small bunch of cherries as she alone of the four looks straight out at us. On the right is Richard Robert who succeeded his father as apothecary at Chelsea. He is playing a serinette or bird charmer and his open, innocent face suggests that he thinks that it is this music rather than the cat on the back of his chair that is frightening the finch in the birdcage. Meanwhile, his other sister appears to be dancing, or at least curtseying, to the music. It is all highly theatrical. The children look as if they could be about to take part in a play. They embody Hogarth's declared aims of treating his picture as his stage and having his characters enact 'a dumb show'. (An early

---

4   Sweet as honey
5   i.e. one.

Figure 6.3   William Hogarth, *The Graham Children* (1742), The National Gallery, London, oil on canvas.

example which combines the stage and the conversation piece is Hogarth's *Children Playing 'The Indian Emperor' before an Audience*, (1731–2). These 'polite children' are not the static, stuffy portrayals of so many commissioned portraits of the time; they are animated by narrative incident and by the life that comes from the depiction, particularly, of their eyes and clothes. This richly painted group portrait has many details to admire from the highly elaborate, superior go-kart to the portrayal of one of the most famous cats in English art. Yet not only is youthful innocence inscribed in the painting by the music and the baby's gesture towards the fruit, but so, too, is its transitoriness by the inclusion of the clock surmounted by the golden figure of Cupid holding a scythe. In all, then, a representation of childhood which, while remaining within the conventions of commissioned portraiture and earning Hogarth his fee, contains none the less a statement about the temporary nature of childhood. An added poignancy is lent to this idea when it is realised that Thomas, the baby, had died before Hogarth completed the picture (Holdsworth and Crossley 1992: 104). Yet, the overall image remains positive and optimistic. Part of the quiet humour of the painting lies in the depiction of how children amuse themselves; part of it also lies in the sense that this balanced grouping of figures, typical of the adult conversation piece, is on the point of collapse under the pressure of childhood energies. In short,

Hogarth's ability to combine amusement with a moralising or educative purpose – so characteristic of his prints and 'progresses' – is just beneath the surface here, too.

It is a combination that John Newbery shared. The advertisement for *The Little Pretty Pocket-Book* states that it is 'intended for the Instruction and Amusement of Little Master Tommy and Pretty Miss Polly'. Indeed, Harvey Darton develops his whole enterprise from this basis when he says that

> the confusion between 'instruction' and 'amusement', and the struggle about them in the minds of purveyors of both (in Newbery's, for instance), are to no small extent the real subject of this book.
>
> (Harvey Darton 1982: 6)

For those wishing to build up a more sophisticated image of childhood from this period than is currently available, a fruitful area of research would be to pursue the relationships between the implied child readers of Newbery's book and those who constituted its actual readership and to compare them with the children constructed in paintings and novels of the same period. To little Master Tommy and Pretty Miss Polly, and the four children of the Grahams, can be added Joseph Highmore's *Pamela Telling a Nursery Tale*, one of his twelve illustrations of Richardson's novel, along with a host of portraits by lesser artists, all of which help to give the mid-eighteenth-century child its image of politeness (Einberg 1987). If any one factor unites such variety it is that, in different ways, they all celebrate the idea of the family.

But this image needs to be read against its opposite.

The impolite child

Hogarth's street children subvert the polite world. The boy peeing on the ground to the wide-eyed amazement of the little girl, thus contributing his own splash of pollution to the picture of *The Enraged Musician* (1741), is one of the many ragamuffins who inhabit the crowded canvases of his anecdotal series. A measure of the innovative shock such images represent can be gained by comparing them with the role of the child in contemporary history painting. Four English *putti* (Prudence, Justice, Temperance and Fortitude) form part of the decorated ceiling of the Aldermen's Court Room, Guildhall, London. *Putti*, of course, don't pee! While Hogarth's father-in-law, Sir James Thornhill, was painting these examples of 'chubby pink infant sausage meat' (to borrow Schama's description of Rubens' *putti*), Hogarth's children appear in a profusion of roles that is not seen in literature until Dickens and Mayhew. These children are not the subjects of polite art; nor are they the English equivalent of the knowing, worldly kids of seventeenth-century Dutch portraiture – children who seem to talk back to the viewer, often with a challenge in their gaze (Schama 1987: 546). Hogarth's children are socially integrated as part of a larger scene. I have selected four to illustrate the range of roles; they will take us rapidly nearer to the point where impoliteness becomes an inadequate description – to the need to acknowledge the image of childhood as a means of representing the human potential for cruelty and wickedness.

But first, the more light-hearted image of a bad-tempered footboy on his reluctant way to church. In 'Morning', the first painting of Hogarth's sequence *The Four Times of the Day* (1736), the child owes something to Shakespeare's 'Whining Schoolboy, with his satchel, / And shining morning face, creeping like snail / Unwillingly to School … ' as he trails grumpily behind the prim and proper figure of his mistress on her way to Covent Garden Church and who, in turn, was to become the model for Bridget Allworthy in Fielding's *Tom Jones* (1749: Book 1, Chapter 11). The humour here is that of innocent entertainment; by contrast, the career of the young, delinquent charity-schoolboy Tom Nero in *The Four Stages of Cruelty* (1751) (Figure 6.4) is a grim indictment of the human capacity for violence driven by explicit moral and educational aims.

Tom Nero and his cronies are shown torturing animals in the street outside the school. These incidents are more than the thoughtless cruelty of young children; the hunched, tense pose of Tom Nero, his back to the viewer cloaking his expression as he maltreats the dog, presents an image of violence that is sadistic and deliberate. This representation of childhood was engraved specifically, Hogarth tells us, 'in the hope of, in some degree, correcting the barbarous treatment of animals'. Its cruelty is enhanced by Tom Nero's insensitivity to another

Figure 6.4   William Hogarth, The First Stage of Cruelty 1751, The British Museum, London, engraving

boy's attempt to bargain for the dog's release by the offer of food; its warning is made more ominous by the gallows chalked on the wall beside him, prefiguring his eventual hanging at Tyburn.

The children of Hogarth's *Marriage à la Mode* (1745), are employed on more sophisticated satirical business. In *The Countess's Levée* (Chapter 5, Plate IV) we see two black figures, the one an older youth serving coffee to the guests, the other a young boy gleefully pointing to the horns of Actaeon, and sharing with us the joke of incipient cuckoldry in the affair that is about to take place between the Countess and the debonair lawyer, Silvertongue. Hogarth's satire problematises the conventional image of the polite child with this elaborately costumed black boy in the role of servant, or the even more demeaning one of plaything. This child is part of the necessary furniture of the fashionable marriage to be paraded at social gatherings such as this and treated on a par with the household pets. The boy has a complex dual role: not only does he make contact with the implied viewer across the proscenium boundary, as it were, to signal the narrative developments and orchestrate the tone in which they should be read; he also embodies an implicit reproof to a society whose prosperity was founded on the slave trade. David Dabydeen (1987: 88) has effectively highlighted the ironic commercial juxtaposition in the period of trade in young black slaves rubbing shoulders with trade in what Hogarth called 'old black masters' – imports of continental paintings which were then in vogue and of which there are examples on the walls. Dabydeen puts it tartly: 'Buying blacks was as much an investment as buying art' and argues that Hogarth was aware of such ironies (Dabydeen 1987: 130–2). Polite society is invaded by such impolite satire – and all through the inclusion of an apparently insignificant child!

The baby's comforter, hanging on the back of the Countess's chair in this Levée scene (Chapter 5, Plate IV) , provides the link with the last picture in the series where the Countess's little girl appears for the only time (Chapter 5, Plate VI). She is a sad, pathetic figure, again with a satirical role that problematises the notion of politeness: for she is the progeny of an arranged marriage between the daughter of a *nouveau riche* merchant, who is cutting his losses on the deal by retrieving the gold wedding ring from his dying daughter's finger, and a syphilitic aristocrat whose inheritance has been passed on to the next generation with tragic consequences. The black spot on the girl's face and the heavy leg-iron create an image of disfigured and crippled childhood with which Hogarth closes his satire of fashionable marriage.

The street children of the engravings and the seemingly more privileged children of the fashionable world offer images of childhood that are sustained by different values from those of polite art. They mostly imply destructive or distorting forces. Tom Nero and the children of *Marriage à la Mode* become the symbols of anti-family values in opposition to the comfortable celebration of family that polite portraiture expresses.

We might expect a parallel literary image of the impolite child in Fielding's novels from the same decade but, in fact, he has little to say about the childhoods of Jonathan Wild, Joseph Andrews or Tom Jones. Fielding seems uninterested in the depiction of childhood: he is content to move rapidly from the oddities of Tom Jones's birth to his teenage years, glossing over his childhood in a couple of sentences (*Tom Jones* , Book 3, Chapter 1), and telling his readers that he has 'left them a space of twelve years' to fill in for themselves. This is another of those Iserian 'indeterminacy gaps' of which the early novelists are so fond. And it was to be followed a decade or so later by the greatest shaggy dog story of them all, *Tristram Shandy* (1762), in which the child-figure is used as a running joke in the repeated images of Tristram's birth as Sterne makes successive attempts to get his hero born.

Towards the end of the eighteenth century the polite/impolite images were superseded by a more dramatically polarised opposition: the innocent and the sinful. Of course, this had existed in one form or another in occasional writings about childhood for some time, but it was only with the shift of sensibilities that heralded romanticism that the child became icon. My second pairing, then, concerns 'little angels' and little devils'. It opposes the child from whom we should learn with the child who needs to be taught its lessons.

The innocent child

Such a description dictates the painting with which to begin: Reynolds' *The Age of Innocence* (1788). The child is now the subject in its own right. She is neither the conventional piece of family portraiture (even though the little girl is Reynolds' own great niece), nor part of social life around her; she has been elevated above mere documentary to become the symbol of an idea. She is presented to us fresh-faced, auburn-haired, bare-foot, fingers loosely entwined before her, looking to the side as if her interest has just been caught by something in the landscape in which Reynolds has placed her. The plain white dress and simple bow in her hair could scarcely be more different from the 'fashionable dressing up of children as little adults' that Peter Coveney reminds us of (Coveney 1967: 43–4).

And what has happened to the *putti*? In Reynolds' *Angels' Heads* (1787) (Figure 6.5) – all pictures of 4-year-old Frances Isabella Gordon – they have lost their lumpy bodies, slimmed their chubby cheeks, grown and blow-dried their hair, and had a wing-transplant from the ankles to some fairly arbitrary location below the ear. Moreover, they are not attendant upon some higher being but on their own, arranged in a harmonious circle, trailing clouds of glory.

These transformations in the portrait and the *putti* signal the main historical shift in representations of childhood. Together with the appearance of Blake's *Songs of Innocence and Experience* and Wordsworth's poems in *The Lyrical Ballads*, both within the last decade of the eighteenth century, we are presented with something new: the child as symbol. Blake's 'innocence' and Wordsworth's 'natural piety' turn conventional Christian imagery around: original sin is confronted by original innocence.

Blake took an uncompromisingly oppositional stance towards eighteenth-

Figure 6.5   Sir Joshua Reynolds, *Angels' Heads*, (1787), The Tate Gallery, London, oil on canvas.

century rationalism and its manifestations in the institutions of his time. The innocent child was the central symbol of this opposition. As the introductory poem to the *Songs of Innocence* makes clear, both the inspiration of and the audience for this sequence are defined in terms of the child.

The often remarked 'deceptive simplicity' of the poems stems as much from the way words are laid on the page like the clear, pure notes of a musical score, as it does from the symbolism of their content. Read aloud (as 'songs', especially, must be) innocence invests the clean structural lines of the poems with a beguiling aural geometry, heard with particular clarity in, say, 'The Echoing Green' or 'Spring'. The poems come alive with all the robustness of children: each has its own autonomous identity. This morphological strength of the poems is complemented by their metaphorical power. It is clear, too, that as Heather Glen has shown, Blake owed much to earlier literary traditions and to the conventions in which they were cast, not least to children's verse. Writing about how contemporary readers would have viewed the two sequences, *Innocence* and *Experience*, she identifies no fewer than six types of verse:

> Some [poems] could be read as *children's hymns* ('The Lamb', 'The Divine Image', 'The Shepherd'). Some are more like the poems about *childish experience* such as Foxton and Watts had written, and the Lambs and the

Taylors were to write ('A Cradle Song', 'The Echoing Green', 'Laughing Song', 'The Schoolboy'). Some, like an increasing number of poems written for children in these years, deal with *social problems* (the two 'Chimney Sweeper' poems, the two 'Holy Thursday's', 'The Little Black Boy', 'London'): others bear more resemblance to straightforward *moral fables* ('The Clod & the Pebble', 'A Poison Tree'). There are *verses about birds and animals*, of which there was a whole sub-genre in the children's books of the late eighteenth century ('The Tyger', 'The Blossom', 'The Fly'). And there are others which seem closer to the *emblem verse* which Bunyan had emulated, and of which Newbery had published a popular collection ('Ah! Sunflower', 'The Sick Rose', 'The Lilly').

(Glen 1983: 14, my italics)

A poem/painting which is perhaps nearest to the last type than to any of the others is 'Infant Joy' (Figure 6.6). A delicate text, largely monosyllabic (only three words with even two syllables), with the repeated vocabulary of a celebratory song, the whole compris-ing a series of transparent statements about the joy of naming a new life. Blake situates this seemingly innocent verbal structure within a strongly delineated, vividly coloured painting in order to explore this concept of 'new life': the new poem is thus enclosed within the body of the painting like the child in the womb. Poem and painting express the concept of 'new life' both structurally and symbolically. For Blake includes two crimson flowers on the plant: one, an unopened bud symbolising the virgin's womb; the other and dominant image is the open flower, the impregnated womb, in which the new born child lies in its mother's lap. Facing them stands a winged messenger with hands outstretched making the scene an 'annunciation'. The poem/painting of 'Infant Joy' encapsulates the central theme of the *Songs*: an affirmation that Innocence is the state of oneness between the Creator and all created things and that the state of childhood is its essential expression.

Where Blake opposes the joy of Innocence with the negative, corrupting power of human nature and society in the *Songs of Experience*, Wordsworth concentrates the whole dialectic into a single poem which stands as the icon for the nineteenth-century idea of childhood – his 'Ode. Intimations of Immortality from Recollections of Early Childhood'. The early stanzas lament the loss of the visionary power of childhood; the later ones argue a theory of human growth to explain the loss. But the vision of innocence is more convincingly portrayed than are the consolations of maturity with which time replaces it. A disingenuous advocacy of 'the philosophic mind' cannot disguise the regret and pessimism which accompany the loss of innocence:

Heaven lies about us in our infancy!
Shades of the prison-house begin to close
Upon the Growing Boy.

Figure 6.6 William Blake, *Infant Joy*, the British Museum, London, hand-coloured copper-plate print

None the less, for Wordsworth, childhood is the key to the full organic develop-ment of the human mind. Here, as in 'Tintern Abbey' and 'The Prelude', he reflects upon his own experiences as a means of exploring the concept of child-hood and , by extension, of establishing general principles of human nature. The child is central to the 'wisdom' he sought to express: the famous epigraph to the 'Ode' makes this clear:

> The Child is father of the Man;
> And I could wish my days to be
> Bound each to each by natural piety.

The shift of consciousness located in the work of Blake and Wordsworth was neither as sudden as this brief account might suggest, nor solely the result of two, albeit influential, geniuses arriving at the same time. Both built upon earlier literary traditions: Blake upon children's verse and Wesley's hymns; Wordsworth on magazine verse (Glen 1983). Both reflected the wider changes of awareness that were taking place in which the significance of childhood experience was acknowledged. John Constable testified to the importance of his 'careless boyhood … on the banks of the Stour' which made him a painter, just as overtly as Wordsworth tells us that the Lake District made him a poet (see Chapter 7).

But what is meant by the innocence of childhood? Certainly its representa-tion in painting and poetry is more than the mere absence of sexuality. In Blake, especially, candour, spontaneity, freedom from routine are celebrated. Such qualities give the innocent child an image of unencumbered honesty; by contrast, the concept of the sinful child is delimited and constrained from birth.

The sinful child

If the concept of *original innocence* derived from the writings of Rousseau and the Romantic poets and is reflected in the work of the painters, that of *original sin* stemmed from the Calvinist belief in innate depravity which retained its power in England through the Evangelical revival well into the nineteenth century. 'Strict discipline, constant watchfulness for sin, the early breaking of the child's will and absolute obedience to parents' (Brown 1993: 6) were the watchwords. *Pilgrim's Progress* (1678, 1684) and James Janeway's *A Token for Children: Being an exact account of the conversion, holy and exemplary lives, and joyful deaths of several young children* (1671–2) remained popular (Harvey Darton 1982: 53). For Janeway children were, in his memorable phrases, 'Brands of Hell', 'by Nature, Children of Wrath'. Yet, as Pattison argues, Janeway is unusual not so much for the extremities of these sound-bites on original sin, but for his insistence that children are capable of rationally understanding and correcting their fallen condition (Pattison 1978: 136). The child figure in chil-dren's literature continued to be used to reinforce Protestant doctrine – in Janeway and Mrs Sherwood with violent enthusiasm; in Isaac Watts, Hannah

Moore, and Ann and Jane Taylor with relative mildness born of the belief that education via good examples would keep children on the straight and narrow. Pattison (1978: 139) and Brown (1993: 40ff.) both show how children's literature softened during the nineteenth century, 'the excessive piety and explicit dogmatism of Janeway ... [giving] way to the subtler, more implicitly doctrinaire technique of telling moral stories like Maria Edgeworth's (Pattison 1978: 139). Later child figures in the work of Lewis Carroll, R.L. Stevenson and Christina Rossetti continue this process, presenting us – in the case of Alice – not so much with representations in which the child is instructed about the folly of the world, as with the child who merely observes these follies (Pattison 1978: 151).

How is the sinful child represented in visual art? Hogarth, as we have seen, presented the cruel unfeeling capacity of childhood in the brutal imagery of Tom Nero – an unidealised, uncompromising picture, protesting at human wickedness and using shock tactics in an effort to correct and reform. While the tradition of graphic satire is a strong one through the eighteenth and nineteenth century (George 1967) the portrayal of children in wicked roles is rare. The emphasis, in painting, certainly, is not upon sinful acts but upon didactic situations; upon prevention rather than cure.

William Mulready's *A Mother Teaching Her Child* (1859) (Figure 6.7) was exhibited with a line from Pope's *Moral Essays*, 'Just as the twig is bent, the Tree's inclined', indicating that the mother's influence upon the child was seen as crucial to its subsequent moral and spiritual development. The mother is poised, calm, serene, with downcast eyes, a governess's hair-do and clad in a simple dress; the naked child is alert and attentive, hands clasped and lips apart, as if repeating a prayer. The iconography is unmistakable: this is the Madonna and Child dressed up as a domestic scene of mother and baby from the 1850s. Mulready is deliberately drawing upon conventional representations of the Virgin and the infant Jesus, on symbolism such as the doves and upon an idyllic pastoral background reminiscent of Renaissance Italy in order to create an image of harmony and piety. There is no wagging finger in this sort of didacticism; rather the mother's hands are supportive, enclosing, part of the nurture that she stands for. The fact that one's response to this painting may well include the unpleasant taste of mid-Victorian religiosity, of an artist exploiting the most fundamental of mother and child images and idealising it to the extent that this 'lesson' appears a piece of meretricious symbolism, leads me to my third pair of representations: the authentic child and the sanitised child.

The distinction I wish to make here is between those painters and writers who created images which tell the condition of childhood as it was, as opposed to those who presented merely sanitised or sentimentalised pictures. Art always mediates the realities it purports to portray ; this interpretative characteristic is a particular problem in reading works of painters and writers who are commonly referred to under the heading of social realism. Victorian England had these in plenty and the child and childhood experiences became prime topics for both exploration and exploitation.

Figure 6.7 William Mulready, *A Mother Teaching Her Child* (1859), The Victoria and Albert Museum, London, oil on canvas.

The authentic child

Victorian England first gained the facts about the condition of its urban poor in the 1840s. Documentation was provided by the *Report of the Commission on the Employment of Young Persons and Children* (1842) and in Henry Mayhew's *London Labour and the London Poor* (first published between October 1849 and December 1850 in a series of 82 pieces in the *Morning Chronicle*). Interpretation came most tellingly in the great novels of this and subsequent decades, notably in Elizabeth Gaskell's *Mary Barton* (1848), Disraeli's *Sybil* (1845) and, of course, in the novels of Dickens. *David Copperfield* (1849–50) is a major portrayal of childhood experiences but, like those other accounts in *Jane Eyre* (1847) and *Mill on the Floss* (1860), it is a scarcely disguised exploration into self; all are novels that diagnose and, to an extent, exorcise the writers' own childhoods.

If we seek the authentic child, these autobiographical novels are best put aside in favour of the social novels of Disraeli and Mrs Gaskell. For, as Coveney (1967: 92) argues, the overriding factor governing the literature of the child from the 1830s was the condition of children in society. The newly publicised image of the victimised, exploited child of early Victorian England did not sit comfortably with the romantic inheritance of innocence and frailty. This is nowhere more apparent than in Disraeli's novel, inspired directly by the 1842 *Report*. In 1843 and 1844 Disraeli travelled widely in the industrial north; in 1845 *Sybil* was published and drew directly upon both the *Report* and his own observations. While the characters of Dandy Mick and Devilsdust are exaggerated creations required to further his polemic, there is no doubt about the social protest that is expressed in his description of these child workers emerging from the mines at twilight:

> See, too, these emerge from the bowels of the earth! Infants of four and five years of age, many of them girls, pretty and still soft and timid; entrusted with the fulfilment of most responsible duties, and the nature of which entails on them the necessity of being the earliest to enter the mine and the latest to leave it. Their labour indeed is not severe, for that would be impossible, but it is passed in darkness and in solitude. They endure that punishment which philosophical philanthropy has invented for the direst criminals, and which those criminals deem more terrible than the death for which it is substituted. Hour after hour elapses, and all that reminds the infant trappers of the world they have quitted and that which they have joined, is the passage of the coal-wagons for which they open the air-doors of the galleries, and on keeping which doors constantly closed, except at this moment of passage, the safety of the mine and the lives of the persons employed in it entirely depend.

Disraeli continues with a biting comment about a painting we have already seen:

Sir Joshua, a man of genius and a courtly artist, struck by the seraphic coun-
tenance of Lady Alice Gordon, when a child of very tender years, painted
the celestial visage in various attitudes on the same canvas, and styled the
group of heavenly faces – guardian angels!

We would say to some great master of the pencil, Mr. Landseer, or Mr.
Etty, go thou to the little trappers and do likewise!

(Disraeli, *Sybil*, Book 3, Chapter 1)

While we know what Disraeli means, what he really lacks is not the painter of
ponies, puppies and *The Stag at Bay*, but the painter of the *Black Paintings* and
The Disasters of War. Where was the English Goya?

Of course, authenticity is not confined to portrayals of the destitute and the
victimised but the fact remains that such children dominate the literary images
of childhood of this period.

What of the authentic child in painting? Sara Holdsworth (1992)
remarks:

> Images of children working down mines or in factories, the horrors of
> which were exposed and publicised by the 1842 Childrens' Employment
> Commission, are rare outside engravings used to illustrate magazine
> features. Such children are absent from paintings. Instead, artists concen-
> trated on the type of work which would be most visible and familiar to
> their urban, middle-class audience: images abound of chimney sweeps,
> flower sellers, crossing sweepers and boot blacks.
>
> (Holdsworth and Crossley 1992: 54)

William Macduff's *Shaftesbury, or Lost and Found* (1863), a tribute to the
philanthropy of the 7th Earl of Shaftesbury, is one of the best known.
Images of rural childhoods were similarly romanticised, for example, in
paintings by Linnell (*Wildflower Gatherers*) and Collins (*Rustic Civility*),
whose titles alone suggest preciousness and sentimentality; but occasionally
one encounters a picture with something of the authenticity of the novelists.
Frederic Shields' watercolour, *One of our Breadwatchers* (1866) (Figure 6.8)
illustrates the exploitation of child labour in the countryside. Julian Treuherz
comments:

> It shows the practice, observed by the artist at Porlock, Somersetshire, of
> leaving children out all day in the snow to scare the birds from the newly-
> sown corn, using wooden rattles. The children sat in shelters rudely
> constructed of gorse and hurdles, and heated by tiny fires. On one occasion
> Shields 'worked for three days in a snow-covered ploughed field sharing the
> privations with his little model and many other boys and girls endured for
> the poorest wage'.
>
> (Treuherz 1987: 38)

Figure 6.8   Frederic Shields, *One of Our Breadwatchers* (1866), Manchester City Art
Galleries, watercolour.

The title, as Treuherz goes on to say, is a pointed comment in itself: its plural
form implicates everyone who eats daily bread in the child's exploitation. But
such images are rare. More often than not exploitation took another form: not
the portrayal of the child used and abused by society, but the exploitation of
childhood by the artists.

The sanitised child

Child-appeal was not new in Victorian times but it was then that it reached its
height. To back-track for a moment, perhaps the best-known examples from the
previous century are Gainsborough's so-called 'fancy pictures', pictures of poor
children set in wild landscapes which date from the 1780s. *Girl with Pigs* (1782),
Girl with Dog and Pitcher (1785) and *A Peasant Girl Gathering Faggots in a Wood*
(1782), each show their child subjects as isolated, wistful figures. The peasant
girl in this latter picture, like the others, presents an idealised version of life for
the poor child of the time. Our attention is drawn to the sad beauty of her face
with its averted gaze, her tumbling ringlets and naked shoulders, all depicted
with heightened detail and colouring compared with the loosely painted clothes
and landscape. The impression she creates is what was described at the time as
'that pathetic simplicity which is the most powerful appeal to the feelings'

(Quoted in Holdsworth and Crossley 1992: 107). Gainsborough's 'fancy pictures' were highly popular; this was, after all, the age of sensibility and such images were carefully constructed to meet public taste. The significance of the subject derives not from any particular event but from the quality of sentiment in the girl's demeanour. Yet she is not painted from imagination alone; Gainsborough used specific studio models, urchins he came across in the street or country lanes whose clothes were appropriately romanticised and who were generally posed with some telling 'prop' such as the bundle of sticks in this painting (Kalinsky 1995: 23; Postle 1998: 14). Emblematic tasks, such as the wood gathering here, it has been argued, signify that the subject should be regarded as one of the deserving rather than the idle poor (Barrell 1980: 35–8) – a discrimination that gathered strength and poignancy in the nineteenth century and can be seen, for example, in Thomas Faed's *The Poor: the Poor Man's Friend* (1867). If Gainsborough's peasant girls give us sanitised portraiture, Faed offers the acceptable face of social realism. The picture shows the labouring poor in the fisherman and his family at the door of their cottage, and the ragged, begging poor in the figures of the blind man and the little girl – a distinction that was written in to the Poor Law (Walvin 1984: 84–9) and that, as the formulation of the title implies, Faed is gently opposing. He does so through softening the imagery of poverty. There is no threat, nothing to fear from these beggars: the quiet dignity of the blind man is balanced by the caring maternalism of the fisherman's wife, while the fisherman himself is flanked by two children whose portrayal suggests they should be regarded and treated equally. They share the same solemnity, their faces are clear and blemish-free, their hair is tidy and neatly parted; they are distinguished only by their clothes – otherwise, Faed implies, these children have an equal right to our concern. Ironically, this cleaned-up image of poverty is a means of making us think about the condition of the poor by engaging our sympathies without risking alienating us with too blatant a social message.

Two ubiquitous images of Victorian art and literature are the dying child and the orphan child. Dickens' description of the death of Little Nell is merely his most affecting and memorable one; in his novels the child mortality rate is high. So it is in the popular poetry of the time, with George Sims' 'Billy's Rose' perhaps narrowly edging out Edward Farmer's 'Little Jim' as the most mawkish. Paintings of sick and dying children are equally common, one of the most celebrated being Luke Fildes's *The Doctor* (1891). Orphans, too, are plentiful from Jane Eyre and Heathcliff to their frequent appearance in children's stories. Penny Brown (1993: 22) describes the orphan as a favourite theme especially among women writers of the time. Another popular painting by Thomas Faed, *The Mitherless Bairn* (1855), unites the literary and painted orphan in that the picture is based on the poem by the Scottish writer, William Thom.

But the child who, above all, demonstrates the three mutually influential factors mentioned earlier (ideology, artistic convention and money) is arguably the most famous of all Victorian child paintings, John Everett Millais's *Bubbles* (1886) (Figure 6.9).

Figure 6.9 John Everett Millais, *Bubbles* (1886), Unilever Historical Archives, Port Sunlight, oil on canvas.

Originally published as a presentation plate with the Christmas number of the *Illustrated London News* in 1887, it was soon turned into an advertisement for Pears' soap – thus giving a fresh and scented meaning to the idea of the sanitised child! The figurative use of soap-bubbles has a long history. As Hall tells us, 'Infants, or *putti*, blowing soap-bubbles symbolise the brevity of life in "Vanitas" pictures and allegories of death' (Hall 1974: 54); and Simon Schama has pointed out the deceptive nature of the soap bubble in Dutch art as it invites 'not merely fascination with its beauty but a poignant foreknowledge of its abrupt end'. He comments:

> By the time that the bubble floated on through the heady stratosphere of Victorian mawkishness, it had not only shed its Renaissance symbolism but actually reversed its sense. Instead of connoting childhood in terms of brevity, poignancy, and doomed grace, it became instead a symbol of its perpetuation of a carefree Peter Pan-like idyll – the never-never land where no bubble pops. ... The Victorian 'Bubbles' – for now there was no distance between the child and his plaything – remained forever uncontaminated by the polluting world.
>
> (Schama 1987: 516)

Millais's *Bubbles* represents the apotheosis of the sanitised child!

Interpreting the image

These representations of childhood indicate that each age reinvents the child in its own image. Historically, my three oppositional pairs have been focused on three decades at intervals of fifty years: the polite/impolite child of the 1740s; the innocent/sinful child of the 1790s; and the authentic/sanitised child of the 1840s. While these decades are commonly regarded as ones of particularly significant activity in art and literature, to pretend that both the categorisation and chronology are wholly susceptible to such tidy formulation is, of course, illusory. Yet, given that the image of childhood is dominated by its aura of holiness, innocence and vulnerability, oppositional readings can help to unpack this stereotype. Pictures of the sanitised child, from Gainsborough's to Millais's, show particularly clearly how painters manipulate the conventions of their medium to produce an image that supports an agreed contemporary mythology of childhood which, in turn, they know has an inherent saleability.

Similarly, while chronology is often a matter of convenience, there is a discernible historical development: the mid-eighteenth-century child is mainly represented within the family or the larger community before being isolated and elevated as a symbol of innocence in the 1790s. And, as the nineteenth century wore on, this symbol itself suffered a steady deterioration. The strong, clear imagery of Blake was eventually replaced by the sentimental child-figures of Victorian genre painting and popular verse. Yet the child as theme and subject proved durable: the interesting distinction in literature and painting lies between those who found in childhood a potent image of growth and understanding, and those who retreated to it as a form of regressive nostalgia (Coveney 1967: 32).

There is evidence, too, in painting in general and in child pictures in particular, that visual art suffered by too close a relationship with literature. Painting is reluctant to show what John Barrell might call the dark side of childhood. As with representations of landscape, so with those of childhood, there is the tendency for the visual image to be a softer, more anodyne one than its literary counterpart. Writing about the so-called 'social realist' painters of the later nineteenth century, Julian Treuherz (1987: 10) argues that 'while the depiction of surface detail may be convincing, the destitution and dirt familiar from written descriptions were usually absent'. Victorian genre paintings owed less to the urgency of the real social problems of the time and more to commercial demands and literary sources – in particular, to the commissioning of artists to provide pictures for the expanding business of illustrated journalism, and to the stimulus of contemporary fiction and poetry which dealt with social issues.

Finally, we must remember, too, that the child paintings of these centuries, whether commissioned for the home of a wealthy patron, like *The Graham Children*, or constructed as a commercial emblem like Millais's *Bubbles*, were usually created in order to please. With the considerable exception of Blake, the image of childhood, in all its manifestations, is generally a construction by adults of the child they want to see. The spectator, whether innocent or experienced, was as responsible for its creation as the artist.

All these issues can be explored in the classroom. Blake's poem-paintings are the place to start. Discussion of *The Good and Evil Angels Struggling for Possession of the Child* (Figure 6.1), as the initial commentary shows, can open up the concept of childhood to conflicting interpretations. *Infant Joy* (Figure 6.6) and *Infant Sorrow* can do the same. As a brief indication of how 17-year-old students respond, here are a few exchanges as three girls, Sally, Jo and Liz, consider a colour reproduction of *Infant Joy*. (I am grateful to Dr Sally Butcher for permission to use these extracts.) The golden radiance in the centre of the flower catches their attention:

Sally:	They're always talking about gold in the Bible and particularly the figures, the figures were actually the first thing I thought of; it's divine and all the colours are like heaven, and because it's also like Jesus' birth.
Jo:	Yeah, it reminds me of the Nativity scene.
Sally:	'Cos it's got the mother, the baby and that angel.
Jo:	And it looks like a halo, well, it *is* an angel 'cos it's got wings and a halo, and the sort of light coming from them, yellow surrounding them.

The colours of heaven, the vocabulary of the Bible, the image of the Virgin and Child all combine to suggest the divinity of the image. Yet, as their discussion continues, the idea of the Nativity is overlaid with other scenes. Their sense of the magical perfection of the sheltered trio of figures evokes the world of fairy-tale and myth: 'I thought they were fairies; they're in a flower', says Liz. The others support this impression, citing *The Sleeping Beauty*, where the prince has to make his way through thorn-laden roses to reach his princess, and *Jack and the Beanstalk*, where Jack has to climb beyond the clouds.

> All these narratives share two aspects: firstly, the realisation of a special, precious realm (the stable, the princess's chamber, the land beyond the clouds) where dreams come true, and secondly, a conflict between good and evil where goodness ultimately triumphs.
>
> (Butcher 1999: 232)

The students' analogies suggest that they have sensed the 'contrairies' within Blake's image: they articulate these explicitly in relation to the shape and colour of the main flower.

Jo:	The petals of the flower sort of enfold and protect the figures, especially this one here.
Liz:	It's almost heart-shaped.
Jo:	Yeah, that's true, it's the colour of a heart, as well.
Sally:	It's more like a pumpkin. *(laughing)* I thought the petals looked like a flame, it's almost like there's a mix between good and evil in it 'cos it's so exuberant, it's touching hell in a way.
Liz:	Actually, the red, yeah.
Jo:	Yes, I know what you mean actually 'cos the plant stems look almost evil in a way.

Petals and flames, the heart-shaped flower and the evil-looking plant stems, protection and threat, heaven and hell – *Infant Joy* takes the students into the complexities of Blake's image of childhood and offers a touchstone against which later images can be read and seen.

There is a wealth of recent and varied resources upon which to draw in order to develop classroom work on the theme of childhood. Mention of two books must suffice:

S. Holdsworth and J. Crossley, *Innocence and Experience. Images of Children in British Art from 1600 to the Present*, Manchester City Art Galleries, 1992.

N. Philip (ed.) *The New Oxford Book of Children's Verse*, Oxford University Press, 1996.

The paintings and poems in these two sources alone offer infinite variations on the Blakean theme and a rich and demanding classroom agenda.

7   Landscape and learning:
Thomson and Wilson; Wordsworth and Constable

The politics of landscape

Landscape is a battlefield. It has been one of the major sites on which two revolutions of art history during the past twenty years have been fought out (Kitson 1994: xii). Significantly, for the present enterprise, both were cross-disciplinary and challenged the assumption that the study of art can be insulated from the culture that produced it; and both were championed largely by historians and critics of literature. In fact, the first was more evolutionary than radical and focused on the study of the sister arts. It was initiated by Hagstrum (1958), taken up by Dixon Hunt (1976/1989), Wendorf (1983) and Heffernan (1985), and concentrated upon the representation of landscape in pre-twentieth-century poetry and painting. The second, reflecting an ideological shift, was a new, radical approach to the study of British art which was concerned with the interaction between paintings and their contexts in political and social history. It was initiated by Barrell (1980) and Solkin (1982), furthered by Bermingham (1986) and Mitchell (1994) among others, and saw landscapes, whether in pictures or the natural world, in terms of cultural studies and practices. These developments, together with other recent publications such as the interdisciplinary studies by Schama (1995) and the work of the Wordsworth Trust, bringing together literature, art and popular tourism (Woof and Hebron 1998), suggest that some signposts will be useful to negotiate this battlefield. The following ten propositions are offered, not as incontestable 'givens', but as issues for discussion, many of which are taken up in the rest of this chapter.

(i) The derivation of the term 'landscape' implies human activity and land use as well as an object of aesthetic pleasure. The word entered the English Language at the end of the sixteenth century from the Dutch *landschap*, was Anglicised into 'landskip' during the seventeenth century, becoming 'landscape' thereafter. That its etymology originally 'signified a unit of human occupation ... as much as anything that might be a pleasing object of depiction' (Schama 1995: 10) tends to be overlooked by those who stress the aesthetics rather than the politics of landscape.

(ii)   Landscape is a construct of the mind as much as a physical construct of earth and water, flora and fauna 'out there'. Poets especially, and Wordsworth in particular, represent the interiority of landscape built up as much from the strata of memory as from the strata of Lake District mountains. Painters, too, reflect the landscape of memory: Richard Wilson's *Valley of the Dee* (c. 1762), or *View of the Thames Near Twickenham* (c. 1762), owe as much to his knowledge of Claude Lorraine and his memories of his visit to Italy as they do to the topography of North Wales or the Thames (Solkin 1982: 213–14).

(iii) All landscapes are culturally modified. Even so-called 'wildernesses' have to be marked off and preserved. The idea of protecting landscape, of nature conservation, means that we have to interfere with it; and there is an ill-defined line between protection and the urge to improve landscape, to make it safe, to domesticate it, to tidy it up and, in extreme cases, to sanitise it into little more than a theme park.

(iv)   The idea of protecting landscape assumes its inherent value and 'natural' purity, both of which are often translated into a sense of its divinity. Both poetry and painting represent this sense of the numinous, most evident in the pantheism of Wordsworth and Samuel Palmer.

(v)   Landscape implies enclosure – not just as a mode of representation (see proposition (vi) below) but as a movement in England's social history (Brewer 1997: 625–6). During the eighteenth century, while the technical case for the enclosure of wastes and open fields may have been strong (Plumb 1950: 82), it effectively dispossessed the English peasantry, ending their common rights, and creating a rural underclass through a form of internal colonisation of the mother country. As Goldsmith writes in *The Deserted Village*: 'But times are alter'd; trade's unfeeling train / Usurp the land and dispossess the swain'. The representation of landscape and the rural poor in the poetry and the painting of the eighteenth and nineteenth centuries in England is intimately bound up with this history (Barrell 1980).

(vi)   Landscape implies framing. Landscape paintings and pictorialist poems are constructions where the boundary lines of their framing (depicted trees or rocks, say, that direct the eye; or the verse paragraph) mark off the selected elements with the uncompromising definitiveness of a garden hedge. The act of looking inside the frame gives a paradoxical sense of both enclosure and expansiveness; the spectator is focused, if not blinkered, by the frame; and, peering through the lens it contains, observes a land of rocks and rivers, fields and woodlands, laid out according to a predetermined schema.

(vii) Landscape creates the illusion of a 'unified scene' (Mitchell 1994: 12–13). The conventional notion is that it took the artists to teach us to see nature as 'scene', that 'until fairly recent times men (*sic*) looked at nature as an assemblage of isolated objects, without connecting trees, rivers, mountains, roads, rocks and forest into a unified scene' (Osborne 1970:

638). Subsequent criticism has subverted this comfortable harmony of 'only connect': Barrell (1980: 6) describes the 'mythical unity' of English paintings of rural life; Solkin (1982: 82) refers to the 'mythic ideal' and the myth of social harmony that they depict. Both locate the reasons why landscape was represented as aesthetically pleasing, unified, ordered and usually serene in terms of the requirements of the patron who commissioned or the purchaser who bought the pictures, and the demands of the artistic conventions that governed the making of the image.

(viii) In the sister arts during the eighteenth and nineteenth centuries, the figures in the landscape changed: the Arcadian swains, the aerial gods and sober statuary, the amorous nymphs and shepherds, the melancholy gentleman gave way to the occupations of the relatively poor, to ragged clothes, muddy boots and agricultural implements. The landscape of leisure was replaced by the landscape of work. This change of emphasis is not unproblematic for, 'as the rustic figures become less and less the shepherds of French or Italian Pastoral, they become more and more ragged, but remain inexplicably cheerful' (Barrell 1980: 16). The treatment of human figures in a landscape indicates the ideology that invests the image.

(ix) Painters and poets of landscape during the eighteenth and nineteenth centuries were continually adapting the inherited conventions of the pastoral genre so that they more closely represented the countryside and rural life with which they were familiar. The classical schema upon which eighteenth-century landscape paintings and pictorialist poems were constructed was steadily modified, not rejected, with the onset of the Romantic movement.

(x) The idea of landscape in both the sister arts is associated with new ways of seeing: the eye is privileged above all other senses. Whether it is Thomson or Wilson controlling our sight lines, Wordsworth recording his impressions upon 'the inward eye', or Constable tempting his potential purchasers with 'a little more eye-salve' (Sunderland 1981: 108), looking and seeing are not only the means of apprehending the work of art, they are also its subject. Spectatorship thus becomes central to landscape painting and literary pictorialism.

The spectator's viewpoint

Beyond the ha-ha: landscape schema in Thomson and Wilson

In the preface to his account of the intimate relationships between poetry, painting and landscape gardening during the eighteenth century, John Dixon Hunt remarks that 'once poets had acquired certain habits of looking and thinking inside a garden they found them equally serviceable beyond the ha-ha'. (Dixon Hunt 1976/1989: xii). It is not too fanciful to extrapolate from his subsequent chapters on Pope and Thomson that the ha-ha can be seen in metaphorical as well as literal terms: not only as the sunken fence bordering a garden or path that allows uninterrupted prospects from within; but also as a symbol of the changing landscape of mind during this period that encouraged poets and painters to emulate the gardener William Kent who, in Walpole's celebrated words, 'leaped the fence and saw that all nature was a garden' (Walpole cited in Dixon Hunt and Willis, 1975/1988: 313). Beyond the ditch lay another sort of landscape, different both from Kent's relatively small-scale garden of serpentine paths, grottoes and statuary and from the controlled perspectives of the vast parks designed by 'Capability' Brown, where the untamed countryside rolled away and where the overwhelming majority of the population lived and worked. James Thomson may celebrate:

> The negligence of nature wide and wild,
> Where, undisguised by mimic art, she spreads
> Unbounded beauty to the roving eye
> > ('Spring', lines 505–7, from Thomson
> > *The Seasons* (1726–44))

but the extent of his interest in and sympathy for those who inhabit it is limited to their roles as decoration. In *The Seasons* human beings are little more than animated statuary. Obliterating the boundaries between the garden and Nature created the sense of a spacious park in front of the manor house. The ha-ha helped to promote the house and its immediate surroundings as a new Arcadia; at the same time, the apparent continuity of landscape it represented symbolised the illusion of harmony in the relationship between land and labour (Schama 1995: 539). Both poets and painters were unwitting conspirators in this illusion.

Perhaps the most coherent statement of the relationship between the arts and Nature is in what Pope called his 'gardening poem', his 'Epistle to Lord Burlington' (1731) in which he invokes the aesthetic spirit which 'paints and 'designs', infusing the work of the gardener with its own mysterious poetry (lines 57–64). 'Consult the Genius of the Place in all', exhorts Pope, for it 'Paints as you plant, and as you work, designs'. This single line, in which poetry celebrates gardening through the metaphor of painting, might be taken as the paradigm for the reading of landscape in the mid-eighteenth century. Here, Walpole's 'three new Graces', poetry, painting and gardening, are combined. Gardens, as much as poems, were texts to be read. When, as Paulson (1975a: 20) argues, eighteenth century landscape taste moved on from the intellectual invitations of what he calls the 'poetic or the emblematic or the learned garden' to the emotional appeal of Brown's 'smoothly-flowing parkland', it is tempting to interpret this shift as a further step beyond the garden gate towards the romantic appreciation of Nature *per se*. But few so-called developments in literary, art or garden history operate with such easy linearity (Heffernan 1985: 12). Each brings its own complex of conventions that practitioners in the other media respond to variously such that efforts to categorise

artists as 'romantic' or 'neo-classic', as if there were some binary division, are
futile as well as misleading (Honour 1979: 11; Butler 1981). Hence, it is not
too surprising to find Wordsworth, a century after Pope, espousing the same
principles as those in the latter's *Epistle*: 'Laying out grounds', he wrote to
George Beaumont, 'may be considered a liberal art, in some sort like Poetry
and Painting; and its object, like that of all the liberal arts, is, or ought to be,
to move the affections under the control of good sense; that is … to assist
Nature in moving the affections' (cited in Heffernan 1985: 13). Yet, despite
these similarities of principle, the continuous and growing interest in the relationship between people and the natural world does lead to a re-positioning of
the spectator and a shift in the ways of looking at landscape. To bring these
issues into focus, the remainder of this chapter will concentrate mainly on two
'pairings' of poets and painters: Thomson and Wilson, Wordsworth and
Constable.

Thomson's *The Seasons* (1726–44) is full of imperatives: words such as 'see',
'behold', 'look', 'come', frequently start his verse paragraphs. They are rhetorical
devices where the notional addressee is either himself, or Nature, or specifically
one of the seasons. Each of the four poems begins with the arrival of the person-
ified season, heralded with a heightened Miltonic invocation as it takes
possession of the natural world. The images are conventionally gendered and
aged as the year goes on, as the hand over from Spring to Summer shows:

> From brightening fields of ether fair-disclosed,
> Child of the sun, refulgent Summer comes
> In pride of youth, and felt through nature's depth;
> He comes, attended by the sultry hours
> And ever-fanning breezes on his way;
> While from his ardent look the turning Spring
> Averts her blushful face, and earth and skies
> All-smiling to his hot dominion leaves.
>   ('Summer', lines 1–8,from Thomson
>   *The Seasons* (1726–44))

Where is the implied reader in respect of such pictures and of those other
exhortations which direct either the eyes to look or the legs to walk through
Thomson's garden of nature? Modern readers peer through the screen of history
and sense the distance (psychologically and in real time) between them and the
scenes of *The Seasons*. Contemporary readers – the implied ones for Thomson's
text – were able to participate more readily with the author and fill out the
'gaps' he left for them, some with enthusiastic detail. Hagstrum concludes his
chapter on Thomson by reference to an eighteenth-century writer in the *British
Magazine* who quoted the following lines from later in Thomson's 'Summer':

> O vale of bliss! O softly-swelling hills!
> On which the power of cultivation lies,

And joys to see the wonders of his toil
      ('Summer', lines 1435–37)

Hagstrum notes that to present-day readers these lines seem 'unvisual' and do not evoke a particular personification in the mind's eye; but the eighteenth century reader who quoted them went on to comment:

> We cannot conceive a more beautiful image than that of the Genius of Agriculture distinguished by the implements of his art, embrowned with labour, glowing with health, crowned with a garland of foliage, flowers, and fruit, lying stretched at ease on the brow of a gentle swelling hill and contemplating with pleasure the happy effects of his own industry.
> (Hagstrum 1958: 266–7)

The passage reveals several of the characteristics that we have touched on so far in reading eighteenth-century landscape. First, as Hagstrum remarks: 'Pictorialist poets breed pictorialist readers.' Thomson's use of the pronoun 'his' is enough to trigger the conventional personification, decked out with all the prolixity of an Arcimboldo fantastic head, and placed in an idyllic landscape. Second, the image, while of hard agricultural labour, is suffused with gardenist overtones: it is 'beautiful', it is 'art', it is contemplative, it is concerned with the genius of the place. And third, as the corollary to this view, it is a falsification in respect of the real world of rural work, telling us more about the reader's familiarity with prevailing artistic conventions than about the world in which he actually lived. To censure such a response is not, of course, to censure Thomson; yet the poet is implicated, for *his* reading and presentation of landscape provide the schema for his readers. Two related aspects of Thomson's internalised representation of the external world are especially pertinent here: his assumptions about time and space in his representation and his difficulties with expressing his affective response.

Generations of readers and painters (Grigson 1959: 27–32), learned to look at the external world through Thomson's lens: the eye dominates Nature poetry during the eighteenth century. The eyes in *The Seasons* are modified in various ways according to their particular functions in widening or narrowing this lens. So here, in a passage from 'Spring', the focal point shifts from the 'middle distance' of a 'bowery walk', to a 'long shot' of distant mountains and the sea, to a 'close-up' of bedding plants flowering in the borders.

At length the finished garden to the view
Its vistas opens and its alleys green.
Snatched through the verdant maze, the hurried eye
Distracted wanders; now the bowery walk
Of covert close, where scarce a spark of day
Falls on the lengthened gloom, protracted sweeps;
Now meets the bending sky, the river now

> Dimpling along, the breezy ruffled lake,
> The forest darkening round, the glittering spire,
> The ethereal mountain, and the distant main.
> But why so far excursive? when at hand,
> Along these blushing borders bright with dew,
> And in yon mingled wilderness of flowers,
> Fair-handed Spring unbosoms every grace.
> ('Spring', lines 516–29)

There then follows a riot of colour: a dozen spring flowers, cunningly augmented by half a dozen early summer blooms, to enchant the spectator and satisfy the gardener in his work:

> and, while they break
> On the charmed eye, the exulting florist marks
> With secret pride the wonders of his hand.
> ('Spring', lines 542–4)

Eighteen flowering plants are enough to propel the description to its painterly climax:

> Infinite numbers, delicacies, smells,
> With hues on hues expression cannot paint,
> The breath of Nature, and her endless bloom.
> ('Spring', lines 553–555)

The 'hurried eye' exercises a wandering viewpoint on the scene: it 'sweeps' the landscape to take in the long shot; it pauses to record details and allows itself to be 'charmed' by their variety and profusion. The spectator's focal length and points of attention are carefully manipulated. The landscape that is created through this representational procedure is spatially delimited and temporally controlled. We are told in which direction to look, what to observe, and for how long to dwell on particular items.

Yet, we are told next to nothing about Thomson's personal feelings about this landscape that clearly moves him to write. As he says, his 'expression cannot paint'; he does not possess the language to enable him to fathom the affective meaning. Instead of personal reflection we are given impersonal, public declamation. He veers away from any attempt at interiority into a grand afflatus in praise of Nature:

> Hail, Source of Being! Universal Soul
> Of Heaven and Earth! Essential Presence, hail!
> To thee I bend the knee; ….
> ('Spring', lines 556–8)

John Dixon Hunt has pointed out the struggle in Thomson over the meeting of the interior and external worlds and discussed some of the ways in which the poet attempts to relate them. He singles out two of these as Thomson's main creative achievements: a meditative focus in relation to the sequence of effects of a landscape garden; and, 'the description of landscape in terms of an eye scanning a picture by Claude or Rosa, where the process of interpreting a landscape becomes part of its structure' (Dixon Hunt 1976/1989: 136). *Ut pictura poesis* ('as a painting, so a poem'), Horace's celebrated phrase, had assumed the status of a critical axiom by this period. Thomson is its most accomplished exponent.

Richard Wilson, sometimes known as 'the English Claude', is the natural corollary to Thomson and enables us to examine the spectator's role before a visual landscape. Inevitably, we look back at his work through eyes more accustomed to the great landscapes of Turner and Constable. It is as well to remember, therefore, that the cultural climate in which Wilson was operating was dominated by Reynolds. Reynolds considered landscapes inferior to history paintings and believed that a landscape painter could meet the criterion of 'perfect form' only by rejecting 'common nature' and creating ideal landscapes as Claude Lorraine had done. 'Claude Lorraine … was convinced that taking nature as he found it seldom produced beauty' (Reynolds (1771), Discourse IV, quoted in Wark 1975: 69–70). The contemporary canon of landscape art is, in fact, mentioned in some lines by Thomson:

Whate'er Lorraine light-touched with softening Hue,
Or savage Rosa dash'd, or learned Poussin drew.
(Thomson (1748) 'The Castle of Indolence', 1: 38)

These painters provided Wilson's models.

Wilson's *Holt Bridge on the River Dee* (c. 1762) (Figure 7.1) is constructed on Claudean principles and exemplifies priorities in the representation of space and the relation of people to the natural world similar to those in the 'prospect poetry' of the period. Indeed, one reason why Claude appealed to Wilson might be that affinity he sensed of a lost Golden Age in Claude's pictures and the feeling they convey that 'nature could be laid out for a man's delight, like a gentleman's park' (Clarke 1956: 83). Nature becomes the subject *per se*, for the land, the water, the sky and the light of which it is composed. In Wilson, as in Claude, the eye is drawn through the landscape towards an area of light; often there is a sense of 'backlighting' (what Constable later called Claude's 'brightness' (Leslie 1845/1951: 307)) suffusing the whole image and investing everything with the same serene mood.

So here, the landscape is viewed from a high angle of gaze, with the light slanting in from the left, silvering the trees in the foreground, illuminating the bridge in the middle distance, and creating a bright centre to the picture above the far horizon. The eye is directed here as astutely as it was in Thomson's Spring landscape quoted earlier: from an elevated position, the spectator's sight lines are focused on the subject of the picture by the framing tree to the left and the cliffs to the right, and by the two converging diagonal lines made by the

Figure 7.1   Richard Wilson, *Holt Bridge on the River Dee* (*c.* 1762), The National
          Gallery, London, oil on canvas.

river bank, left, and the rocks and bushes, right. That it is a construction according
to Claudean conventions and that Wilson paid little heed to strict topography
is vouched for by Martin Davies, who

> 'could not get to the right spot' from which the view might be seen: the
> foreground seems clearly to have been invented; and the general character
> of the scene has been somewhat changed by Wilson, the hills in particular
> being made to look higher than they do.
>
> (cited in Parris 1973: 31)

Nature, in other words, has been improved upon, in line with the aesthetic
ideology of the eighteenth century, and the vertical and horizontal 'holds' (to
speak in televisual terms) stabilise and control our viewing. Within this framework, how are we to read the figures in the landscape? Curiously, none of the
four is looking at the view. The reclining couple appear to be precariously
placed on the edge of the drop: she shades her eyes from the sun, he lies
propped on his elbows, both look up at the young man standing nearby sere-
nading them on a flute. The fourth figure, a passer-by only discernible by his
head and shoulders, carrying some equipment (a fishing rod or gun?), has his
attention taken by the music and looks across at the other three as he emerges
from beneath the lip of the hill. Just as in Thomson, people are part of the

garden furniture of an artificially constructed depiction in which adherence to conventional iconography is more important than attempting to say anything significant about them individually. The central trio are a way of establishing the foreground; the gaze of the internal spectator – the passing countryman – serves to focus us upon the group, especially on the standing figure of the flute-player who acts as a sort of viewfinder for the external spectator. The clothes are eighteenth century, but the pose is classical: the source of this image is nearer to the shepherd playing his pipes in an Arcadian landscape than to the realities of rural life in Wilson's native North Wales. Significantly, this is not the tone of Wilson's preparatory sketch (reproduced in Parris 1973: 31) where, in a diminished foreground, a mother and child stand casually in this central posi-tion looking at the view – a further indication of the dominance of artistic convention over narrative incident in the process of composition. Familiarity with the con-ventions of both arts, particularly in the representation of space and in the assumed relationships between painter/poet, their viewers/readers and the depicted scene, are essential prerequisites in reading eighteenth-century land-scapes. How do the conventions and schema develop as we move into the romantic period?

Interior landscape in Wordsworth and Constable

The bridge between the formalised, idealised landscapes of the eighteenth century and those of Constable and Wordsworth is the Picturesque. But it is a slippery bridge. The term covers a set of ideas about, and attitudes towards, real landscapes and their representations in painting and gardening in the period from about 1770–1820. The Picturesque was not a coherent aesthetic theory, more a cult associated, amongst other things, with the rise of tourism particu-larly to Wales and the Lake District (Andrews 1989). As a fashionable cult, it became the subject of satire in Jane Austen's *Northanger Abbey* (Chapter xiv) and in Rowlandson's send-up of picturesque tourism in his *The Tour of Dr. Syntax in Search of the Picturesque* (Brewer 1997: 615–17). More significantly, it reflected the need for the landowners to maintain control of the landscapes. 'It was a holding operation', says Leslie Parris, 'by and for the squirearchy which had lost ground and continued to lose ground in the dynamic of country life' (Parris 1973: 58). The politics of the Picturesque were thus an integral part of the way people, especially tourists, travellers and amateur artists, armed with the essays of William Gilpin as their guide, were encouraged to read the coun-tryside around them. Landscape was seen through art, in particular that of Claude. Indeed, the traveller keen on sketching would take along a 'Claude glass' in order to compose picturesque views. This was a portable, black convex mirror whose weak reflection diminished the landscape to look like a painting by Claude. The positioning of the mirror, as the artist stood with his back to the landscape, was used as an aid to composition. By such means the British land-scape was reduced to images in a Claudean theme park. The schema was thus established but so, also, were the contents of the landscape. Not just any bit of countryside would do. There had to be elements of roughness and wildness. In a remarkable account by Uvedale Price, elaborately entitled, *An Essay on the Picturesque, As Compared with the Sublime and the Beautiful, and on the Use of Studying Pictures, for the Purpose of Improving Real Landscape* (1794), the author goes into detail about what constitutes the picturesque in trees (the 'rugged old oak' not the 'smooth young beech'), animals (the donkey rather than the horse; the rough water-dog rather than the greyhound; sheep are to be ragged and woolly not shorn), and buildings where mossy ruins and broken-down hovels were in vogue. But it is when he comes to describe the role of people in such landscapes – as opposed to those other people who were the viewers and his readers – that the politics and these formulaic artistic conventions unite. Price says:

> In our own species, objects merely picturesque are to be found among the wandering tribes of gypsies and beggars; who in all the qualities which gave them their character, bear a close analogy to the wild forester [i.e. pony or horse] and the worn out cart-horse, again to old mills, hovels, and other inanimate objects of the same kind.
>
> (cited in Parris 1973: 60)

Neither the view of people as on a par with 'inanimate objects' nor the conventions through which landscape was itself viewed could survive unchanged into the Romantic period. The Picturesque outlook focused upon the composition of a pleasing prospect and expected the spectator to recognise and appreciate the elements in it that reflected classical painting and literature. The Romantic interest centred on the effect of landscape on the feelings of the artist, poet or spectator. Both were concerned with expressing response to the natural world; but their schema, conventions, and ideological priorities steadily shifted.

The Romantic artist adopts a different viewpoint, in both senses, and invites a 'reading' of landscape much altered from what had gone before. There is more freedom in the positioning of the viewer/reader and more variety in the angle from which a scene is observed. Equally, there is a sense of greater involvement and personal knowledge in the landscapes of Wordsworth and Constable such that, because their ownership of the scene is part of its creative expression, the viewer/reader feels drawn in affectively rather than kept at a distance. Even so, both poet and painter operate according to inherited schemata which they adapt to their own purposes. The similarities in Wordsworth's and Constable's art have long been recognised, particularly in respect of the importance both attach to their childhood experiences of landscape and, therefore, to the power of memory and its formative, moral function (Clark 1956: 86–91; Heffernan 1985: 95–101).

The 'reading viewpoint' that Wordsworth takes upon those remembered epiphanies that he records in *Tintern Abbey* and *The Prelude* is clear from his description of the celebrated 'spots of time' in the latter poem (*The Prelude*, 12: 208–86). The 'ordinary sight' of the beacon, a windblown woman, and the pool is charged with significance not only because the self he recalls as a boy has just

left the place where a murderer has once been hanged, but also through Wordsworth's characteristic practice of mixing a straightforward narrative viewpoint
with an overlaid viewpoint from another source in his personal history. Memory
holds endless potential for such experiences; but 'spots of time' are only realised
where the viewpoints of several (usually three) recollections intersect. So here,
the episode is framed visually in the memorial formulae Wordsworth typically
favours, a sort of personalised version of 'once upon a time': 'I remember well
that once, …' is concluded 41 lines later with:

> And think ye not with radiance more sublime
> For these remembrances and for the power
> They had left behind?

Outside this frame there are lines to interpret the depicted incidents (lines
208–25; 269–86). Inside the frame, three viewpoints are set at angles, as it were,
to each other to create the spot of time: the 'I' of the mature poet, the youthful
Wordsworth walking the landscape with Mary Hutchinson, and the poet as a
boy becoming lost and frightened in the mountains leading his horse past the
ancient gibbet. The reader as spectator is offered a verbal triptych. Wordsworth
encourages a painterly reading, by conveying his sense of depression when lost
as a boy with the words:

> …but I should read
> Colours and words that are unknown to man
> To paint the visionary dreariness …
> (lines 254–6)

and by constructing the landscape of boyhood memory with both picturesque
sightlines and details. Hence, his schema for the scene is expressed as he climbs
up to a high vantage point to look back:

> Then, reascending the bare common, saw
> A naked Pool that lay beneath the hills,
> The Beacon on its summit, and, more near,
> A Girl who bore a Pitcher on her head,
> And seemed with difficult steps to force her way
> Against the blowing wind.
> (lines 248–53)

Foreground, middle distance and horizon are all clearly imaged as the eye ('I')
takes a leisurely look at the landscape and settles on the moving figure. Prior to
this view from the hill-top, the focus of the experience in the valley bottom was
the 'casual glance' at the carved letters of the murderer's name beneath the
'gibbet mast'. The gibbet itself 'had mouldered down, the bones / And iron case
were gone'; it is presented as a picturesque detail giving access to 'former times'
with their burden of violent local incident. The landscapes within the frame

comprise both a graphic sense of place and an inscribed sense of time through Wordsworth's technique of transforming the schema of the single classical viewpoint into one which contains multiple perspectives. The reflections outside the frame, where Wordsworth, as it were, considers the interrelationships in this picture he has created, show him reading the narrative of his own history and arguing that this transformation is more than a technical device; it is a reading of self in which significance is bestowed by the perceiver and is sustained by the power of the individual's reflective imagination (lines 219–23; 275–7); it has a 'renovating virtue' which is both pleasurable in itself and psychologically restorative (lines 210–18). This, of course, is the interior exploration that we never get from Thomson. As we have seen, while both poets make the conventional reference to the inadequacy of language to convey their experiences of landscape, there is a radical development in the spectator's role in Wordsworth. The poet looks 'in' as well as 'at' and the reader follows him, gaining access to a landscape that is composed of external and internal elements fused together – the present 'glimpses' (line 281) of an old man constructed into a coherent and balanced picture from the mental imagery stored inside his head. In this sense, Wordsworth's landscapes are as much concerned with learning about himself as they are with learning about the natural world. As such, this passage expounding and illustrating the 'spots of time' is a microcosm of the whole of *The Prelude*: separate episodes are developed from events in Wordsworth's own life but, rather than describing these incidents as they seemed at the time, they are arranged spatially and expanded or contracted temporally, as the distant retrospect of old age inevitably dictated, and as the interpretation of the narrative pattern of his long life demanded.

Earlier it was argued that the conventional approach to landscape in the eighteenth century was to produce pictures that were usually idealised and sanitised images, based rather more upon the artists' study of other pictures than upon their study of actual countryside. Constable rejected this approach. Like Wordsworth, he was aware of breaking new ground, of creating a new pictorial language just as Wordsworth was attempting a new poetic language (Wordsworth 1802; Constable cited in Sunderland 1981: 5–6).

Constable, like Wordsworth, was aware that originality meant not the wholesale rejection of his predecessors Claude and Wilson – painters whose work he held in high esteem – but a rethinking from first principles of the received pictorial grammar. From London in May 1802, Constable sent this famous progress report to John Dunthorne:

> For these two years past I have been running after pictures and seeking the truth at second hand. ... I shall shortly return to Bergholt where I shall make some laborious studies from nature – and I shall endeavour to get a pure and unaffected representation of the scenes that may employ me. ... there is room enough for a natural painture.
>
> (Constable cited in Parris 1973: 95)

If Wordsworth's life-long preoccupation, as recorded in the 50-year history of *The Prelude*'s composition, was to interpret the growth of the poet's mind and show how 'The Child is father of the Man', Constable's corresponding life's work was to realise 'natural painture' on canvas. More specifically, how was he to read the landscape of the Stour Valley and represent that reading in such a way that contemporary viewers could share its power?

Constable's *The Cornfield* (1826) (Figure 7.2) invites us to make links backwards to eighteenth-century visual conventions, and sideways to Wordsworthian poetic innovation. The painting depicts the lane from East Bergholt along which Constable walked to school as a boy; the lane dips away to the right, the eye is directed through the field gateway towards a distant village and church, so located for compositional effect. Michael Rosenthal (1987: 156) is tough in his criticism of this picture as 'one which virtually parodied the conventional Picturesque'. He notices, amongst other things, the interpictorial references to Gainsborough's *Cornard Wood*, the dead tree, the broken gate, and the unshorn sheep at harvest time. He might also have mentioned the donkey. Certainly, *The Cornfield* contains picturesque elements, maybe reflecting Constable's concern to sell the picture. It is evident, too, as Rosenthal implies, that he is 'seeking the truth at second hand' in so far as he incorporates motifs like the sheep or the dead tree from his own or others' previous work. Yet neither issue should surprise us: the original style he sought did not entail severance from past landscapists, nor exclude the re-use of particular details in several paintings which was his habit. As Sutherland remarks, these reappearing details

> underline the fact that Constable's large paintings, and especially his later ones, were created in the studio from sketches and recollections and memories. They were not the result of one direct confrontation with a landscape, but of a gradual build up in his mind over many years of his experience of nature.
>
> (Sunderland 1981: 118)

Substitute Wordsworth's fourteen books of *The Prelude* for 'Constable's large paintings' and these sentiments are equally appropriate. But what matters in the present context is the degree to which Constable reworks the schema and conventions of landscape art and how far the analogy with Wordsworth can be taken.

Heffernan makes a sophisticated case for reading *The Cornfield* as 'something very like a Wordsworthian "spot of time"' and asks what this 'carefully assembled configuration of elements', some of which are noted above, 'is meant to signify' (Heffernan 1985: 98–101). Referring to the facts that Constable often used to call this picture 'The Drinking Boy' and to his famous remark about his 'careless boyhood' on the banks of the Stour that made him a painter, Heffernan infers that the boy represents Constable's boyhood self. So far this seems plausible. But Heffernan's whole argument rests upon the figure of the farmer just

Figure 7.2   John Constable, *The Cornfield* (1826), The National Gallery, London, oil on canvas.

inside the field gate seemingly looking back towards the boy and, as it were, towards the viewer. He interprets this figure as 'the mature Constable contemplating his own past'. Heffernan says:

> this surrogate self gazes back on the circle of a world in which a boy lies down to drink, donkeys nibble leaves, sheep saunter along, and the shepherd dog who is supposed to guide them momentarily forgets his duty. The picture is a spot of time in which the present is revitalised by the past, in which Constable represents himself in the very act of seeing again the boy

he once was in one of the scenes that 'made me a painter'.

(Heffernan 1985: 100)

Here, then, we have another spectator in the picture, a mirror presence walking through the scene, much as the passing countryman does in Wilson's landscape, but employed to substantiate an autobiographical reading of the painting along Wordsworthian lines. The case is subtle, attractive but ultimately speculative. However much we may like to see this 'subliminal figure standing at the gateway to the world of man's work' as the mature Constable looking back and 're-creating the life of the boy', the burden of picturesque convention that the picture carries and, by extension, the emphasis upon the pastoral beauty of the landscape rather than the labour needed to produce it – an issue which Heffernan does not confront with conviction – together outweigh the plausibility of Constable consciously encapsulating his own history in the farmer at the field gate. None the less, Heffernan's account does sharpen our sense both of the personalised, poetic reading of landscape that the painting offers and the way in which Constable was a painter of the particular and momentary rather than the generalised ideal landscape. Constable, like Wordsworth, rethought the conventions inherited from the eighteenth century and created a new schema of representation that included the spectator as an 'insider', the spectator whose affective participation was artistically valid, morally valued, and directly sought.

Educating the eye

In the opening contribution to Richard Wendorf's *festschrift* for Jean Hagstrum, the acutely titled *Articulate Images*, Lawrence Lipking forcefully restates one of the central messages of Hagstrum's *The Sister Arts*. He says: 'to put it bluntly: the vast majority of modern readers are blind to eighteenth-century poetry. We do not see poems well; we do not make the pictures in our minds that the poets direct and excite us to make' (Lipking 1983: 5). He goes on to acknowledge that while complacent ways of reading may partly explain the difficulty, the power of artistic conventions, as Gombrich made us realise, is also a significant factor. He explains:

> No eye is innocent. Nor can descriptive poetry ever escape the prison-house of visual habit and protocols in which the brain has caged the sight. If eighteenth-century poets do not project clear pictures into modern minds, on this line of thought, the reason may be less that we are blind than that they wore blinkers: rigidly restricted formulas for seeing
>
> (Lipking 1983: 10)

In the educational context the eighteenth century has long been out of fashion and its poetry, in particular, has been by-passed for years in school and university courses. There is a growing sense, too, that, with the notable exception of

Blake, this malaise has now spread into the nineteenth century and that the reflective thinking of, say, *The Prelude* is as remote from modern students as is the way of seeing and representing the world in Thomson's *The Seasons*. The canon wars of recent times and the revised curricula that have ensued have made it easier for older students to negotiate their way round such poetry; course structures, with their brave new rationales and multiple options, have legitimised their doing so. Gains in student choice and motivation are offset by a bewildering diversity of texts and justifications for studying them. Augustan and, increasingly, Romantic poetry are often the first casualties. That there has been a reaction against these trends on the part of government in the last few years, notably in the prescriptive requirement to teach pre-twentieth-century literature in the National Curriculum for English in England and Wales (1995), serves only to emphasise the pedagogical problem. The rehabilitation of this literature entails, as Lipking indicates above, re-educating the eye.

The cross-disciplinary developments noted at the outset suggest how this task may be approached. For example, comparative study of, say, the opening thirty-five lines of Wordsworth's *Tintern Abbey* and Constable's *Fen Lane, East Bergholt*, might focus upon the relationship between the implied spectator and the landscape and discuss the positioning of the reader/viewer, the angle of gaze, the selection of details and the composition of the scenes. Similarly, photographs of Stourhead, Richard Wilson's *View of Croome Court* (c. 1762) and *View of Wilton from Temple Cross* (c. 1762) can be juxtaposed with the description of Hagley Park in Thomson's 'Spring', lines 904–62. Classical park landscapes can then be studied in three media – as gardens, paintings and poetry – and the 'imitative picture reading' that characterises this whole prospect passage in 'Spring' (and so much else in *The Seasons*) quickly becomes more comprehensible from being contextualised within the other arts.

Ideological as well as aesthetic issues are embedded here, of course, but these are more easily approached through looking at the biographical impetus and the role of human figures in the landscapes of Wordsworth and Constable. Memories of childhood experiences are the source of the emotive power in both poet and painter. Writing of his boyhood in the Stour Valley, Constable remarks in one of his most famous letters: 'The sound of water escaping from mill dams, … willows, old rotten banks, slimy posts, and brickwork. I love such things … I shall never cease to paint such places. They have always been my delight … I associate my 'careless boyhood' to all that lies on the banks of the Stour. They made me a painter' (Beckett 1962–8: 7–8). Similarly, these Lake District scenes made Wordsworth a poet:

> I cannot paint
> What then I was. The sounding cataract
> Haunted me like a passion: the tall rock,
> The mountain, and the deep and gloomy wood,
> Their colours and their forms, were then to me
> An appetite: a feeling and a love

That had no need of a remoter charm,
By thought supplied, or any interest
Unborrowed from the eye.
> (*Tintern Abbey*, lines 76–84)

The significance of these early, formative experiences is easily pursued in Wordsworth's 'Intimations Ode', in extracts from *The Prelude*, Book One, and through study of Constable's paintings of the Stour Valley, including *The Haywain*, the painting that has achieved iconic status in representations of English landscape. Perhaps its appeal is associated, in part, with the role of the figures, harmonised as they are into the scene such that the spectator has to play hide-and-seek to find them all. The haywain has been driven into the river at noon to allow the horses to drink and the wooden spokes to swell into the wheel rims, while the two men rest. The woman doing the washing outside the farm and the fisherman half-hidden in the river bank to the right seem literally parts of the landscape; while four blobs of white paint in the distant fields above the fisherman indicate a line of hay-makers, presumably working to the hay cart to their left against the trees. Constable may be known for his working landscapes but here, as elsewhere, agricultural labour is kept at a distance; the working men and women are absorbed into the landscape.

Wordsworth characters in the *Lyrical Ballads*, the farmers and shepherds, vagrants and children, are all foregrounded more explicitly, yet their overall function is the same: to serve as examples of the virtues of the simple, pastoral life lived close to Nature. The final lines of 'The Old Cumberland Beggar' sum up the idealised unity between man and landscape with a picture of this poor 'old Mendicant', seated on the roadside grass beneath the trees, sharing his scraps with the birds, and suffused with sunlight that he can no longer see: he is merged into the landscape as fully as Constable's figures in *The Haywain*. So, Wordsworth concludes:

As in the eye of Nature he has liv'd,
So in the eye of Nature let him die.

Such comparative study of landscape paintings and nature poetry opens up the rich classroom agenda of issues set out at the start of this chapter. Taken together, the biographical, cultural, aesthetic and political dimensions listed there offer opportunities for that education of the eye that is necessary if we are to learn from, as well as taken pleasure in, looking at the landscape.

8 Turner our contemporary:
'poetic painting'

Painting and Poetry flowing from the same fount mutually by vision, constantly comparing Poetic allusions by natural forms in one and applying forms found in nature to the other, meandering into streams by application, which reciprocally improved reflect and heighten each others' beauties like … mirrors.

(J.M.W. Turner, *Royal Academy lecture*, 1812)

His use of poetry, his close and indeed indissoluble connection with it, help us to understand in many ways how he developed his aesthetic, his sense of nature as a ceaseless process out of which endless patterns emerge, harmonious and violent, stable and unstable.

(Jack Lindsay (1985) *Turner. The Man and his Art*)

Turner continued to feel an urge to unite the visual and the literary, and it should never be supposed that he was, on any level, anything other than a poetic painter.'

(John Gage (1987) *J.M.W. Turner. 'A Wonderful Range of Mind'*)

Three spectator-poets

Throughout the 50 years of his working life, from the 1790s to the 1840s, Turner was an inveterate scribbler of verses and notes, often in the margins of his drawings. These *aides memoire*, together with his *Verse Book*, his illustrations for editions of poems by Scott, Rogers and Campbell, and his use of works by Milton, Pope and Byron as symbolic subject matter for his paintings, all provide ample evidence for Turner's affinity with poetry (Wilton 1990). Yet, this data of the literary dimension in Turner is generally not what viewers are referring to when they describe his paintings as poetic. Rather, the term appears to reflect several related characteristics: the sense that Turner's paintings, like poems, suggest more than they state, evoke more than they record; that they possess qualities of insight into the elemental and unknowable in nature that are associated with poetry, not mere verse; and that, above all, as a painter of colour and light, Turner gives us access to *how* we perceive the world, not just to what we are invited to look at.

This chapter asks: What can recent poetry tell us about Turner's 'poetic painting'? Three modern ekphrases offer different perspectives upon this concept.

In doing so, the first two re-work now familiar ideas of spectatorship and the third extends it. The first poem, about Turner's *The Shipwreck* (1805), exemplifies the gallery experience of 'seeing in'; the second in response to his *Snowstorm – Steam-Boat off a Harbour's Mouth* (1842), using words like brush-strokes, explores the materiality of its medium in the act of representation (cf. Chapter 2, this volume). The third poem problematises the notion of spectatorship as it re-reads Turner's *Slavers Throwing Overboard the Dead and the Dying – Typhoon Coming On* (1840) and its history through the lens of black consciousness and its history. In all three of these dramatic marine pictures, there is the vertiginous sense of Turner drawing the spectator in: the storms envelop us in their wind and wet, and seas seem about to sweep us into their sliding waves. This feeling is, perhaps, most powerful in relation to *Snowstorm* where, as Paulson has commented, 'viewer and artist (whom he [Turner] equates) are both participants inside the storm that whirls about them as they look at the painting and actors at the centre of the landscape, tied to the mast of the ship that is rocked by the storm' (Paulson 1982: 82). But, just as we know that the spectator–participant role may be defined by the artist through the construction of his painting (cf. James's comment on the reader's role, Chapter 1, this volume), we also know that the spectator retains a degree of detachment. In what follows, three spectator-poets – John Wain, Pauline Stainer and David Dabydeen – respectively reflect on the aesthetic process, recreate the visual in the verbal, and resist the implications of Turner's image.

Reflection, re-creation and resistance

Figure 8.1   J.M.W. Turner, *The Shipwreck* (1805), The Tate Gallery, London, oil on canvas.

John Wain's lengthy poem (it runs to 75 lines) 'The Shipwreck' (1986) is about Turner's painting of that name from 1805 (Figure 8.1). Wain's reading of the picture moves from the technical to the philosophical; from how Turner's colours create sound to a consideration of how art can catch a momentary beauty at the point of death. The narrative framework is established by situating this reading in the reverential atmosphere of the gallery. The *sotto voce* murmurings of the spectators are drowned out by the noise of the silent canvas:

> This canvas yells the fury of the sea.
> Across a quiet room, where people murmur
> their poised appreciations, it shrieks out
> the madness of the wind.
>> (John Wain, 'The Shipwreck' (1986),
>>> lines 1–4)

'How can that be?' Wain asks, since the painting is 'woven of voiceless threads'. The conceit of linking the canvas of the picture with that of the ship's sail is laid down here for later use. His answer is that:

> ... the colours hold
> the secret. They are noise, and tilt, and steepness.
> The colours are trough, and crash, the cry of gulls
> lifted and blown away like part of the spume.
> The colours are the bawling of the wind.
>> (lines 11–15)

After a long central section speculating on the deaths and afterlives of the ship-wrecked figures, Wain introduces Turner's interpolated voice into the narrative to express the meaning of the picture:

> and Turner here seems to be saying *Now*
> *I will show you how terror and agony*
> *and the utterly final arrival of death can distil*
> *an essence of beauty-in-terror, an enrichment*
> *in the moment of final relinquishment of all.*
>> (lines 53–7)

The interplay of the technical and the philosophical in the poem culminates near the end with the image of 'the frantic slap / of the saturated sail' and with the re-assertion of the narrative frame as the engrossed viewer returns from his absorption in the image to his awareness of the gallery.

> Canvas to canvas. Sound
> to silence, through the artist's compassionate mind,
> and back to sound again, as I stand here.
>> (lines 66–8)

This intoning, punning repetition of 'canvas' which commits the figures to their watery death is daringly done; the materiality of the picture and its depicted scene are caught in this single word which then 'flaps' in the artist's/viewer's/reader's mind as 'sound', 'silence', 'sound' alternate in the lines that follow. The poem closes by refusing to allow that the impact and meaning of the picture can be accounted for simply in formal terms:

> Oh, it has 'painterly values' too, and can be discussed
> in purely abstract terms: but not now, not now.
>
> (lines 69–70)

We can infer that the poetic qualities Wain finds in Turner are those that his poem has explored: the ability of the painting to provide a special sort of aesthetic experience in the spectator. Wain's gaze has certainly been drawn into the rhombus-shaped space of wild, white water that Jack Lindsay also remarks upon: 'A strong diagonal, given a series of inner tensions by the lines of masts, stays, spars and waves, leads down into a central vortex, a kind of exploding lozenge full of local whirls and surges' (Lindsay 1985: 44). Form, light, colour all contribute to the sense of instability, of moving space; yet these 'painterly values' are but half the story. Wain extrapolates also on Turner's subject matter and records his response to the fate of the shipwrecked people. His poem thus dramatises the act of viewing. It expresses the experience of responding to both the marked surface and the represented scene. It is a poetic evocation of Wollheim's 'twofoldness' (Wollheim 1987: 72).

The story behind the next picture (Figure 8.2) is one of the best-known and contentious in relation to Turner and one that has a bearing upon what the ekphrasis reveals about the artist's poetic painting. The titles are significant: Turner's painting was exhibited as *Snow-Storm – Steam-Boat off a Harbour's Mouth Making Signals in Shallow Water, and Going by the Lead. The Author Was in This Storm on the Night the Ariel Left Harwich* (1842). Pauline Stainer's poem, discussed below, is called 'Turner is lashed to the Mast'.

Turner further elaborated his direct involvement with this scene in some much-quoted remarks to Ruskin's friend, the Rev. William Kingsley, who told him that his mother had had a similar experience and understood what he was depicting. Turner replied:

> I did not paint it to be understood, but I wished to show what such a scene was like; I got the sailors to lash me to the mast to observe it; I was lashed for four hours, and I did not expect to escape, but I felt bound to record it if I did. But no one had any business to like the picture.
>
> (Cited in Butlin *et al.* 1974: 140)

The title and this gloss provide as tantalising and obscure a narrative as the painting itself. Lindsay (1985: 146) comments that the details of the event have usually been misread, that Turner had mistaken the name of the ship for 'The

Figure 8.2   J.M.W. Turner, *Snow Storm – Steam-Boat off a Harbour's Mouth*, 1842, The
Tate Gallery, London, oil on canvas.

Fairy', which sank in a storm off Harwich in November 1840, and that anyway
he does not claim to have been actually on board either vessel. If anything,
Gage (1987: 67–8) is even more sceptical, pointing out that Turner is not
known to have visited the east coast during this period, doubting whether even
a man as robust as Turner could have withstood four hours' exposure to the
elements at the age of 65, and concluding that Turner was simply teasing his
critics with a painting they were to describe as 'soapsuds and whitewash'.
Whatever the truth of the story, there is little doubt that Turner witnessed the
intensity of a storm at sea at close quarters and that the resulting image conveys
the impact of this immediacy. Here is Turner's vortex seeming to suck in the
spectator by the giddy instability of its design. The horizon – such as it is – tilts
steeply to the right; the foreground shows layers of water sliding over and into
each other; the whole left side of the painting shoots spray and snow together
upwards into the clouds to merge with the spiral of smoke from the labouring
vessel. The bowed mast, with its tattered flag and taut cables is set in a circular
area of light. It is both the focus of the composition, the point around which
the intersecting areas of dark and creamy pigment are ranged, and it is the
fulcrum of the tension that pervades the whole scene and its narrative incident.

It is with the incident and the anecdotes surrounding it that the ekphrasis
begins. Pauline Stainer's poem is given here in full.

Turner is Lashed to the Mast

I did not paint it to be understood
but to show how water
makes the wind visible,
how the sea strikes
like a steel gauntlet

I scent the blizzard
lashed like Odysseus
the air laced with diamond,
salt-pearl at my wrist

indistinctness is my forte
a gauze backdrop,
a ship hulling
to the hiss
of the vortex

I would fix
such sirens,
before unseen currents
disperse their dissolve.
            (Stainer 1994: 53)

Unlike Wain, self-consciously looking at a picture in a gallery, Stainer casts her poem as a first-person statement from a fictional Turner, a representation of the imagined thought-track of the artist as a latter-day Odysseus lashed to the mast, which in turn becomes a quasi-commentary on what Turner was expressing in his painting. Two quotations of the artist's own remarks (though the second is disputed), initiate the two halves of the poem. In each, words are used like brush-strokes of varying weight, colour and texture. Here, the painting's materiality is inscribed in the language: the impact of the sea that 'strikes/ like a steel gauntlet', the hard brilliance of the blizzard with 'the air laced with diamond' are embodied in the vocabulary. In the second half of the poem the imagery changes to represent Turner's ability to capture the evanescent, the indistinct, the flux of natural phenomena. So here, Turner is portrayed as wanting to 'fix/ such sirens' as the swirling wind and waves before everything relapses into formlessness: the vocabulary of formlessness thus opens ('indistinctness', 'gauze') and closes ('disperse', 'dissolve') these two short sections, seeming to envelop the ship in the vortex of the storm.

  The poetic in Turner is thus identified directly with art's ability at 'showing' – the verb that both painter and poet use in place of 'understood'. Both set out to re-create, not to explain; to fix in a pictorial construct – whether in oils or words – the colours and forms of natural phenomena and to imply their transience. Hence, the movement of the poem is from strong, hard, 'visible' imagery of metal and precious stones to opaque, indistinct, 'unseen' imagery of hissing air and invisible currents. The ekphrasis itself represents this movement towards dissolution as the vocabulary is drawn ineluctably into its own verbal vortex in the final two lines.

From hero to anti-hero; from Turner as Odysseus to Turner as captain of a slave ship. With David Dabydeen's poem 'Turner' (1994) we are given a complex reading of another of the late marine paintings, which, in effect, deconstructs the culture from which the image was born and questions the motives of the artist in creating it. The notion of the 'poetic' is exposed as a cruel indulgence on Turner's part: the challenge of Dabydeen's poem is to look at *Slavers Throwing Overboard the Dead and Dying – Typhoon Coming On* (1840) (Figure 8.3) through the eyes of black history and recognise that there is no easy reconciliation between the artistic radicalism of Turner's technique and the moral radicalism that the painting is conventionally thought to express. A year before the publication of Dabydeen's poem, in an otherwise powerful and informed account, Lukacher (1993: 135) remarked: 'In *Slavers*, Turner's lifelong passion for nautical disaster and blood-red sunsets found its perfect expression in a near contemporary subject of moral outrage and social conscience'. Dabydeen's 'Turner' implies that such a formulation is facile.

The origins and development of both the painting and the poem themselves offer a complex of narratives that help to elucidate the ambivalent responses that this image provokes.

Figure 8.3   J.M.W. Turner, *Slavers Throwing Overboard the Dead and Dying – Typhoon Coming On* (1840), Museum of Fine Arts, Boston, oil on canvas.

The three factors through which any close study of the painting is mediated are the literary influences upon its composition, Turner's own lines from *The Fallacies of Hope*, which accompanied the picture on exhibition, and the eulogy by Ruskin, the first owner of the painting, in *Modern Painters I* (1843).

John Gage comments that 'the superabundance of imagery in this dazzling canvas brings together the fruits of an extraordinarily wide-ranging reading' and he goes on to discuss Turner's debts to Thomson's 'Summer' (lines 980–1025), Gisborne's *Walks in a Forest* and Beale's *Natural History of the Sperm Whale* which, he argues, provided the imagery of the sharks, the teeming fishes and the typhoon for the painting (Gage 1987: 194). Above all, Turner knew the recently published second edition of Clarkson's *History of the Abolition of the Slave Trade*, with its notorious account of the captain of a slave ship *Zong* who ordered the sick and dying to be thrown overboard because insurance could only be claimed for those lost at sea, not for the diseased or for the dead on board ship. More recently, McCoubrey (1998: 319–53) has mentioned further publications that appeared between 1838 and 1840, including a biography of William Wilberforce and his correspondence, as evidence of the urgency of the abolitionists at this time. He argues that the painting needs to be seen in the context of the contemporary campaign to abolish the international slave trade – officially banned in Britain in 1807 and elsewhere in 1838 but, unofficially pursued by some nations, notably Spain and Portugal, who were still 'trafficking in the trade in violation of their treaty obligations to desist'.

If the impetus for the painting derived from this reading and the urgency of the abolitionists' cause, Turner's own lines extend its effect.

> Aloft all hands, strike the top-masts and belay;
> Yon angry setting sun and fierce-edged clouds
> Declare the Typhon's coming.
> Before it sweeps your decks, throw overboard
> The dead and dying – ne'er heed their chains
> Hope, Hope, fallacious Hope!
> Where is thy market now?
> ('The Fallacies of Hope', in Wilton 1990: 180)

Turner's ekphrasis is located earlier in this evil narrative than the situation shown in the painting. It is closer to the point of the captain's decision, the issuing of orders and the preparation for the storm. The reader is pitched into the midst of dramatic action, whereas the viewer sees the results as the sharks gather and the ship is hit by the typhoon. In the final lines the reader is also projected into the future when the shipping company can hope to collect on the insurance. Turner's attitude to this particular 'fallacy of hope' is unequivocal in its condemnation.

By 1844 the painting belonged to John Ruskin, who had recently written enthusiastically about Turner's colours and composition:

beyond dispute, the noblest sea that Turner has painted, and, if so, the noblest certainly ever painted by man, is that of the Slave Ship. ... Purple and blue, the lurid shadows of the hollow breakers are cast upon the mist of night, which gathers cold and low, advancing like the shadow of death upon the guilty ship as it labours amidst the lightning of the sea, its thin masts written upon the sky in lines of blood, girded with condemnation in that fearful hue which signs the sky with horror, and mixes its flaming flood with the sunlight, and, cast far along the desolate heave of the sepulchral waves, incarnadines the multitudinous sea. I believe, if I were reduced to rest Turner's immortality upon any single work, I should choose this.

(Ruskin, cited in Butlin *et al.* (eds) 1974: 145)

The inflated pretension of this description, culminating in its re-working of a famous Shakespearean image of bloody murder (*Macbeth*, Act II, Scene ii, lines 60–2) is revealing. Death, blood, guilt, horror may be the key ideas but they are elements of a poetic set-piece, in praise of Turner's mastery of colour, introduced by the thought that this is Turner's 'noblest sea' and concluded by the judgement that this testifies to his greatness. In other words, Ruskin has assimilated the social and economic evil that provoked the picture into his appreciation of Turner's colours and composition and celebrated it in his own word-painting. As McCoubrey (1998: 338) suggests, Ruskin selects his areas for comment carefully, leaving out distasteful details like the drowning woman and displacing them into metaphoric descriptions of the sea. Is this assimilation characteristic only of Ruskin? Or might Turner also be guilty of a similar confusion of ideas in his poetic painting? Dabydeen's poem, as will be argued shortly, suggests that he was.

The moral condemnation is inscribed in the geometry of the painting for, as Heffernan (1985: 180–1) has suggested, Turner forgoes his favoured vortex in exactly the subject where we would expect to find it and instead gives us a 'burning cross'. The light from the setting sun forms the vertical axis which is bisected by the uneven horizon with its turbulent masses and violent changes of colour. 'Here', Heffernan concludes, 'the sun becomes an infinitely blazing cross on which – in effect – the slaves are crucified'. This symbolism is further supported by McCoubrey (1998: 320), who comments that the painting should be seen 'in the context of abolitionist poetry in which the wrecking of slave ships by storm was a metaphor for divine intervention'. The top-left quadrant is dominated by the slaver, its blood-red masts and spars echoing the overall design, as it faces into the typhoon; by contrast, the top right has the conventional calm of sunset with the subtle gradation of colour found in Turner's 'colour beginnings'. In the lower left quadrant, the sea is littered with manacled bodies and the desperate hands of the victims reaching above the waves, while fish and gulls prey upon the flesh. But the dominant feature in the sea is in the lower right where, balancing the slaver, the swollen body of a female slave sinks below the surface, her shackled leg grotesquely pointing after the ship. There is sensuality as well as horror in the shoal of fish that swim sinuously round the body ready to feed. Perhaps it was this area of the painting particularly that led Dabydeen to the view he expresses at the end of the Preface to his poem: 'The intensity of Turner's painting is such that I believe the artist in private must have savoured the sadism he publicly denounced.' Dabydeen implies that Turner's public stance has to be judged alongside the personal relish he took in painting such horrific details and the commercial gain he stood to make from depicting these 'losses at sea'.

The genesis of Dabydeen's ekphrasis is relevant to understanding the type of narrative that he develops in his poem. In an unpublished interview, given in 1995 to Dannet Parchment, he said that the poem did not begin with Turner's painting but with the account of the slave ship 'Zong' which he had known for some years. 'The story began before the painting; it was only a little way into the poem that I realised that one could connect up the painting with it ... they just jelled'. The challenge of writing about a painting, the very art of ekphrasis, is an act of translation which, he explains, is analogous to the status of being a 'West Indian' immigrant in Britain who must constantly translate himself into a new way of life. The poem is about Turner and his picture, but it is also sugges-tive of the history of black people, fractured and severed from their birthright, in which journeyings and forced emigration are central symbols. In the poem, as in this history, the land, the family, the role of the mother are the keys to iden-tity and to a sense of rootedness in a personal culture. The poem offers no easy solution to the effects of the black diaspora initiated by the slave trade. It ends with a bleak vision of alienation whose insistent negatives create a tragic beauty of their own in the final lines:

> There is no mother, family,
> Savannah fattening with cows, community
> Of faithful men; no elders to fortell
> The conspiracy of stars; magicians to douse
> Our burning temples; no moon, no seed,
> ... No savannah, moon, gods, magicians
> To heal or curse, harvests, ceremonies,
> No men to plough, corn to fatten their herds,
> No stars, no land, no words, no community,
> No mother.
>   (Dabydeen 1994: 39–40)

The nihilistic imagery is as intense as the abandonment and depersonalisation suggested by the body parts sinking in the lurid waters of Turner's painting.

Against this background, what role do Turner and his picture have in the poem? Two fictional Turners figure in the narrative: the captain of the slave ship and a stillborn child tossed overboard from a future ship. But the protago-nist in this mythic narrative is the drowning slave in the right foreground of the picture. Dabydeen's poem moves with the heavy swell of big seas through its twenty-five sections. His Preface contains a summary of its development.

My poem focuses on the submerged head of the African in the foreground of Turner's painting. It has been drowned in Turner's (and other artists') sea for centuries. When it awakens it can only partially recall the sources of its life, so it invents a body, a biography, and peoples an imagined landscape. Most of the names of birds, animals and fruit are made up. Ultimately, however, the African rejects the fabrication of an idyllic past. His real desire is to begin anew in the sea but he is too trapped by grievous memory to escape history. Although the sea has transformed him – bleached him of colour and complicated his sense of gender – he still recognises himself as 'nigger'. The desire for transfiguration or newness or creative amnesia is frustrated. The agent of self-recognition is a still-born child tossed overboard from a future ship. The child floats towards him. He wants to give it life, to mother it, but the child – his unconscious and his origin – cannot bear the future and its inventions, drowned as it is in memory of ancient cruelty. Neither can escape Turner's representation of them as exotic and sublime victims. Neither can describe themselves anew but are indelibly stained by Turner's language and imagery.

(Dabydeen 1994: ix–x)

The figure of the still-born child constantly floats into the poem, constantly floats towards the partially submerged African but never gets there. This image, Dabydeen says, is the dominant idea of his poem. This failure to connect, to become whole, represents the negation of Caribbean consciousness by colonialism. Dabydeen continues in the Interview: 'Slavery is a form of child abuse which runs throughout the poem but in a symbolic way it is also about stifling life'. The poem thus juxtaposes the image of Britain's historical prosperity from the slave trade with the image of violated childhood. The portrait of Turner, the slave ship's captain, employs both images to imply the buggery of black nationhood:

> he sketches endless numbers
> In his book, face wrinkled in concentration
> Like an old seal's mouth brooding in crevices
> Of ice for fish, ...
> ... He checks that we are parcelled
> In equal lots, men divided from women,
> Chained in fours and children subtracted
> From mothers. When all things tally
> He snaps the book shut, his creased mouth
> Unfolding in a smile, as when, entering
> His cabin, mind heavy with care, breeding
> And multiplying percentages, he beholds
> A boy dishevelled on his bed.

(Dabydeen 1994: 17)

Turner the artist is implicated by association. Dabydeen can accept neither Turner's creative enjoyment in depicting this subject as a wholly innocent act nor, despite the contemporary concerns of the abolitionists, Turner's exhibition of the painting as a public protest when it came so late, years after Britain's slave trade had been abolished. 'Therefore', he says, 'I've put Turner back into his painting; I've just put him back and made him responsible for his painting'.

McCoubrey's view is quite the opposite: 'There is no reason to doubt that Turner painted *The Slave Ship* in good faith as an act of protest in a cause he supported' (McCoubrey 1998: 332). The spectator of this painting and poem is, thus, situated between two interpretations of history, both of which wrestle with 'the perplexing issue of aesthetics versus message', an issue that will reappear in other contexts in Chapters 10 and 11.

Three violent seascapes evoking three narrative ekphrases, each representing its reading of the painting in the rhythm and symbolism of its language. Each, too, contains a poetic construct of Turner suggested by Wain's interpolated speech, Stainer's quoted remarks, and Dabydeen's fictional characters. Equally, each poem constructs an image of the poetic in Turner, Wain locating it in the spectator's aesthetic response, Stainer in the artist's re-creation of our way of perceiving the flux of the natural world. If there is a hint of idolisation in either of these poems, Dabydeen's remarks provide the corrective. 'There is no sacred Turner', he asserts; and, certainly one dimension of his poem is its deconstruction of the whole concept of Turner's poetic painting.

Turner now and then

McCoubrey (1998: 353) concludes his account of *The Slave Ship* by describing his approach as one that 'has found a more complete artist in Turner, one who thinks in words and images as well as paint'. The sentiment holds true more widely and suggests the emphasis that pedagogy might take in cross-curricular work on Turner.

The three paintings discussed above are surrounded by texts of various kinds, some of which we have drawn upon – extended narrative titles in two instances, Turner's own remarks in prose and verse, contemporary criticism, as well as the recent poems. Juxtaposing late twentieth-century poems with the words and images from 150 years earlier encourages the sort of reading insights that were noted at the end of Chapter 4, where, it was argued that the 'then' is apprehended through the 'now'. The reverse is also true, as the third example shows, implying, as it does, that a current understanding of the situation of black people in a predominantly white society can only be achieved with a knowledge of the history of slavery. Indeed, it was the pressure of this relevance that suggested the title for this chapter. Contemporary is an adjective that elides past and present: it can signify either an earlier period in history, or the modernity of the present day.

Turner is our contemporary, too, in another group of paintings, which through their connection with one of the major Romantic poets, give his work a European dimension. It is only relatively recently that Turner's Byronic paintings and illustrations have become the subject of a full study. David Brown's *Turner and Byron*, The Tate Gallery (1992) is the essential guide. Both Turner and Byron were great travellers; both sought and were looking to express the broad, encompassing patterns of human history in their work; and both found inspiration for these patterns in the history of peoples and places. The six paintings that Turner created on explicitly Byronic themes raise the questions of verbal–visual relationships and the nature of Turner's poetic qualities from another angle. They pose the issue of how we are meant to read the images in relation to *Childe Harold* (Byron (1812–1818), the poem to which all are directly linked. Do Turner's paintings illustrate, interpret, develop, subvert the Byronic views embodied in the selective quotations from the poem which Turner appended as extended captions? How far do the paintings reflect an originating or implied narrative? Do they depict a whole episode in the poem or just a detail? Or is the rela-tionship just a matter of association? Conversely, are the pictures comprehensible without some knowledge of their stories in Byron and the titles Turner gave them?

Byron's *Childe Harold's Pilgrimage* appeared between 1812 and 1818, a poetic travelogue narrated by a passionate, melancholy, well-informed tourist whose fictitious title did little to disguise the fact that the protagonist was the author himself. Two of Turner's paintings relate to Canto 3 (1816), the other four to Canto 4 (1818) and were exhibited over a period from 1818 to 1844. They picture the carnage of Waterloo, the sparkling landscape of the Rhine near Coblenz, a bright, optimistic Italian landscape, a view of Rome, and two views of Venice. While there is no evidence that poet and painter met, it is clear that Turner was conscious of following in Byron's footsteps when he visited Waterloo and the Rhineland in 1817. As Brown (1992: 26) neatly puts it: 'While Turner drew the Rhine, Byron was in Venice, at work on *Childe Harold IV*'.

Three of Turner's Byronic paintings, together with the relevant lines from *Childe Harold*, will take students into the issues raised above. They are:

- *The Field of Waterloo* (1818), originally exhibited with Byron's stanza from *Childe Harold*, III, 28, slightly adapted. Painting and poem are explicitly connected (Lindsay 1985: 86; Brown 1992: 92). Both resist the triumphalism of victory over Napoleon and focus on the grim realities of mass slaughter.
- *Childe Harold's Pilgrimage* (1832), originally exhibited with seven lines from *Childe Harold*, IV, 4. Turner is here illustrating not a text (despite the quoted lines) but a concept – Italy as a rich, fertile land of beautiful build-ings in decay. The picture attains its poetic character less from its title and caption than through its Claudean composition, light, and sense of serenity.
- *Venice, the Bridge of Sighs* (1840), originally exhibited with lines either misremembered or deliberately changed from the celebrated opening of

Childe Harold, IV: 'I stood in Venice, on the Bridge of Sighs, / A palace and a prison on each hand'. Turner's prosaic version, leached of its Byronic music, reads: 'I stood upon a bridge, a palace and / A prison on each hand'! Here, the relationship between words and image is merely referential. Turner's interest is in the play of sunlight on buildings, the merging of stone, sunshine, air and water.

As Brown suggests, Byron certainly contributed to Turner's Europeanism and credits him with 'Turner's transformation from a relatively insular artist to one of the most widely travelled of the British Romantics' (Brown 1992: 56). Turner accorded no other contemporary poet the distinction of having his name and the title of his work alongside his paintings. However, he did revere the poets and painters from the previous century and celebrated their work in both verse and pictures.

Finally, then, a group of paintings, with accompanying verses by Turner himself, which focus on the symbolism invested in the Thames of Pope and Thomson. The essential source book here is Andrew Wilton's *Painting and Poetry. Turner's 'Verse Book' and his work of 1804–1812* (Tate Gallery 1990). The three paintings are:

- *View of Pope's Villa at Twickenham during its Dilapidation* (1808), together with Turner's verses, 'On the Demolition of Pope-House at Twickenham' (Wilton 1990: 150. See also, pp. 129–30). In 1807 an act of desecration took place on the banks of the Thames: Pope's house was demolished, apparently, because the new owner could not tolerate the succession of visitors to this cultural shrine. The literariness of the subject is also present in the metaphorical details of both painting and poem.
- *Thomson's Aeolian Harp* (1809), together with the longest poem Turner every published (32 lines), 'On Thomson's tomb the dewy drops distil … ' (Wilton 1990: 134). The painting was constructed on Claudean principles to create a landscape deliberately associating Britain with the harmony, prosperity and culture of the Golden Age. The poem is a Thomsonian pastiche whose words mirror the picture and simultaneously reflect Turner's respect for the poet and painter he most admired.
- *London* (1809), together with Turner's six-line poem, 'Where burthen'd Thames, reflects the crowded sail … ' (Wilton 1990: 135). The painting shows one of the most famous views across the city, a panorama from Greenwich Park. The pastoral foreground and architectural grandeur celebrated in the picture are subverted by the 'commercial care and busy toils' that characterise the poem.

What do these three Thames pictures and their verses tell us about Turner's 'poetic painting'? Clearly, the ekphrastic relationship of the poems to their respective pictures differs: the lines on *Pope's Villa* stay close to a descriptive reading of the visual image before venturing into symbolism; those on

Thomson's Aeolian Harp read more like public homage to Thomson and Claude where the music of the one and the landscape schema of the other are implicit in the poem; those on *London* appear more like a rejection of description in favour of an interrogation of the picture through the reflective, probing power of verbal imagery. Yet, what they have in common is more important than what differentiates them. For, in so far as the verses show Turner interpreting his own paintings by means of symbolic details, personification, metaphor, allegory and other figurative devices, they all indicate modes of representing experience which characterise not only his poetry but also his painting. Poetry, for Turner, was part of the creative process; it was his 'working' – a verbal means to an end.

The notion of Turner's 'poetic painting' with which we began can thus be explored through these three complementary groups of pictures and poems that direct attention, respectively, to perspectives of and from each of the past three centuries. In studying these paintings and texts, our roles as spectators assume different guises and afford different insights. We learn about the early nineteenth-century canon and see the influence of Claude and Thomson on the sister arts. We watch Turner follow in Byron's footsteps, painting European scenes observed on his travels, yet seeing them through Byronic eyes. We look back at Turner from the late twentieth century, sensing how his art continues to speak to modern spectators, reading with or against his visual texts according to how we balance their aesthetic appeal with the ideas they embody. Looking at Turner is to study a contemporary now and then.

9   Painting Shakespeare

Illustration

Illustration is the reverse of ekphrasis: unlike the poem 'speaking out' for a silent picture, paintings which illustrate literature 'read silently' the poetry to which they refer; and these 'visual readings' remain on view, available as texts to complement that literature. But one cannot overlook the dependency in the origins of illustration. The visual image comes into existence in response to a verbal stimulus, its orientation controlled and its details dictated to a greater or lesser extent by its original in another medium. There is a measure of freedom in the translation; and how painters exercise it is of significant interest to aesthetic education in two ways. First, in illuminating how the two media create their effects; and second, for the pedagogical benefits that flow from using paintings in literature teaching, especially in relation to older texts.

For the best part of two centuries, from Hogarth's *The Beggar's Opera* (1728) to Waterhouse's *The Lady of Shalott* (1888), English painting is liberally punctuated with famous images based on literary texts. Shakespeare, Milton, Keats and Tennyson are perhaps the most popular poets with painters. In comparative art history, these literary subjects hold particular interest when the same text is depicted by different artists. From an educational standpoint, the relationship between word and image is the more productive. It is a problematic one, raising a list of tricky questions: Do paintings extend or close down our readings of literary texts? Are there different modes of 'reading' required of the two arts? Is there a type of reading available to us via the visual image, one inexpressible in language, that exists alongside the literary text to which it refers? How does the illustrative painting deal with matters of description and narration in respect of its literary source?

Turner's Byronic paintings raised some of these questions but nowhere are they more starkly posed than in paintings of Shakespearean scenes. As Merchant points out in his account of the Boydell Shakespeare Gallery, a project that was intended as the foundation of a British school of history painting, it was Alderman Boydell himself in 1789 who, with disarming honesty, put the case against the illustration of Shakespeare: 'he [Shakespeare] possessed powers which no pencil can reach … it must not, then, be expected, that the art of the

Painter can ever equal the sublimity of the Poet'. Charles Lamb was more bluntly critical:

> What injury did not Boydell's Shakespeare Gallery do me with Shakespeare. To have Opie's Shakespeare, Northcote's Shakespeare, light headed Fuseli's Shakespeare, wooden-headed West's Shakespeare, deaf- headed Reynolds' Shakespeare, instead of my and everybody's Shakespeare. To be tied down to an authentic face of Juliet! To have Imogen's portrait! To confine the illimitable!
>
> (Merchant 1959: 67)

This intemperate outburst ignores the fact that, far from being a means to confine or tie down, painting a Shakespearean scene is itself an interpretation; at its best, it can open up elements of the literary text, and be viewed as a sort of performance which offers its spectators a form of understanding akin to that reached through watching a scene in production. The rest of this chapter sets out to substantiate this claim.

The traditional literary critical argument over Shakespeare has been whether to treat his plays as extended poems or as acting scripts. In educational contexts, this argument resolves itself into a further sub-division between script and performance, since schools and colleges, of necessity, make clear distinctions between play-readings in the classroom and play productions for public view. These distinctions are useful in exploring what sort of understandings are available to the spectator of Shakespearean paintings. Three well-known paintings, representative of poem, script and performance, respectively, will indicate the variety of insights that a study of such paintings can offer. They are: *Ophelia* (1852) by John Everett Millais, *Lady Macbeth Seizing the Daggers* (c. 1812) by Henry Fuseli and *The Play Scene in 'Hamlet'* (1842) by Daniel Maclise. The first depicts a scene that is not staged in Shakespeare but evoked with such descriptive power in the poetry that the artist is led to *augment* his image with his own visual rhetoric. Drama is subdued by painterly detail. The second depicts a scene that is staged in Shakespeare but where the artist *abstracts* the essential theatrical tension and re-dramatises it through representing it in this different iconic medium. The third depicts a scene that is not only staged in Shakespeare but one where the artist is at pains to *document* a notional performance by representing the proscenium arch as a compositional principle and by including references to contemporary styles of acting and production. Of course, these are not discrete categories of illustration; but they do reflect the emphases of a great many pictures and are helpful in teasing out the aesthetic appeal of painting Shakespeare.

Poem: the female muse

Pre-Raphaelite painting was linked with poetry from the time of its inception just four years before Millais's *Ophelia* was first exhibited at the Royal Academy in 1852. Shakespeare's plays provided the source for what became one of the Pre-Raphaelites' most absorbing interests: women. As Jan Marsh (1987) has shown, their fascination took many artistic forms. On the one hand, they elevated women to an instantly recognisable type of goddess – long-necked, with flowing tresses and a soulful expression; on the other, they reduced women to a series of roles which were the constructs of the predominantly male painters – virgins, mothers, fallen women and femmes fatales. Similarly, though their view of women is idealised and celebratory, it is also invested with Victorian values that were accustomed to promoting the passive, decorative woman as the centre of moral and domestic influence within the home. Favourite Shakespearean women painted in this period are Ophelia, Juliet and Miranda. These three women have much in common; they are all very young, desirable, naive, and essentially powerless. They also all experience deep romantic love. In each case their lives are ordered and their futures decided by an older, male generation. The Pre-Raphaelite painters would have been attracted by them as nubile young women under the influence of romantic love that was to be (in two cases) shattered by death. Moreover, the contemporary model of marriage was moving away from a union determined by considerations of class and property to a relationship that was expected to involve the deepest sexual and romantic feelings of the participants. Whilst similarity of background and interest was seen as desirable, the ideal union – which is in many places enshrined in Victorian literature – was based on a shared romantic commitment. However, it was also a relationship which was vulnerable to untimely death, most often of the wife, in childbirth. Thus, from this Victorian pairing of love and death with youth and beauty springs the choice of Shakespearean heroine and the elegiac quality of many contemporary paintings.

Uniquely, in his picture of *Ophelia* (Figure 9.1), Millais expresses these themes in both art and life. The construction of this image is well documented: Millais spent nearly four months from July to October 1851 painting the background on the bank of the River Hogsmill at Ewell in Surrey. In December he returned with the canvas to London where he inserted the figure, with Elizabeth Siddal portraying the tragic heroine. The short career of Elizabeth Siddal as a super-model – or 'stunner' to use the Pre-Raphaelites' term – and her early death are surrounded by an aura of romantic myth which vies with that of the fictional figure she portrays (Marsh 1991; Surtees 1991). By re-inventing the Shakespearean woman in these visual terms, Millais was giving form and substance to the Pre-Raphaelites' Muse. Painting Shakespeare as poetry could scarcely have had a more propitious narrative in art history from which to spring for, though frequently chosen by later artists, Ophelia was at this time a highly original subject.

Millais' painting is faithful to Shakespeare's text in providing an imaginative recreation of Gertrude's lines describing Ophelia's death:

> There is a willow grows aslant a brook
> That shows his hoar leaves in the glassy stream;

Figure 9.1   John Everett Millais, *Ophelia* (1851–2), The Tate Gallery, London, oil on canvas.

> There with fantastic garlands did she come
> Of crow-flowers, nettles, daisies, and long purples
> That liberal shepherds give a grosser name,
> But our cold maids do dead men's fingers call them.
> There, on the pendent boughs her coronet weeds
> Clambering to hang, an envious sliver broke;
> When down her weedy trophies and herself
> Fell in the weeping brook. Her clothes spread wide,
> And, mermaid-like, awhile they bore her up;
> Which time she chanted snatches of old tunes,
> As one incapable of her own distress,
> Or like a creature native and indued
> Unto that element. But long it could not be
> Till that her garments, heavy with their drink,
> Pulled the poor wretch from her melodious lay
> To muddy death.
> > (*Hamlet*, Act IV, Scene vii, lines 167–84)

The imagery is intensely visual and Millais's interpretation is correspondingly rich in precise natural detail. The willow grows 'aslant' the stream, its branches entwined with a nettle and a robin perched on its bough. This recalls the 'bonny Sweet Robin' of Ophelia's song in Act IV, Scene v. The dog roses on the bank, the one by Ophelia's cheek, a further pink rose by the hem of her dress may refer to Laertes having called Ophelia the 'rose of May'. Purple loosestrife in the upper right-hand corner of the painting reflect the 'long purples' of Gertrude's speech, while the violets encircling Ophelia's neck recall those which ' withered all when my father died'. They also carry the meanings of faithfulness, chastity and death. Other flowers in the painting are introduced by Millais: daisies figure innocence, the poppy symbolises death and the forget-me-nots half-way up the figure on the right, and also bottom left, are chosen for their name. The image of woman-as-flower is also one which is pervasive in Pre-Raphaelite painting; woman as fragile, fragrant and passive. The natural colouring of the picture, blending with the silvery-brown of Ophelia's dress and its stylised flower pattern, suggests that she is returning to a fertile, natural element into which she will gradually be absorbed. There is no sense of an individual young woman, despite the well-known account of Elizabeth Siddal's long-suffering role as Millais's model (Wilson 1990: 83), but rather woman as an example of tragic heroine; a sacrificial victim who is all the more alluring because at the point of death. Her facial expression is empty of all meaning, the eyes unseeing because she has passed beyond any visual awareness of her surroundings. The impact of the painting rests in the poignant contrast between the bright Spring flowers and the defencelessness of the drowning girl. There is no sign of the 'envious sliver', no dirt under her finger nails, no mud on her dress; she is a mermaid in her element, belonging to water not earth, and associated, as her parted lips suggest, with an unearthly music.

Given the painstaking, botanical fidelity, the presentation of the figure, and the deliberate exclusion of any details suggesting a stage, this example of 'painting Shakespeare as poem' has a curiously ambiguous effect. The spectator is faced with an image in which the background is in danger of overwhelming the subject in a way that is impossible when a Shakespearean text is considered as either script or performance. In pursuing a portrayal of the poetic description, Millais has achieved a vivid tableau. If one covers the hands, bosom and head of the figure, the remaining nine-tenths of the picture is a display of technical virtuosity – a brilliant rendering of botanical detail, an almost two-dimensional flatness in the spatial organisation, aqueous effects, and subtle lighting. This prolixity is neither present nor needed in Shakespeare. The weight of detail 'stills' Millais's image, whereas in Gertrude's lines the natural scene is infiltrated by the sequence of actions describing Ophelia's last moments. Moreover, the figure, on the visible evidence of her head and hands, appears healthy and serene, not deranged as the play describes. The spectator might well feel that there is more of the actual Elizabeth Siddal than of the poetic Ophelia. Here, too, the attempt to illustrate the poetry is subverted by the artifice of the different iconic medium; as a result, the spectator is left with the sense that this image says more about Millais's construction of Victorian womanhood than it does about Shakespeare's Ophelia.

Millais's *Ophelia* must stand as the representative of the many other nine-teenth-century painted Ophelias; and she exists, too, along with Dante Gabriel Rossetti's multiple images of Elizabeth Siddal, as the female ideal that can be found and reconstructed in the real world. Together, fictional Ophelia and actual Lizzie become the icon for the myth of womanhood that the Pre-Raphaelite painters especially pursued. Women inspired them, in particular, the young and always beautiful women of Shakespearean and Romantic poetry. In one sense this was the ordinary desire of male painters to paint decorative women but, as indicated above, 'woman' became a dominating metaphor for their creative psyche; a blend of muse, cultural ideal and spiritual icon. It is rewarding to examine the extent to which a character is granted autonomy, something which Shakespeare had no trouble in assigning to his women, and the extent to which subjects remain simply that – prisoners of the artist. A comparison of these areas shows Shakespeare vigorously reclaiming the wider spectrum of human behaviour. By contrast, Millais and his fellow Pre-Raphaelites had little time for Benedict's Beatrice, Petruchio's Kate, Portia, or Lady Macbeth – difficult char-acters, to a woman. For their representative, we need to look elsewhere.

Script: the 'painted devil'

With Fuseli's *Lady Macbeth Seizing the Daggers* (Figure 9.2), illustration takes a step nearer to the stage. Fuseli concentrates on the visual representation of an episode of heightened psychological tension. Whereas Millais's picture 'lives off' its original text, presenting a richly jewelled surface that is essentially parasitic upon Shakespeare's words, Fuseli's picture interprets and expresses the obsessive and perverted relationship between the protagonists that drives the whole of *Macbeth*.

Again, the genesis of the picture is helpful in understanding the nature of the image. From the 1760s onwards, Fuseli was, in Lucy Oakley's words, 'England's most prolific and influential eighteenth-century artist-interpreter of Shakespeare' (Oakley 1986: 5) and *Macbeth* was the play to which he returned most frequently. Two particular theatrical interpretations together with many depictions of episodes from the play over a forty-year period appear to have influenced this final painting. The immediate inspiration may well have been Mrs Siddons's last performance in her celebrated role as Lady Macbeth on 29 June 1812, the year in which Fuseli's picture was first exhibited. Years before, however, Fuseli had watched David Garrick and Mrs Pritchard in the leading parts and produced a watercolour of this same scene. Comparison of this 1766 drawing (reproduced in Oakley 1986) with the later oil painting is instructive. Although the concentration upon the figures is essentially similar, the treat-ment is dramatically different. Against a more realistically painted stage set with paved floor, screens and curtains, the two figures are elaborately clothed – Macbeth in buckled shoes, knee breeches, shirt and long jacket; Lady Macbeth in shoes, underskirt, a voluminous farthingale and adorned with a light shawl and various items of jewellery. Macbeth's stance and face express a melodramatic stage horror which, no doubt, reflected Garrick's performance, as he points the daggers towards his wife. She, in turn, leans slightly backwards, her left index finger to her lips to quieten her husband and her right hand, open-palmed, extended towards him in the manner of a reproving mother dealing with a naughty boy.

The final painting strips the image of this stagy naturalism: the curtain to the right is reduced to a dark shape tied back; the door jambs to the left function more as a psychological cage pressing in claustrophobically on Macbeth than as an actual door frame. Fuseli has no other interest in the stage set. His attention is upon the walking, haunted ghost that Macbeth has become and the intensity that he is greeted with by his wife.

> Infirm of purpose!
> Give me the daggers. The sleeping and the dead
> Are but as pictures; 'tis the eye of childhood
> That fears a painted devil.
>   (*Macbeth*, Act II, Scene ii, lines 53–6)

Fuseli gives us Macbeth as 'a painted devil': the bloodied daggers are now angled towards himself, the naked evil of his crime exposed in his portrayal as a tense,

Figure 9.2   Henry Fuseli, *Lady Macbeth Seizing the Daggers*, c. 1812, The Tate Gallery, London, oil on canvas.

inhuman skeleton. The overall atmosphere achieves its intensity also through areas of black and dark brown contrasted with the use of a ghastly white. We know that the murder of Duncan takes place at night but here Fuseli creates a Stygian darkness that effectively conveys appropriately mythological intimations of hell. In Fuseli's interpretation of the scene, Macbeth and Lady Macbeth are both living within a nightmare of their own creation and are already fatefully depicted as the lost souls they are destined to become.

As is often typical of Fuseli's more mature painting, he does not extend his picture to the borders of the canvas, thereby attaining a heightened concentration on its central focus. The two protagonists confront one another but there is little doubt as to where the balance of power lies. Conspirators in action, they are irrevocably connected and psychologically divided. Macbeth, a skeletal, stooping figure stumbles through a doorway transfixed by the horrific evidence of his crime. As Fuseli's depiction suggests, he has already become a hollow shell of a man, manipulated by his ruthless wife. The Greek mask of terror that his face resembles is noted by Jean Hagstrum (1978: 27) as Fuseli's 'regular symbol of oppression and tyranny'. The blood that covers his dagger and hands, and that can also be seen within Macbeth's torso, indicates the extent of his moral compromise with evil, suggesting a cancerous process that cannot now be reversed. Lady Macbeth's stance is contrastingly bold and vigorous; her strong movement emphasises Macbeth's paralysis – it conveys the body language of power. Unlike her stance in the early drawing, she now leans energetically forward, the angularities of her form clad only in the ghostly drapery of an evening dress. She now gestures silence with her right index finger, allowing Fuseli both to balance the two figures by extending her left arm along the same line as Macbeth's and to infuse Lady Macbeth with the urgency of dramatic movement that Shakespeare's scene demands of her: within two lines she has left to incriminate the grooms.

What does the foregoing account imply about 'painting Shakespeare as script'? Clearly, Fuseli's painting depends in a fundamental sense upon Shakespeare's play and yet it has the ability to encapsulate theatrical and dramatic meanings that lead from both the stage and the page. Fuseli's work inhabits the area between a theatrical production and a literary reading, since it develops from both art forms to establish its own independent dimension. This dimension is achieved by going beyond mere theatricality and introducing surrealistic elements which are either unacceptable or unworkable on stage. The spectator is drawn into the interior, psychological world of *Macbeth*, not by the painterly elaboration of details, but by the rigorous exclusion of naturalism in favour of an expressionist image of the play's central conflict. Such illustration is far removed from being a decorative response; it is an interpretative act of critical insight.

Performance: 'the play's the thing'

In a fascinating essay on 'Shakespeare and the Theatre of Illustration', Cary Mazer describes the idiom in which nineteenth-century productions of

Shakespeare were staged as 'pictorial realism' (Mazer 1986: 24). He goes on to explain how this 'theatre of illusion, of spectacle, of picture, of geographical and historical specificity' shared an aesthetic kinship with the art of the easel painter and the book illustrator. This idiom was at odds with the theatre for which Shakespeare wrote his plays where the players and the poetry set the scene. In contrast, the theatre of pictorial realism set out to create an illusion of an actual place and time. Mazer continues: 'The proscenium arch, behind which the action took place, was like a picture frame setting off a pictorial composition, or a window through which the audience viewed an illusionary world.' Yet this was not another variation on the theme of the sister arts with, in this instance, theatrical productions and Shakespearean paintings imitating each other; for, despite the abundance of portraits of actors in their roles and depictions of scenes from their performances, 'the vast majority of paintings on Shakespearean subjects were not based on the Shakespeare of the theatre, but on the Shakespeare of the study'. Mazer argues that the theatre of pictorial realism was a theatre of illustration. Stage performance was a way of elaborating upon the literary text, of telling the Shakespearean stories 'in the language of living pictures'. He concludes: 'The features that Shakespearean painting and Shakespearean performance of the nineteenth century have in common, then, are not so much the product of their interrelationship as of their parallel relationship to literary, rather than theatrical, sources' (Mazer 1986: 28). Against this background, when we look at Maclise's painting of *The Play Scene in 'Hamlet'* (Figure 9.3), how much do we read 'backwards' to Shakespeare's text and how much 'sideways' to contemporary theatrical practices?

Maclise's picture is a history painting on the grand scale. It is a huge canvas (60 x 108 ft) yet, despite its size, there is a firmly controlled compositional

Figure 9.3   Daniel Maclise, *The Play Scene in 'Hamlet'* (1842), The Tate Gallery, London, oil on canvas.

scheme to organise the host of characters and to depict the play-within-a-play. The frame of the painting – with the aid of two curved reminders of the actual theatre in the top corners – creates a proscenium; 'and the play-within-a-play is staged on a proscenium-within-a-proscenium' (Mazer 1986: 26). The spectator views the action from the best seat in the house, slightly raised above stage level and centrally placed. The dramatic moment that the painting depicts is at the climax of the play-scene, just before Claudius's departure, when Lucianus pours poison in Gonzago's ear. Yet, when originally exhibited, Maclise chose Hamlet's lines to Horatio before the start of the play-within-a-play with which to accompany the painting:

> There is a play tonight before the king;
> One scene of it comes near the circumstance
> Which I have told thee, of my father's death;
> I prithee, when thou seest that act afoot,
> Even with the very comment of thy soul
> Observe my uncle …
>   Give him heedful note,
> For I mine eyes will rivet to his face.
> (*Hamlet*, Act III, Scene ii, lines 71–6; 80–1)

The reason for this is clear: the caption quotation clearly directs us to the narrative performance of the play-within-a-play and, particularly, to its effect on the spectators. The meaning of the painting lies in the intelligibility of the internal gazes of the characters. Maclise translates the final lines of the caption quotation into visual terms: spectatorship, or more precisely, observation is the theme. Courtiers, guards, ladies-in-waiting and children form the outer audience watching the action with a variety of emotions: to the left, one apprehensive lady, hands clasped together, receives an explanation from the man behind her; to the right, two women stare at the stage, seemingly transfixed by the simulated murder. The inner audience comprises Horatio and Ophelia to the left, Claudius, Gertrude and Polonius to the right, and a recumbent Hamlet between them below the recessed stage. It provides, simultaneously, both a cross-current of gazes to capture the psychological tension, and a strong compositional framework to encapsulate the dramatic climax. Of the six principals, only Gertrude appears to be watching the play; the rest are watching each other. Horatio thoughtfully observes the King, Ophelia's eyes are cast down sadly towards Hamlet, while her father stands, head bowed, watching his daughter; but the core of the tension is inscribed in the triangulation that connects the murder of Gonzago happening on stage at its apex, with Hamlet watching Claudius, and Claudius, turned away, staring into his own soul. Neither Hamlet nor Claudius needs to watch the play at this point; they know what is happening. The tension that flows along the lines of this central triangle scarcely needs the dramatic chiaroscuro on the clothes and faces, nor the touch of melodrama in the shadow of the hooded Lucianus, the poisoner, which rears up across the back wall. Also consistent with the idea that the theatre of pictorial realism was a theatre of illustration is Maclise's introduction of visual symbolism to add the moral weight of historical precedent to the drama. Hence, in the background are ranged a series of allegorical emblems: Ophelia sits beneath a figure whose hands are in an attitude of prayer; the statue of Justice with sword and scales stands over Claudius. The tapestries are similarly balanced. That on the left wall depicts the temptation and expulsion of Adam and Eve from the Garden of Eden; that on the right wall shows 'The Sacrifice of Abel' and 'Cain Murdering Abel': all refer to the play's themes of murder and disinheritance. Such visual representations of Biblical stories add an intertextual layer of meaning to the picture.

'Painting Shakespeare as performance' is clearly more complicated than the straight translation from theatre to canvas. While the stage and the spectator's angle of gaze may provide the schema, the substance of the image is likely to derive from various literary and visual sources and to reflect the artistic conventions of more than one medium. Shakespeare's text, contemporary productions of *Hamlet* that Maclise attended, other pictures of the play with which he was familiar such as those by the German artist Moritz Retzsch (Anderson 1986: 71) – all contribute to the final image. Visual representations of stage performances, whether notional or actual, are constructs that may beguile by their seemingly innocent appearance as theatrical documentary; in fact, they are doubly representational, affecting to represent on canvas what has already been represented on stage with the illusion of verisimilitude that is neither possible when painting Shakespeare as poem, nor sought after when painting Shakespeare as script.

Text and image

Implicit in the examples we have discussed is the triangular relationship between Shakespeare's texts, stage performances and the painter's visual representations. The substantive words and images, constantly open to our inspection, are joined by the ghosts of past performances. The aesthetic problems that this series of relationships sets the spectator are not only complex in themselves as the above account shows but also pose issues of classroom methodology. The 'double status' of the text – as script and as poem – complicates the study of Shakespeare for scholars, painters and teachers alike. This is why, when considering the range of Shakespearean paintings, it is helpful to discriminate further between the 'visual script' such as Fuseli's that constitutes a psychological metaphor, and the 'visualisation' offered by Maclise that, for all its tension, reflects the conventions of the theatre of illustration whose purpose was to tell tales from Shakespeare in the idiom of living pictures.

In respect of classroom methodology, the exploration of various aesthetic relationships is opened up by such cross-curricular study. For example, Millais's *Ophelia* is one among many. Students' own visualisations of the scene can be compared with those of a range of artists where the contrasts in the representation of her character, the precise moment of her death scene that is depicted, and the relationship between the figure and the setting offer a variety of interpolations that serve to direct the spectator back to the poetry of Gertrude's lines. To Millais's tragic heroine might be added Arthur Hughes's elfin-faced, Madonna-like girl and any of John Waterhouse's three Ophelias, dated respectively, 1889, 1894 and 1910. Waterhouse's first image is of a tousled and provocative girl lying in an abandoned attitude in the grass, a seductive Ophelia whose innocence has been corrupted. The second is an enchanting, medieval damsel from the age of romance and Arthurian quests, dressed in period costume, with the look of a tragic princess waiting to be rescued by her knight. The third reflects the Edwardian fashion for a more statuesque figure and this full-bosomed girl appears both pensive and sensuously beautiful. Whether lying down, sitting or standing – at whatever the supposed moment in the scene – Waterhouse's Ophelia gives no sense of a deranged mind. The comparative deconstruction of such images in relation to Shakespeare's text offers insights into how description and narration operate in the two media. Considered alongside Shakespeare's poetry, these images expose the delimiting effects of illustrating unstaged scenes, as the painter is driven to compensate for the narrative restrictions of the medium, either by increasing specificity of detail (Millais), or by portraying his subject as a sort of costume drama in ancient or modern dress (Waterhouse).

Other questions were raised at the outset to do with 'reading' the two arts. Fuseli's reading of *Macbeth* as seen in the particular painting discussed could be extended to include other drawings, sketches and paintings he produced of scenes from the play, notably, *Lady Macbeth* (1784), *The Weird Sisters* (c. 1785), two versions of Macbeth and Banquo meeting the witches on the heath (1798 and 1817), and his *Shakespeare Cycle: Macbeth* (1777–8), a set of six ink sketches on paper of different scenes (Merchant 1959; Weinglass 1994). More significantly, in the light of the questions raised on p. 147, this long preoccupation with the play appears to deepen both his aesthetic appreciation of its meaning and his capacity to express it on canvas. His late great painting *does* possess the quality to stand alongside Shakespeare's lines and communicate the evil intensity and existential horror of the scene in a visual language unavailable to the playwright. Shakespeare gives us a narrative of evil; Fuseli paints evil itself. Word and image complement each other in a unique relationship.

These are big claims and should not be advanced without evidence. A few excerpts from the tape-recorded comments of four 17-year-old girls discussing Fuseli's painting and Shakespeare's text must suffice. (I am grateful to Dr Sally Butcher for permission to use these extracts from her unpublished PhD thesis.) They indicate, in turn, how the students read the visual language of the painting, especially in the portrayal of Macbeth's figure; the students' awareness of being positioned in a spectator role that, imaginatively speaking, is dangerously close to these murderers; and, third, their appreciation of the complementarity of text and picture.

Their discussion of the painting began with some remarks about the facial expressions and bodily positions of the characters. There then followed an interesting exchange that showed their sense of the visual language of the picture, where the stillness and silence demanded by Shakespeare's scene became the stillness and silence of the visual medium.

Liz:	There's a lot of kind of suppressed movement in it as if they've been running around and suddenly they're almost trying to ... still it.
Julia:	Yes – it's their life. They're both sort of mid-movement, aren't they?
Liz:	Yeah, she's trying to silence the picture, silence him, silencing the picture almost.

This feeling of tense immobility led to a series of comments on the significance of the characters' body language. It culminated in the following exchanges about the depiction of Macbeth, which show the students translating the visual language of colour, shape and form into a sense of the symbolism at the heart of the whole play, as Liz's final remark in particular suggests.

Julia:	His whole body is weird; it's like a cross between armour and a skeleton, I think.
Jo:	He looks like death itself, I think, 'cos his hair is so grey and ...
Julia:	And his face is wild, isn't it?
Jo:	Yeah, ... it's like electricity flowing through his hair.
Julia:	But, don't you think that, if you look right down the front of him, that looks like ribs?
Jo:	Yeah, his ribs and all his muscles you can see in his arms like the strings.
Julia:	And look at how his right leg turns into some sort of bone and you can barely see the rest of his leg.
Liz:	As if what he's done has stripped him of all his human nature.

The image on the canvas, like the corresponding scene on the stage, is one of the most powerful theatrical moments of the whole play. It owes its intensity, in part, to the fact that the spectator is positioned as a privileged but unacknowledged observer of an encounter where no witnesses are wanted. The students sensed the virtual danger that the painting evoked:

> *Liz:* Psychologically, it does give you a bit ... makes you a bit scared, just looking at their faces. ... I'd straight away just shut up, just looking at her, it'd make me stop and think as if I was in the room, and just watch.
>
> *Julia:* You're looking on a level with them, I think.
>
> *Liz:* I think we're in darkness.
>
> *Julia:* You're certainly in the room with them, I think, almost like you're in the corner just watching what's going on.
>
> *Liz:* But it makes me want to shut up in case he saw me and came at me with a dagger.

As spectators, they have been placed very close to the action, silently and covertly watching, hidden 'in the darkness'. Significantly, as Julia says, they are 'in the room', not in the wings: the space they imaginatively occupy is the secondary world of Macbeth's castle at Inverness, not the primary world of a stage set. For these students, Fuseli's picture thus achieved the illusion that theatre constantly seeks.

But, did the painting add anything to the text? More pertinently, what can the painting convey that the text cannot, and *vice versa*? Here is what the students said:

> *Liz:* I think it's really appropriate that she's the dominant one just as she is there [i.e. in the text] and also she looks so angry with him.
>
> *Julia:* Yeah, it gives you an idea of what they're feeling.
>
> *Jo:* And of their relationship.
>
> *Liz:* The painting shows the stance they're in, their action gives you an idea of where they've come from and what they've done and what they're about to do. But also I mean ...
>
> *Julia:* It can't tell you what's going to happen, can it?
>
> *Liz:* No.
>
> *Julia:* In the text you know that she's going to go and she's going to take the daggers.
>
> *Jo:* But here in the picture you don't know.
>
> *Julia:* If I had to choose one or other to get a clearer picture, I'd choose the text, 'cos in the text you get the picture and you also get more in depth. You know, when you look at this [the painting] you're thinking, 'well, perhaps she could be feeling this' and 'perhaps he could be thinking that', whereas with the text you know it's there.
>
> *Jo:* I think that the text and the painting complement each other.

Julia:	Yeah, I do as well.
Jo:	Because the text has some bits which you couldn't tell from the painting, and the painting has some bits which … I think the picture in a way is almost … I don't know if it's more powerful but …
Julia:	It's more of an instant thing, isn't it?
Jo:	Yeah, it's very much visually … Ooh! … striking!
Julia:	You look at it!
Jo:	Their eyes, you know, his are so full of fear and hers are so full of rage and *that* is not an instant thing which you get from the text.
Julia:	Yes, it's definitely a more immediate reaction you get from the painting.

Even these short extracts indicate the extra dimensions that such comparative study offered. The students' awareness of their spectator role and of the complementary qualities of the three different art forms of theatre, painting and poetry clearly extended their knowledge of how these arts create their effects and enriched their experience of Shakespeare.

If studying Fuseli's *Macbeth* painting can deepen the concept of reading in these ways, the pictorial realism exemplified by Maclise offers different benefits. In particular, the parallel relationship between theatrical practices and visual illustrations on canvas or in books, gives ready access into how nineteenth-century aesthetic principles interpreted early seventeenth-century dramas. Maclise's painting is less important for the details it documents about the staging of Victorian productions of Shakespeare than it is for what this documentation signifies about these principles. To read the positioning of the characters, the symbolic areas of light and shadow, the allegories on the walls, is to read the Victorian mind and how it interpreted a canonical text in the light of contemporary values.

Paintings of Shakespearean scenes thus offer singular sorts of 'performances'. They are not to be viewed as mere 'stills', as it were, from an ongoing production, but as representations that have distilled influences and ideas from far beyond the confines of the particular image and from outside the medium in which they are made. Conversely, such concentrations of meanings into a single image lead to paintings of Shakespeare – whether of poem, script or performance – that offer rich insights into the plays themselves.

10 Images of war:
Spencer, Nash and the war poets

Earth and air

In the public mind, the emblem of the First World War is the trench; that of the Second World War is the bomb. The First World War was mainly a land war. Soldiers fought and died in their tens of thousands over patches of ground that were still recognisably fields of battle. The names we remember are Passchendaele, the Somme, Flanders Fields. ... The Second World War was dominated from the air. Between the atrocities of Guernica in the Spanish Civil War in 1937 and Hiroshima and Nagasaki in 1945, tens of thousands of civilians were subjected to aerial bombardment in their own homes. The other names we remember are the blitzes of London, Coventry, Dresden. ...

Anthologies of poetry and pictures recording these conflicts are legion and need no rehearsal here. This chapter has a deliberately narrow focus upon works by two artists who each depicted images of both wars and which, among other things, reflect this change in emphasis from earth to air. Stanley Spencer's paintings in Sandham Memorial Chapel (1927–32), drawing upon his experiences in the First World War, are earth-bound in the human scale and often domestic nature of their subject matter; yet, their spiritual orientation is heavenwards. Paul Nash's 'aerial creatures', his own phrase for the paintings of aircraft he produced between 1941 and 1944, are an exploration of his life-long interest in flight; yet, they are painted by a man who himself never took to the air and whose most memorable achievement is a picture of wrecked German planes in a dump at Cowley – the dystopian landscape, *Totes Meer, 1940–41* (Figure 10.2). These works by Spencer and Nash set the agenda for the two parts of this chapter: how the sister arts represent what happens when the Christian faith 'goes to war'; and how painters and poets reconstruct the conventional idea of landscape as a means of conceptualising their relationship with war.

The spiritual dimension in Spencer is complemented by Wilfred Owen's well-documented struggle 'as a conscientious objector with a very seared conscience' (Owen and Bell 1967: 461, Letter no. 512). Yet painter and poet express strikingly different perceptions of the relationship between war and Christianity. Owen frequently draws upon Christian symbolism as in his celebrated 'Anthem For Doomed Youth'; and 'Strange Meeting', with its subterranean vision, provides a spiritual pessimism about death in war as a worthwhile sacrifice which counters the naive optimism of the central painting at Sandham, *The Resurrection* (Figure 10.1), where dead soldiers rise from their graves and happily greet their comrades in arms. The complements to Nash's painting are Keith Douglas's three linked poems, 'Landscape With Figures' (1943) written by a poet who was later killed in action. Keith Douglas's changing viewpoint perfectly conveys his ambivalent sense of involvement in and detachment from the theatre of war – its inner and exterior landscapes.

This range of time, place and purpose, even within such a limited selection of examples, means that spectatorship manifests itself in a variety of ways. In particular, in this chapter, there will be an emphasis upon the soldier-poets and the soldier-painters themselves as spectators of and participants in the actual conflicts, as well as upon the spectatorship of their readers and viewers. There is an uneasy relationship between the two. Those who suffer war are separated, by their experiences, from those who do not. The warring loyalties to his beliefs and to his fellow soldiers, felt, for example, by Owen and, albeit less acutely, by other combatants can be only partially understood by the majority of us, far removed in time and place from the action. Furthermore, there are several unique factors to keep in mind about how the arts represent the two world wars. One curiosity is that wars have their officially appointed artists but their unofficial poets. Paul Nash, Stanley Spencer, Christopher Nevinson, Eric Ravilious and others were all appointed by Government ministries to make a visual record of the conflicts. Wilfred Owen and Siegfried Sassoon in the First World War, Keith Douglas and Alun Lewis in the Second World War were all on active service of which Sassoon was the only survivor. The variety of roles and differences in status also influence their work and, in particular, have a bearing on the stances they assume. The spectator-participant role thus has a singular meaning in these representations of war. For the poet or painter, it may be as recorder (officially or otherwise), as propagandist, or as protester – stances which may change in the course of a conflict under the pressure of actual rather than artistic participation, as occurred, for example, with Sassoon and Nash. For the reader or viewer, spectatorship may involve similarly unstable or conflicting features: for example, revulsion at the depicted scene yet admiration for the skill that portrays it; or the guilt that accompanies responses to the aesthetics of suffering; or the sense that what the war poem or painting represents for its maker is something quite 'other', and inaccessible to us.

'Onward Christian Soldiers … ': Spencer and Owen

While Stanley Spencer was working as a medical orderly at Beaufort Hospital, Bristol from July 1915 to August 1916, Wilfred Owen, having joined up in the Artists' Rifles in October 1915, was undergoing military training prior to being commissioned as a Second Lieutenant in the Manchester Regiment in June 1916. Painter and poet then experienced 'different wars'. Stanley Spencer volunteered for overseas service and, in August 1916, was assigned to the 68th Field Ambulances in Macedonia. The following year he transferred to the 7th Battalion of the Berkshires and spent several months in the front line before the war ended. Wilfred Owen, meanwhile, left for France in December 1916 and by New Year was on the Somme. For the first six months of 1917, Owen fought in France until, diagnosed with shell-shock, he was sent to Craiglockhart War Hospital near Edinburgh in June. Then followed a year in Britain on light duties during which time he met Sassoon and wrote some of his finest poetry (Hibberd 1973: 35). He returned to France in August 1918 and was killed in action on 4 November 1918, one week before the war ended.

So much for the biographical outline. The issue here, however, is how painter and poet represented their war experiences and, in particular, the way in which their Christian visions of service and sacrifice were affected. An early indication of Spencer's vision lies in the painting he completed in 1919 after being invalided home with malaria, *Travoys Arriving with Wounded at a Dressing-Station at Smol, Macedonia, September 1916*. It depicts wounded soldiers being transported from the Front into a field hospital on mule-drawn stretchers, or travoys. The atmosphere is calm, the composition orderly with none of the mud and blood that would have been encountered on the battlefield. Spencer was explicit that his picture was 'not a true war picture but brought me nearer the truth'. And he goes on to explain that he saw the experience as

> a kind of lesser crucifixion. I mean, not a scene of horror but a scene of redemption from it, and I was right in making it a happy picture as the early painters were right in making the crucifixion a happy painting as they often did.
>
> (MacCarthy 1997: Plate 7)

It appears that, during the two and a half years that Spencer was based in Macedonian hills north of Salonika, he invested the landscape with the same religious vision as his native Cookham (Harries and Harries 1983: 110). The peace of God, even in the depths of suffering, is Spencer's subject.

Spencer placed the following inscription on the west wall of the Sandham Memorial Chapel:

> These paintings by Stanley Spencer and this oratory are the fulfilment of a design which he conceived whilst on active service 1914–1918.

The pictures on the North and South walls are of three types: eight arch-topped panels, painted at the easel and installed above eight rectangular 'predellas' as Spencer called them (small paintings usually – though not here – beneath an altar piece); along each upper wall, over the four panels on either side, Spencer painted a panoramic mural. These two pictures, like that of *The Resurrection of the Soldiers*, which fills the East wall, were painted *in situ*. Nineteen pictures in all, the whole enterprise took nearly four years to complete of which one year alone was devoted to the *The Resurrection*: 'What Ho, Giotto!' was Spencer's enthusiastic response to the commission! (MacCarthy 1997: 22).

Spencer's pictures, even when they depict active service in Macedonia, stress the human companionship and daily routines of war. All eight predellas are homely, mostly interior scenes of hospital activities – scrubbing floors, sorting laundry, filling tea urns and the like which, according to his own account, he invested with spiritual energy. 'When I scrubbed floors', he said, 'I would have all sorts of marvellous thoughts, so much that at the last, when I was fully equipped for scrubbing – bucket, apron, and "prayer mat" in hand – I used to feel much the same as if I was going to church' (Robinson 1991: 8). Of the eight panels, five depict soldiers on active service in Macedonia, where again his main interest lies in comradely activities – soldiers dressing and shaving under mosquito nets, filling water bottles, map-reading, making a protective fire-belt round the camp. Only *Dug-out* shows us soldiers in the trenches and even here the physical horrors are stylised away in favour of aesthetic and spiritual considerations. The overall impression of the pictures on the North and South walls is of domestic service as much as military service. Spencer invested the menial with a sense of sacred purpose and associated himself directly with the privations and routines of a soldier's life by painting himself into several scenes. He appears in the predella *Bedmaking*, not as an orderly but as a patient recording a time when he was hospitalised with malaria in Salonika. As Private Spencer, he appears, too, in the North wall panorama, *The Camp at Karasuli*, depicting himself on litter duty, spearing newspapers with his bayonet. Most obviously, he includes himself in *Making a Fire Belt* where, as Duncan Robinson remarks (1991: 10), 'The resemblance to the artist of the figure crouching in the foreground is unmistakable and confirms his statement that "all my figures are simply *me*, putting myself in places and circumstances in which I want to be". Given this self-referential, not to say egocentric, sentiment and the fact that the Sandham pictures were retrospective images a decade after the war was over, the idea of celebrating service to one's fellow men in any practical sense seems less important than his need to represent and thus exorcise his wartime experiences. Service, for Spencer, appears as a religious duty, contentedly undertaken and optimistically portrayed. It is all one, aesthetically and ideologically, with the celebration of Christian sacrifice and the belief in life after death that are represented in the whole concept of the Sandham Chapel and epitomised in its dominant painting, *The Resurrection*, discussed below. The paintings on the North and South walls, arranged as they are in their three different configurations, avoid a straightforward, sequential account and, instead, offer a symbolic narrative with what Spencer described as 'a mixture of real and spiritual fact' (Robinson 1991: 8). Their purpose is both to provide a supportive context for the message of *The Resurrection* and to reflect its meaning through their visual glorification of mundane experience.

In Owen's case, his upbringing and his dedication to the men under his command were linked and help to explain the complications of his attitude to war. He was brought up in the culture of evangelical Anglicanism and, under the influence of his mother, took an unpaid post as a lay assistant to a country vicar. As Hibberd (1973: 20) says: 'It is important to be aware of the *sort* of religion Wilfred was brought up in: it explains much in his poems – the theme of sacrifice, his fondness for Biblical language, the reality of Hell.' A belief in service to others that develops with such a background could have had no sterner test than at the Front. It led to the inner conflict that lies at the heart of his poetry, the resolution of which has been seen as the prime motive for his writing (Welland 1960: 84–9). When Owen's well-known self-assessment, quoted earlier, as 'a conscientious objector with a very seared conscience' is set alongside his fatal decision to return to France in August 1918, we can only conclude that his sense of service outweighed his knowledge of the evil that awaited him and was likely to kill him. Service, for Owen, was a belief that an officer should be with his men. It is documented in his letters and his verse. Writing of the 'strange ... incomprehensible look' on the faces of the soldiers in the camp at Etaples, Owen says:

> It was not despair, or terror, it was more terrible than terror, for it was a blindfold look, and without expression, like a dead rabbit's. It will never be painted, and no actor will ever seize it. And to describe it, I think I must go back and be with them.
>
> (Owen and Bell 1967: 521, Letter no. 578)

And in the final version of his poem 'The Calls' in May 1918, revised during the months before his return to the Front, he adopts the stance that Heaney has called 'the poet as witness' (Heaney 1988: xvi) and makes explicit his belief that, for him as a poet of war, writing and combat are two sides of the same coin. The poem ends:

> For leaning out last midnight on my sill
> I heard the sighs of men, that have no skill
> To speak of their distress, no, nor the will!
>   A voice I know. And this time I must go.

The voice of conscience tells him that service has two complementary aspects: the reflective role of the writer – albeit one who warns, protests, pities – is not enough; actual, not just imaginative, participation is demanded. As he said in another of his letters:

> I came out in order to help these boys – directly by leading them as well as an officer can; indirectly, by watching their sufferings that I may speak of them as well as a pleader can.
>
> (Owen and Bell 1967: 580, Letter no. 662)

Both Owen and Spencer came to the battlefield in 1917 with a belief in service founded on their Christian faith, yet there is a selflessness and a sense of struggle in the writer's letters and poems that are absent in the painter. The question of sacrifice distinguishes them further: Owen, spiritually challenged, feeling faith is literally on the line, criticising the established Church for betraying Christ ('At a Calvary near the Ancre'; 'Le Christianisme'); Spencer, apparently depicting a comfortable war, believing in the power of faith and the strength it gives to the human spirit, and subsequently celebrating both in the construction of a memorial chapel. Their juxtaposition sharpens one of the central questions about the war and the way it was represented in words and images: How could Christ and Flanders Fields be reconciled?

On 4 July 1918, while training troops in England and himself preparing to return to the Front, Owen wrote to Osbert Sitwell:

> For fourteen hours yesterday I was at work – teaching Christ to lift his cross by numbers, and how to adjust his crown; and not to imagine he thirst till after the last halt; I attended to his Supper to see that there were no complaints; and inspected his feet that they should be worthy of the nails. I see to it that he is dumb and stands at attention before his accusers. With a piece of silver I buy him every day, and with maps I make him familiar with the topography of Golgotha.
>
> (Owen and Bell 1967: 562. Letter no. 634)

Ironically, there is an affinity with Spencer in the domestic details of meal times, foot inspection and map-reading, all of which he depicted at Sandham; but, where the paintings of British soldiers obediently carrying out their tasks are projections of a seemingly uncomplicated, if idiosyncratic, faith, the point of Owen's extended metaphor is the role he gives himself. Both painter and poet see Christ in the ordinary soldiers, but it is Owen who here sees himself in the role of crucifier, betraying these Christ-soldiers. The notion of soldiers as Christ-figures was both contentious and common during the war. Many parallels were drawn:

> The soldier waiting behind the lines was like Christ in Gethsemane. As he carried burdens up the communications trenches, he was Christ carrying the cross. He was 'crucified' in a place of skulls, where, like Christ, he might feel that even God had abandoned him. Laying down his life for his friends (either the nation or his comrades), he saved humanity and earned eternal life – or so he was often assured.
>
> (Hibberd and Onions 1986: 17)

How far Owen was following this conventional practice and how much should be concluded from an incidental paragraph in a letter are inconclusive matters. A similar uncertainty characterises 'Strange Meeting' in so far as some passages, and hence parts of its argument, remain obscure (Hibberd 1973: 45). However, what it does achieve is a memorable representation of an unresolvable dilemma: the dramatisation of the doppelganger theme as the symbol of the Christian soldier who is both Christ and crucifier. To be killed and have death interpreted as a sacrifice on the altar of 'greater love ... ' was one thing; to do the killing, either by proxy in sending British Christ-soldiers to their deaths, or directly with gun and bayonet against German Christ-soldiers on the Front line, was quite another. 'Strange Meeting' faces up to this issue which resonates elsewhere in his letters and poems (Letter no. 512; 'Greater Love'). It may not be as well-wrought as 'Anthem for Doomed Youth' or have the bitter dynamism of 'Dulce et Decorum', but it grapples with a tougher problem: how to resolve the paradox of 'the Christian soldier'.

The imaginative force of 'Strange Meeting' lies in its representation of the trench as the mouth of Hell and of the act of killing others as the death of self. The narrative setting symbolises the first; the dialogue between the soldier and his *alter ego* develops the second. 'It seemed that out of battle I escaped / Down some profound dull tunnel, ... ': the dream narrative leads the soldier underground into one of the chambers of Hell, where the noise of battle cannot be heard nor the blood of soldiers seep. One of the corpses springs up 'with piteous recognition in fixed eyes' and, smiling in friendship, appears to bless the soldier. At the end of the poem, the soldier learns the identity of the dead man who addresses him:

> I am the enemy you killed, my friend.
> I knew you in this dark: for so you frowned
> Yesterday through me as you jabbed and killed.

In the middle section of the poem, the dead enemy identifies himself with his killer: 'Whatever hope is yours, / Was my life also' and mourns the 'undone years, / The hopelessness'. The tenor of regret and loss focuses upon two concepts: the 'truth untold, / The pity of war, the pity war distilled' – Owen's sense that individuals and nations will not learn from their suffering without the soldier-poet to diagnose the truth of their experiences; and, second, that war has killed the ideal of service, which as we have seen, was at the heart of Owen's personal credo. Hence, the conditional phrasing of the lines:

> I would have poured my spirit without stint
> But not through wounds; not on the cess of war. ...

and the final line suggesting the psychological and spiritual damage that war inflicts: 'Foreheads of men have bled where no wounds were.' It is this telling combination of elements – narrative momentum, archetypal symbolism, dialogue, and the discursive exploration of ideas and feelings about war that led Sassoon to describe 'Strange Meeting' as Owen's 'passport to immortality'. Its message has all the power of Owen's experiences of the trenches behind it: death on the battlefield is not a worthwhile sacrifice.

'Strange Meeting' illustrates one of the spectatorship issues raised at the end of the first section. It arises from the way the reader is positioned during this narrative. The discussion in the long middle passage where Owen through his narrator is, in effect, talking to himself, is framed between two short sections so that we are never allowed to forget that this is a construction, a story exploring the meaning of war experience, not a poem that sets out to involve us in partic-ular experiences *per se*. The reader eavesdrops upon the intimate struggle between the twin personae of the 'soldier-poet', and is constantly kept aware of the distance between those who suffered the obscenity of trench warfare and those, then and now, whose non-participant role was or is to look on. The narrative never draws the reader in, never allows the reader the indulgence of assimilating its experiences; instead, its job is to construct an objective correla-tive in order to represent and understand them. The reader may be haunted by the symbolic narrative of 'Strange Meeting', and feel the deep pessimism that pervades each line. Yet, at the same time, the poem seems to keep the reader at a distance. Ironically, the act of constructing a metaphor of sufficient resonance to carry the weight of Owen's war experiences simultaneously creates a sense of alienation in the reader from those very experiences that occasioned the poem. Imaginative participation in such circumstances is strictly delimited.

There is no hint of the resurrection of the soldier in 'Strange Meeting'. By contrast, Spencer's dead soldiers rise from their graves and are shown meeting and greeting their resurrected comrades and carrying their crosses to their saviour, Christ (Figure 10.1).

Owen's battlefield is a vision of Hell-on-earth; Spencer's battlefield is a vision of Heaven-on-earth. Owen's metaphor is a Dantesque journey into the underworld; Spencer's motif is the Cross. Instead of a picture of carnage and slaughter, Spencer gives us a scene of recovery and reunion where the dead are whole, strong, clean-limbed and robustly-painted. The Cross is central to both the composition and the theme. Spencer has transformed the iconography of the war cemetery: the serried ranks of identical white crosses, each marking the grave of a dead soldier, laid out on the grass with due military precision, are here translated into a state of controlled disorder. The effect is twofold: it reminds us of the chaos of the battlefield but, overriding this, it asserts the belief in redemption through self-sacrifice. Hence, the crosses are neither broken nor even soiled. As Duncan Robinson (1991: 10) comments, Spencer chose to paint the crosses 'on the Day of Judgement, uprooted by their owners and piled as tokens of their sacrifice throughout the landscape and down, so that they appear to rest on the actual altar of All Souls'. The balance of weight and movement in the picture is based on a complex pattern where the composition reflects the theme. The design is conical with, at its base, several clearly delin-eated figures, seeming to rise up from behind the altar, each roughly framed in the arrangement of crosses, and making the link with the actual space in the chapel in which they are placed. Beyond and above them is the pile of crosses deposited by the soldiers coming out of the ground and, in the centre of the picture, a collapsed mule waggon. The heads of the two mules are turned away from the viewer directing the eye towards the seated figure of Christ receiving the soldiers' crosses at the apex of the design. While the weight of the picture lies with the clutter of figures and crosses at its base, the movement of the resur-

Figure 10.1   Stanley Spencer, *Resurrection of the Soldiers* (1927–32), Sandham Memorial
Chapel, Burghclere, oil on canvas-covered wall.

rection follows the conventional arrangement upwards from Death, through
War, to Christian Redemption. There is no sense of protest neither here nor
elsewhere in the Sandham Chapel paintings. Instead, Spencer offers the viewer
a message of contemplation: placed centrally in the design near the feet of
Christ is a young soldier, lying alone on the boards of the waggon, studying
intently the only cross in the picture which carries the image of Christ. The

crucifix stands as the symbol of faith's triumph over death and the reward for the ultimate sacrifice that the soldier can expect in heaven.

Dystopian landscapes: Nash and Douglas

Though Spencer, like Nash, served as an official war artist for a time in both world wars, their visual responses to the conflicts were strikingly different. Spencer spent the period from May 1940 to May 1946 working on a commissioned series of shipyard paintings, *Shipbuilding on the Clyde*, an experience which led to his taking up the theme of the resurrection once more in the *Port Glasgow Resurrection* series. Just as at Sandham where he had glorified the mundane, routine tasks such as map-reading and scrubbing floors, so in *Shipbuilding on the Clyde* he again focused on everyday work – in this case, the technicalities of riveting, welding, bending the keel plate and so on (MacCarthy 1997: Plates 44, 45). Partly because they lack the immediacy of actual wartime experiences and partly because there was no unifying concept such as the Sandham Chapel, the Port Glasgow paintings do not have the impact of the earlier series.

Until relatively recently Nash, too, has been considered primarily as an artist of the trenches. Paintings such as *The Menin Road* and the ironically titled, *We Are Making A New World* are the visual complements of the poems of the soldier-poets of the First World War. These pictures convey a message similar to that of Owen's: Nash's letter home to his wife from Flanders of 16 November 1917 (Nash 1949: 210–11) vividly puts into words both the scenes of such paintings and his attitude to the war. 'Evil and the incarnate fiend alone can be master of this war, and no glimmer of God's hand is seen anywhere'. Sunset and sunrise are seen as 'blasphemous … mockeries', setting and rising over a landscape which is 'one huge grave, and cast upon it the poor dead'. His letter concludes:

> It is unspeakable, godless, hopeless. I am no longer an artist interested and curious, I am a messenger who will bring back word from the men who are fighting to those who want the war to go on for ever. Feeble, inarticulate, will be my message, but it will have a bitter truth, and may it burn their lousy souls.

This is the voice of protest from a 28-year-old official war artist who, as Owen and Sassoon had done in their different ways, rethought his role as artist and revalued it as messenger.

Nash was fifty at the outbreak of the Second World War. Both the style of his paintings and their purposes as images of war show marked changes. In 1942 he wrote: 'I first became interested in the war pictorially when I realised the machines were the real protagonists … ' and 'for me, the airplanes seemed paramount' (Nash 1949: 248). His paintings of these 'aerial creatures' enabled him to blend his continuing interest in landscape with an avant-garde fascination with Surrealism in which different aircraft were playfully seen as predatory creatures, ranging from the Wellington bomber as a killer whale to the Hampden bomber as a pterodactyl! (Nash 1949: 248–53). His ideological emphasis changed, too. His Second World War pictures, such as *The Battle of Britain* (1941) and *Battle of Germany* (1944), are not so much visual diatribes against war itself as visual propaganda directed against the ideology of Nazism. Yet, while their titles reflect Nash's patriotism, their style shows a more abstract way of handling pictorial space. The horizon is lowered and the spectator given a higher vantage-point on these aerial scenes; there is a greater concern for the relationships between colour, line and mass for their own sake – especially in the latter picture – and correspondingly less interest in literal illustration.

Totes Meer 1940–41 (Figure 10.2) stands centrally in Nash's art as a major painting that combines elements of his First World War style with his later fascination with aircraft: earth and air are brought together in death. The landscape is a dehumanised tangle of metal wreckage which, in common with most of Nash's landscapes, has no human figures, alive or dead. The motif is the sea, not The Dead Sea; there is 'nothing grand or biblical about it' (Hall 1996: 22).

From Nash's own account, *Totes Meer* is a mixture of fact and fantasy, propaganda and poetry. It is based on photographs Nash took of the wreckage of German planes at the Cowley dump – a documentary record of Germany's defeat in the air that Nash was keen to have used for propaganda purposes (Hall 1996: 14). Yet both the resulting image and Nash's own description of it have a dream-like quality which conveys the elegiac atmosphere of the scene and implies its allegorical connotations. Nash's account catches these contrasting elements and is worth quoting at some length:

Figure 10.2   Paul Nash, *Totes Meer 1940–41*, The Tate Gallery, London, oil on canvas.

The thing looked to me, suddenly, like a great inundating sea. You might feel – under certain circumstances – a moonlight night for instance, this is a vast tide moving across the fields, the breakers rearing up and crashing on the plain. And then, no; nothing moves, it is not water or even ice, it is something static and dead. It is metal piled up, wreckage. It is hundreds and hundreds of flying creatures which invaded these shores (how many Nazi planes have been shot down or otherwise wrecked in this country since they first invaded?). Well, here they are, or some of them. By moonlight, the waning moon, one could swear they began to move and twist and turn as they did in the air. A sort of rigor mortis? No, they are quite dead and still. The only moving creature is the white owl flying low over the bodies of the other predatory creatures, raking the shadows for rats and voles. She isn't there, of course, as a symbol quite so much as the form and colour essential just there to link up with the cloud fringe over head.

(Hall 1996: 31)

Formally, the lines of the picture lead the eye towards the top right corner where the cloud-edge peters out on the horizon and the waves of wreckage lap the sandy-coloured land in the foreground. But the mood of the painting is created by the harsh outlines and shadows of the aircraft parts under the ghostly light of the moon, complemented by the white, low-flying owl. From a propagandist point of view, *Totes Meer* can be read as a patriotic celebration of effective British resistance. But the overwhelming feeling is the deep sadness of a visual elegy. Although the painting was completed in 1941, its sense of an ending has the death-like finality of the 1945 photographs of Hiroshima and Nagasaki. Everything, even violence itself, has come to an end in *Totes Meer*, stilled in this chill, glinting graveyard.

Whereas the horizon line is high in *Totes Meer*, stressing its relationship with Nash's First World War pictures of brutalised landscapes, his later paintings increasingly adopt an aerial perspective. Hall (1996: 34) puts it neatly: 'after *Totes Meer* the worm's-eye-view is gradually displaced by the bird's', and he goes on to note that, by 1941, Nash was enquiring if there were any security objections to his making a painting 'based on "an aerial map" or photograph of the Thames Valley'. This led to the remarkable, panoramic *Battle of Britain* (1941) (Figure 10.3) – a combination of topographical and symbolic detail.

Again, Nash's own comments point to the mixture of propaganda, documentary and the selection of metaphoric details:

The painting is an attempt to give the sense of an aerial battle in operation over a wide area and thus summarise England's great aerial victory over Germany. The scene includes certain elements constant during the Battle of Britain – the river winding from the town and across parched country, down to the sea; beyond, the shores of the Continent, above, the mounting cumulus concentrating at sunset after a hot brilliant day: across the spaces of sky, trails of airplanes, smoke tracks of dead or damaged machines falling,

Figure 10.3   Paul Nash, *Battle of Britain* (1941), The Imperial War Museum, London, oil
on canvas.

floating clouds, parachutes, balloons. Against the approaching twilight new
formations of the Luftwaffe, threatening.

(Hall 1996: 34)

Furthermore, Nash is explicit about the necessity of symbolism, the aerial viewpoint from which the landscape is observed, and the moment of the narrative.
He goes on:

> To judge the picture by reference to facts alone will be unjust to the experi-
> ment. Facts, here, both of Science and Nature are used 'imaginatively' and
> respected only in so far as they suggest symbols for the picture plan which
> itself is viewed from the air. The moment of battle represents the impact of
> opposing forces, the squadrons of the RAF sweeping along the coast and
> breaking up a formation of the Luftwaffe while it is still over the sea.

(Hall 1996: 34)

Battle of Britain moved Kenneth Clark to describe it as 'one of the most
thrilling works of art yet produced by the war' and to tell Nash that ' in this and
Totes Meer you have discovered a new form of allegorical painting' based upon
'making ... symbols out of the events themselves' (Hall 1996: 34–5). Both
paintings can be read as the official artist's contribution to the war effort, yet
the images could scarcely be more different: the dead landscape viewed from
ground level is replaced by an action-packed vista seen, as it were, from the

cockpit; instead of subdued browns and greys, there is the vibrant use of orange, yellow and red; static, geometric design gives way to the dynamic whorls of black and white vapour trails set against patches of cumulus cloud above a glowing evening sky. However distinct in mood and composition, the symbolic nature of these two landscapes – like those of Spencer's Macedonia and Owen's Somme – suggests a common characteristic of war experience: a sense of unreality, the awareness of being an inhabitant of another world, like the dramatised narrator of some horrific fiction who both participates in the action and can also observe it from a distance. Keith Douglas, as we shall see, explores this aspect of spectatorship in a way that exposes this sense of aesthetic alienation through juxtaposing the exterior landscape of the battlefield with the interior landscape of the soldier's mind.

Keith Douglas fought in the Battle of Alamein; his images are those of a desert war. His 'Landscape With Figures' appears most frequently as two, loosely connected, irregular sonnets (Hughes 1964: 54–5; MacBeth 1967: 256). Occasionally (Graham 1978: 103–4), a third, apparently unfinished 15-line poem is included which, as is suggested below, creates both a coherent sequence and a link with the First World War poet whom Douglas most admired. The initial vantage point and the poet's relationship with the landscape of death are both reminiscent of Owen's 'The Show', which begins:

> My soul looked down from a vague height, with Death,
> As unremembering how I rose or why,
> And saw a sad land, weak with sweats of dearth,
> Gray, cratered like the moon with hollow woe,
> And pitted with great pocks and scabs of plagues.

The poem moves from this foul, cancerous landscape, crawling with hideous, grotesque creatures devouring each other, to an ending where Death shows Owen his future – the half-buried corpse of one of these creatures, 'And the fresh-severed head of it, my head'. In Keith Douglas's three poems the relationship of parts to whole is necessarily more tenuous. The imagery is more sophisticated, but the poems exhibit a similar development, as their opening lines indicate.

The first poem views the tanks and vehicles of the desert landscape from an aerial perspective:

> Perched on a great fall of air
> a pilot or angel looking down
> on some eccentric chart ...

The second closes in on the corpses that litter the landscape:

> On scrub and sand the dead men wriggle
> in their dowdy clothes ...

The third shifts to the interior landscape of the poet's mind, possessed by all the 'angels and devils' of war:

> I am the figure burning in hell
> and the figure of the grave priest
> observing everyone ...

Observation, in fact, is the common quality of these poems, with the narrator looking on in detached fascination at both the scenes in front of him and those imprinted in the mind's eye. Their imagery shifts correspondingly from the aerial view of wrecked tanks and trucks 'squashed' or 'stunned / like beetles'; to the dead soldiers enacting their final and fatal mimes; to the mind populated by all the figures of a war-torn imagination. The middle poem is the fulcrum of the sequence and ends with a dramatic switch of perspective that gives yet another variation on the spectator–participant role.

This second poem in the sequence blurs the formalities of the sonnet through its informal, impressionistic style, through eliding the octave and the sestet, and through its use of Owen-like half-rhymes. The running metaphor plays upon the notion of the theatre of war: the dead are silent, petrified actors arrested at some arbitrary moment in their grotesque mimes; their blood-smeared make-up is death's handiwork; the decor of this scene 'is a horrible tracery / of iron'. Eleven lines elaborate this image, viewed as it were, from the auditorium. Then, in the last three lines, with shock tactics reminiscent of the ending of Owen's 'The Show', there is a startling shift of perspective:

> A yard more, and my little finger
> could trace the maquillage of these stony actors:
> I am the figure writhing on the backcloth.

The narrator is not watching from the comfortable, safe distance that the reader had assumed. In this landscape with figures he is both spectator and participant: he is part of the action, imaginatively the figure painted on the theatre back-cloth, observing and suffering as he both watches and participates in this tableau of the dead. Ted Hughes (1964: 13) hinted at the significance of this stance when he identified two related qualities in Keith Douglas's last poems: the poet's 'foreknowledge of his own rapidly-approaching end', one that is here worked out as an active foresuffering of death; and, second, the realisation that 'the truth of a man is the doomed man in him or his dead body'. The idea that the moment of dying contains the truth about our living, that we are what we are in the snapshot of death, has particular poignancy for those killed in battle. The poem is dated January 1943; six months later, Keith Douglas was killed in action, aged 24.

Cross-curricular issues

Does art aestheticise the horrors of war? In one sense, the answer is an obvious and inevitable 'yes'; but the question is usually posed pejoratively, as it has been (as we shall see in Chapter 11) over Seamus Heaney's poetry about the conflict in Ireland, carrying with it the implication of a failure to engage. Such an implication overlooks the basic paradox of representation, which remains as true for the subject of war as it does for anything else: the very process is, simultaneously, a means of understanding, of coming to terms, and a means of shaping words or paint into an appropriate artistic image. It is both exploration and communication. War poets and painters face this endemic aestheticisation more acutely than most in dealing with the ugliness and atrocities of man's inhumanity to man. The most pertinent question posed to the reader/viewer by their work is whether the figurative language or visual symbolism advance our understanding of war, or merely retreat into nostalgia and escapism. How far do the worlds of dream-like fantasy created by Owen, Spencer, Nash and Douglas in their different ways, facilitate, through their imaginative withdrawal from the immediacy of battle and the evocation of image and symbol, a more profound engagement with their subject matter? The conclusion must surely be that the soldier-poet or soldier-painter needs, more than most, the distance conferred by the spectator–participant stance in order to represent the experience of war as truthfully as the conjunction of memory and art will allow.

These issues of representation and stance can be taken up in the classroom through the two themes upon which this chapter has concentrated. That of war and Christianity can be explored and extended by studying, say, the seven poems of Owen mentioned earlier ('Strange Meeting', 'Anthem for Doomed Youth', 'Dulce et Decorum', 'Le Christianisme', 'At a Cavalry near the Ancre', 'Greater Love' and 'The Show'), together with the relevant letters in Owen and Bell (eds) (1967) *Wilfred Owen. Collected Letters*, Oxford: Oxford University Press. A slide pack, booklet and other information about Stanley Spencer are available from The Custodian, Sandham Memorial Chapel, Burghclere, Newbury, RG20 9JT. The most useful biographical sources are Stallworthy (1974) on Owen and MacCarthy (1997) on Spencer.

The landscape theme can be usefully linked to the material in Chapter 7. The intellectual battlefield described there is here replaced by the actual one. Several of the initial propositions in Chapter 7 remain relevant, notably those concerning the representation of a 'unified scene' (vii), and the 'predetermined schema' (vi) invested with a particular set of beliefs (iv). Useful autobiographical sources here are Nash (1949) and Douglas (1946).

Ekphrasis offers another angle. The approach to Paul Nash's *Totes Meer* and Anna Adams' two-poem ekphrasis of the same name, outlined in Benton and Benton (1995a: 45–9), can be adopted with other pairings: for example, Seamus Heaney's 'Summer 1969' linking Goya's pictures to 'the troubles' in Ireland (Benton and Benton 1990: 104–8); R.S. Thomas's poem about Ben Shahn's painting of refugees, *Father and Child* (Benton and Benton 1995a: 37); and Pauline Stainer's group of eight poems, under the title 'Modern Angels', after paintings by Eric Ravilious (Stainer 1992: 76–80).

Resources are plentiful to enable students to pursue this topic – from the ubiquitous First World War posters to the paintings, exhibitions, films and archive documents at the Imperial War Museum. Anthologies continue to appear: two to be recommended are Hibberd and Onions (1986) and Graham (1998). The most useful and accessible classroom text, which combines poems and pictures is Martin (1991). It lists a number of background books and other accounts of the two world wars. Two books that are particularly appropriate in the cross-curricular study of war are, Taylor (1966) and Harries and Harries (1983). Within the two contexts of such a fully documented history and the localised, but no less horrific, wars of today, the study of how poets and painters have represented war retains its awful relevance.

11 Myth:

Hughes's 'crow' and Heaney's 'bog poems'

Myth-making

In the 1970s two writers, whom many regard as the major poets of their generation, each created a symbolic representation of the destructive potential within
the natural order and its manifestations in human history. Hughes's 'crow' and
Heaney's 'peat bog' have come not only to stand for some of the prevailing
anxieties of the late twentieth-century to which conventional religious symbolism
offers an inadequate response, but also to show how such imagery develops the
status of contemporary literary myth. Both have their origins in the visual
image.

Ted Hughes's *Crow* (1970) is a poetic sequence intended to form a composite
book, with poems by Hughes and engravings by the American artist Leonard
Baskin whose image of 'Crow' dominates the dust cover. Seamus Heaney's
development of the bog symbolism can be traced back to his first book, *Death of
a Naturalist* (1966) with the seminal poem 'Digging' and is to be found also in
his most recent, *The Spirit Level* (1996), in 'Tollund'; but the focal point is
'Tollund Man' (*Wintering Out*, 1972) and the sequence of bog poems in Part
One of *North* (1975) arising from Heaney's response to the photographs of
exhumed Iron Age bodies in Jutland in P.V. Glob's *The Bog People* (1965, trans.
1969). Both poets seek to develop an image of sufficient resonance and flexibility to carry their ideas of the dark and violent forces within human nature. In
doing so, they mythologise their subject matter, exploiting the visual images of
Baskin's 'Crow' and the Danish bog-bodies in characteristically different ways,
and making new demands upon both themselves and their readers to collabo-
rate (to widen the reference of Heaney's words to embrace Hughes) in the
'search for images and symbols adequate to our predicament' (Heaney 1980:
56). Hughes's myth is cosmic, impersonal, expressing the anxieties of a post-
Christian age: crow is born(e) out of deep space on vast, black wings which cast
their shadow over planet Earth. Heaney's myth is earth-bound, deeply personal,
digging down into the atrocities of an early and pre-Christian age: bog-bodies
preserved in centuries of peat reveal their secrets slowly and painstakingly
through his poetry's verbal archaeology.

Both sequences of poems have had their critics. Even the admirers of *Crow* acknowledge its unevenness (Sagar 1975: 145; Gifford and Roberts 1981: 114); but few have been so readily seduced by the journalistic sound-bite as Adam Thorpe, in his 'Review of *New and Selected Poems, 1957–94* by Ted Hughes' (*The Observer Review*, 5 March 1995: 20), who dismisses Hughes's writing of the early seventies as 'full of sub-Amerindian apocalyptic gibberish'. Where Hughes has been attacked for the variable quality of the poems and the formlessness of the sequence, critics have found Heaney's care over language and form and his construction of *North* to be major virtues of his bog poetry (O'Donoghue 1994: 68–76; Morrison 1982: 53). Adverse criticism has taken a predictably political turn. David Lloyd (1997: 174) in particular, has taken Heaney to task for what he calls 'the aestheticisation of violence' of the bog poems, arguing that Heaney is too concerned to produce well-wrought pieces of symbolism and that the very process of mythologising his essentially political and historical subject-matter is reductive and serves to distance the reader. The controversial nature of *Crow* and the bog poems is a pedagogical advantage. Readers will develop their own sense of whether some of the *Crow* poems are 'crude' or 'facile' (two favourite adjectives of Hughes's critics); or whether, with David Lloyd (1997: 172), they judge Heaney's poems as representing 'a metaphorical foreclosure of issues'. There seems little doubt, however, that both sequences have the power to rise above particular criticisms, not least because of their symbolic and mythic character.

What happens when we read a poem from *Crow* or one of the bog poems? Behind the act of reading lies an act of viewing: whether reproduced on the page or visualised through the words, Baskin's drawing and Glob's photographs are more than mere points of pictorial reference. Their mythic presence permeates the two sequences. They ensure that the reading of an individual poem forms part of a larger symbolism. In such circumstances of what may be called intratextuality, the reader as spectator is constantly aware of the imaginative context in which any single act of reading takes place: one in which visual and verbal elements together compose a myth to interpret our times. Such myth-making is both grounded in traditional forms and a modern translation of them. For example, both poets mythologise landscape. Yet, Hughes's *Crow* debunks the comfortable English view of Nature; the landscape over which Crow flies is not the romantic Wordsworthian one but an image of Earth that symbolises 'the horror of Creation'. And Heaney's peat bog exists not merely as the cultural landscape of Ireland but forms a symbolic landscape that holds together personal and national 'memory and bogland and … our national consciousness' (Heaney 1980: 54–5). In reading *Crow* or the bog poems, we are reading landscapes against the background of those discussed in Chapter 7 and the dystopian landscapes of war in Chapter 10 (where the violence of earth and air is uncannily paralleled in Heaney's and Hughes's symbolism). Such intertexuality, too, adds another dimension to the experience of reading these two sequences. Accordingly, the purposes of this chapter are to explore the nature of the two symbols, their development as literary myths, and to suggest ways in which the themes of *Crow* and *North* can be approached in the classroom by first examining the visual images from which they spring in relation to a representative selection of poems from each sequence.

The 'horror of Creation'

The body of Baskin's 'Crow' (Figure 11.1) has the solidity of dense matter. It is black with striations and dark patches round its frame but empty in its centre – an inchoate and featureless lump save for the shock of its human male genitals. The head seems to grow out of the body's mass as if Crow's identity is in the very process of being born. The aggressive eye, the crude open beak, the suggestion of stubble – all give the image a startling physicality. Supporting the body, the legs are rigid and muscular, animal – not bird-like, the claws of the three-toed feet echoing the curve of the beak. The whole drawing has the massive, hard resilience of metal sculpture. Indeed, Hughes said of Baskin: 'He regards himself as first and foremost a sculptor, and in all his graphic images the "wiry, bounding line", the sheer physical definition, is sculptural.' He went on to diagnose this feeling of muscular effort in Baskin's drawings as deriving from the expression of external forms in which the spectator senses the internal map of their life force. Hughes continued:

> His (Baskin's) imagination is innately kinaesthetic. It projects itself exclusively in tensile, organic forms, which are, moreover, whole forms – images

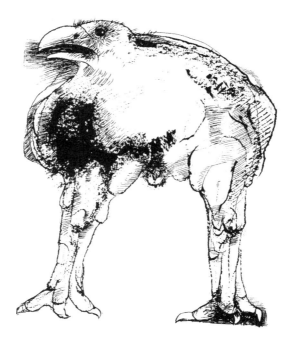

Figure 11.1   Leonard Baskin, *Crow* (1970), London, Faber and Faber, engraving.

of the whole being. At the same time, as he feels out the contours and balance of these forms, he receives an X-ray of their insides. His graphic image reproduces this complex of sensations as a blueprint: the translucent womb-life of an unborn sculpture, flattened onto the paper.

(Hughes 1994: 86)

These last six or seven words can serve as a summary description of Baskin's 'Crow'.

Hughes was also explicit about the genesis of the crow poems and the invitation by Leonard Baskin 'to make a book with him simply about crows'. Hughes remarked: 'As the protagonist of a book, a crow would become symbolic in any author's hands. And a symbolic crow lives a legendary life. That is how *Crow* took off' (Hughes 1994: 243). Earlier in the same piece, Hughes identified the source of this 'legendary life' as trickster literature: 'the Trickster Saga was my guiding metaphor when I set out to make what I could of Crow'. Distinguishing the trickster tales of oral and folk literature from black comedy, Hughes characterises them as having an 'unkillable, biological optimism'; as making repeated 'attempts to live and to enlarge and intensify life, however mismanaged; … ' as 'founded on the immortal enterprise of the sperm'. The tales themselves are a 'playful-savage burlesque of trickster's inadequacies and setbacks'. And, in a description that most nearly characterises Crow, the Trickster, Hughes said of the series of tragicomedies that comprise the Trickster saga:

It is a series, and never properly tragic, because Trickster, demon of phallic energy, bearing the spirit of the sperm, is repetitive and indestructible. No matter what fatal mistakes he makes, and what tragic flaws he indulges, he refuses to let sufferings or death detain him, but always circumvents them, and never despairs … he rattles along on biological glee.

(Hughes 1994: 241)

This goes some way towards explaining why Hughes chooses a crow as his protagonist but, as Keith Sagar (1975: 105–7) points out, crows are legion in folk-lore and their symbolic character is largely derived from the characteristics of the real bird – intelligent, omnivorous, solitary yet common, black, harsh in its call. It is little wonder that the collective noun for the largest and most strident of British song-birds is 'a murder of crows'. Hughes's mythology of Crow is deeply rooted in legend yet deliberately free from specific cultural references. Hughes's concern was to create something 'as it might be invented after the holocaust and demolition of all libraries, where essential things spring again – if at all – only from their seeds in nature' (Sagar 1975: 105).

If the above suggests the character of Crow and the orientation of the poems, their style, too, befits the 'legendary life'. Hughes describes the language of most of the *Crow* poems as 'determined by the fact that it is a song-legend' and by the adoption of a voice that 'tends again to select for itself an elemental vocabulary – one that has, like music itself, kinaesthetic or at least physical roots' (Hughes 1994: 242).

So, by Hughes's own accounts, his verbal creations reflect their visual origin: the sheer sculptural muscularity that he identified in Baskin's drawing of 'Crow' is the very quality he represents in the language and style of his *Crow* poems. We can expect Crow's voice to be harsh and grating and for his songs to be deliberately unmusical and unpoetic: for the conventional beauties of English verse scarcely suit this anti-aesthetic persona. Instead, Hughes turns to more primitive forms of address, to incantations, lists, questions and answers, repetitions and the like, as in the first three poems in the sequence, the third of which, 'Examination at the Womb-door', begins:

> Who owns these scrawny little feet? *Death*
> Who owns this bristly scorched-looking face? *Death*

and continues its litany with a dozen or more questions before concluding:

> But who is stronger than death?
>
> *Me, evidently.*
>
> Pass, Crow.

thus establishing Crow as the primal power beyond life and death. Crow is born out of the original blackness, a symbol of the primitive energy that initiates existence – amoral, constantly changing, indestructible and, as such, 'stronger than death'.

The sequence of sixty songs shows Trickster–Crow in all sorts of guises. The main theme may be seen as a version of Creation mythology: it is expressed with characteristic black humour in 'Crow Alights' and 'Crow Blacker than Ever'. In the first poem, Crow approaches Earth from the depths of space and inspects it through the lens of his black eyes:

> Crow saw the herded mountains, steaming in the morning.
> And he saw the sea
> Dark-spined, with the whole earth in its coils.
> He saw the stars, fuming away into the black, mushrooms of
>   the nothing forest, clouding their spores, the virus of God.
> And he shivered with the horror of Creation.

The pristine beauty of the earth is bound in the serpent's coils; the stars in the heavens are mere symptoms of the virus of a diseased Creator. The shock of these images hits Crow with the power of hallucination. When he alights and inspects what has been done to this landscape, he finds a waste land of unconnected, random objects and an image of faceless, alienated man. He is left bemused, staring uncomprehendingly at the evidence. Later in the sequence, in 'Crow Blacker than Ever', Crow tries to solve the puzzle of creation by uniting Heaven and Earth. It is a comic yet serious, naive yet knowing version of the Christian allegory of Creation. It begins:

> When God, disgusted with man

Turned towards heaven.
And man, disgusted with God,
Turned towards Eve,
Things looked like falling apart.

But Crow   Crow
Crow nailed them together,
Nailing Heaven and earth together — ...

The agony of human existence is thus, literally, nailed down; man and God are condemned to exist in this relationship of painful imperfection; and Crow has the gleeful satisfaction of having cobbled together a symbol of anti-Creation in this makeshift bit of repair work which, having 'creaked at the joint', decomposes into a rotten crucifixion – 'a horror beyond redemption'. The poem ends with lines that are simultaneously celebratory yet sardonic in their Biblical resonances:

Crow
Grinned
Crying: 'This is my Creation,'
Flying the black flag of himself.

One of the main variations on the creation theme is that of language: words are both subject and style in *Crow*. As Hughes says: 'Words are continually trying to displace our experience. And in so far as they are stronger than the raw life of our experience, and full of themselves and all the dictionaries they have digested, they do displace it.' (Hughes 1967: 120). Words are dangerous things, ever ready to make a take-over bid for real experience. There is something of this in *Crow* but our anti-hero is having none of it. In 'The Battle of Osfrontalis', Crow proves himself immune to the power of words; words retire defeated, reduced to a superficial gloss on experience:

Words retreated, suddenly afraid
Into the skull of a dead jester
Taking the whole world with them —

But the world did not notice.

And crow yawned – long ago
He had picked that skull empty.

Elsewhere, Crow turns his back on the seductive beauty of words. In 'Crow and the Birds', Hughes builds up fourteen lines of subordinate clauses each depicting the aesthetic appeal of a separate bird, from the majesty of the eagle to the sauciness of the blue tit, only to deflate this word-picture with the bathetic finale of

Crow spraddled head-down in the beach-garbage, guzzling a
                                        dropped ice-cream.

If these poems show the dangerous beauty of language, none the less, Crow – true to his trickster nature – cannot resist using what seems to be this best available means of understanding experience. 'Crow Goes Hunting' is the down side of Hughes's seminal essay 'Capturing Animals' (and, incidentally, the antithesis of its much-quoted 'The Thought-Fox') where words are celebrated for their sensuous qualities (Hughes 1967: 15–31). By contrast here, Crow sets off with his 'lovely pack' of well-trained, sharply imagined words to hunt down a hare. Naming it should capture it. But, in a series of images typical of the shape-changing trickster, the hare eludes him; the reality of experience cannot be caught in mere words and Crow is left, gazing after the hare as it bounds away, 'speechless with admiration'.

Teaching *Crow* poses the problem not only of making a selection from sixty poems but also of how to handle these in relation to their origins in Baskin's drawing and the trickster tales. The foregoing brief account suggests part of the answer: start by gathering students' responses to Baskin's 'Crow', follow up by explaining and illustrating the trickster character and then focus upon, say, half a dozen poems like the ones mentioned here, which are both accessible and which explore the central theme of the sequence. Yet, this approach may easily founder if we fail to take account of the problem that Hughes himself raises in 'Myth in Education'. He cites the story of Christ as an example of the way a single word can switch us on to the whole myth.

> No matter what point of that story we touch, the whole story hits us. If we mention the Nativity, or the miracle of the loaves and fishes, or Lazarus, or the Crucifixion, the voltage and inner brightness of the whole story is instantly there. A single word of reference is enough.

These verbal triggers may well be all that an educated, older generation needs; but what of the average 16-year-old today? Hughes asks us:

> to imagine for a moment an individual who knows nothing of it (the Christ story) at all. His ignorance would shock us, and, in a very real way, he would be outside our society. How would he even begin to understand most of the ideas which are at the roots of our culture and appear everywhere among the branches?
>
> (Hughes 1976: 80)

We cannot make the easy assumption that the Genesis story upon which a significant number of poems in *Crow* depend is known to today's students. Teaching *Crow* requires some background in this third area in addition to the two sources noted above. Students need some familiarity with the main characters of the myth – God, Adam, Eve, and the Serpent – and then, within this context, they might read 'Apple Tragedy' or 'A Childish Prank'. This latter poem both gives trickster Crow's version of the Garden of Eden story and implies the existence of some primal cause beyond God, something that constantly reasserts itself as a potent, mocking, destructive force. Here, as God sleeps, Crow is God's nightmare.

Given the approach suggested above, 'A Childish Prank' is a good poem with which to start since it introduces many of the main characteristics of the whole sequence. Its subject also has student appeal. In 'A Childish Prank', Crow invents sex. God has created Adam and Eve and drops off to sleep wondering what to do with them. Enter Crow, the villain who gives the Genesis story a touch of melodrama. Here is the poem with an 18-year-old student's initial responses (Figure 11.2), typed for clarity, but otherwise numbered and placed exactly as she wrote them, together with her indication, via the dotted lines on the left, of how her reading related to her note-making.

A Childish Prank

Man's and woman's bodies lay without souls, (6) soul - sexuality
Dully gaping, foolishly staring, inert (7) activity comes with sexual desire
On the flowers of Eden.
God pondered.

The problem was so great, it dragged him asleep

Crow laughed.
He bit the Worm, God's only son, (8) Why is the Worm God's son??
Into two writhing halves.

He stuffed into man the tail half
With the wounded end hanging out. (1) Pathetic, pitiful manhood

He stuffed the head half headfirst into woman
And it crept in deeper and up
Wormy (10) To peer out through her eyes (2) woman's sexual power over men
eyes   Calling its tail-half to join up quickly, quickly
Because O *it was painful*. (3) sexual longing. The strong need for man &
                                    woman to unite.

He awoke being dragged across the grass. (4) as if he gets dragged by his
Woman awoke to see him coming. (5) as if   sexuality, the Worm - his penis
Neither knew what had happened.   woman is never overcome with sexual desire:
                                       as if she just lies and waits for man to
                                                            come along.

God went on sleeping.
Crow went on laughing.

                    TED HUGHES.

(9) Sexual desire is painful. Every time man and woman are not united in the
     flesh they are only half, and the separation leaves a big bleeding wound.
     They are forever doomed to be painfully apart relieved only with few
     sporadic moments of unity. But the Worm will remain parted; man and woman
     used to be one, but can never become one again.

(11) I wonder why T.H. has chosen the head half to go into the woman and the tail
     half into the man. The tail is worse off without a head, than the other way
     around. Does this mean that man's desire and hence suffering is greater
     than woman's?

Figure 11.2   Student's notes on Ted Hughes's, 'A Childish Prank'.

The student read the poem through twice and then, half-way through a third reading, began to annotate the text. She took about twenty minutes in all to produce these eleven jottings. Her movement around the poem shows how her attention focused on the central, sexual image (lines 10–17) of the Worm invading the two bodies; all but three of her comments relate directly to these lines. Interpretatively, she has travelled some distance in a short time. Comments 1–5 show that she has felt the power of the symbolism which reduces man and woman to soulless and loveless creatures who experience only the painful urge to join the two ends of the internal serpent together. And in comments 5 and 11 she is already questioning a text that implies a passive role for woman. Her other question is the equation of the Worm with God's son, which perhaps indicates that, without the advantage of reading the poem in its sequence, she has not yet had the chance to tune into the trickster humour which typifies the whole tone of *Crow*. Even so, her longest comment, 9, acts as a summary statement and shows a clear grasp of the main idea of Crow despoiling God's creation of man and woman.

Preparing the visual and verbal context, using individual jottings as a prelude to discussion, focusing upon a selection of, say, six poems – these strategies together can open up one of the most powerful poetic myths of our time. In doing so, they are true to the mythic character of *Crow* since, as Hughes himself said, the 'epic folk-tale' into which the poems were intended to develop was not completed. Hence, 'the story is not really relevant to the poems as they stand. … I think the poems have a life a little aside from it' (Hughes 1971: 18). None the less, commentators have not been able to resist interpolating a mythic narrative from the wide range of sources and allusions upon which *Crow* draws in order to provide a framework for the sequence of poems (Sagar 1975: 106; Gifford and Roberts 1981: 116). Yet the fact that they simultaneously deny its necessity as a way-in to the poems indicates a useful delimitation of the term 'myth' in respect of *Crow*. For *Crow* offers not a coherently developed narrative myth; it is not a modern equivalent of ancient stories. Instead, it comprises a series of poetic fragments in which the reader's sense of the mythic is continuously fed by the style and the substance of the poems. In turn, this feeling of reading a fractured narrative reflects the tough, imperfect, yet indestructible universe that has spawned Baskin's 'Crow' as its graphic representative.

Crow is not the only instance of Hughes's collaboration with Baskin. In fact, subsequent books brought Hughes's poems and Baskin's images into a fuller and more complex relationship. *Under the North Star* (1981) is an anthology of paired poems and water-colour paintings about the creatures of the Arctic where the verbal and the visual complement each other in such a harmonious relationship that it all but deflects the question: Is this ekphrasis or illustration? We do not know the answer; indeed, the sequence could encompass both. In *Cave Birds* (1978) this intermingling of the two categories as an integral part of the composing process actually seems to have occurred. In a study of the textual history of the book, Loizeaux (1999: 92) reveals that '*Cave Birds* is *not* an illustrated book, or not entirely: it was composed in three stages, two of ekphrasis and a final one of illustration'. Baskin produced nine drawings for which Hughes wrote poems, followed by a further ten drawings for which again Hughes wrote accompanying poems. Hughes then composed twelve poems, which Baskin subsequently illustrated. The interplay between word and image during this process effectively blurs the distinction between ekphrasis and illustration since the later poems and pictures would inevitably be composed with the existing ones in mind. The implications for spectatorship, further complicated by the existence of a first-person narrator in the poems, are similar to those involved in reading a picture-book. Do we read text or pictures first? Do we flit back and forth between them? … Read the whole or in parts? … Re-read words and images with different sorts of attention? Just how do we build up a concept of the relationship between the two media? Hughes's and Baskin's collaboration in these books offers pedagogy unique material through which to explore the interdependence of the sister arts.

'Writing for myself': the poet as witness

> I have always listened for poems, they come sometimes like bodies come out of a bog, almost complete, seeming to have been laid down a long time ago, surfacing with a touch of mystery.
>
> (Heaney 1980: 34)

The Tollund Man (Figure 11.3) is the heart of Heaney's myth. This picture in Glob's book (1965), which Heaney first saw in 1969, the year 'the troubles' restarted in Northern Ireland, arrested the poet's attention with the force of revelation. Heaney became a fascinated spectator, for here was one of Glob's 'unforgettable photographs' that held, within its deceptively serene image, the meeting-point of several narratives that were to develop into a metaphor for the condition of Ireland.

Heaney himself has commented upon the source of his bog poetry in 'Feeling into Words' (Heaney 1980: 41–60) and in an interview with James Randall where the effect of these different narrative threads coming together is apparent. Heaney said:

> The Tollund Man seemed to me like an ancestor almost, one of my old uncles, one of those moustached archaic faces you used to meet all over the Irish countryside. I felt very close to this. And the sacrificial element, the territorial religious element, the whole mythological field surrounding these images was very potent. So I tried, not explicitly, to make a connection between the sacrificial, ritual, religious element in the violence of contemporary Ireland and this territorial religious thing in *The Bog People*. This wasn't thought out. It began with a genuinely magnetic, almost entranced relationship with those heads. … And when I wrote that poem ('The Tollund Man') I had a sense of crossing a line really, that my whole being

Figure 11.3   Photograph of 'The Tollund Man', whole body (1969), Silkeborg Museum, Denmark.

was involved in the sense of – the root sense – of religion, being bonded to something, being bound to do something. I felt it a vow.

(Heaney, quoted in Randall 1979: 18–19)

Taken along with the more extensive account in 'Feeling into Words' (Heaney, *Preoccupations*, 1980) these comments suggest that four interwoven narratives had combined to evoke an experience akin to one of Wordsworth's 'spots of time': the cultural history chronicled in the bog landscapes of Ireland and Jutland; the violent, sacrificial killings common to the ritual practices in the Iron Age and modern Northern Ireland; the rhetorical power of Glob's archaeological account in *The Bog People*; and Heaney's autobiographical narrative – his sense of 'crossing a line' in his personal quest to understand and express his relationship with his country and its history. Edna Longley has remarked upon the significance of the visual image: 'His (Heaney's) reaction to the Man's photograph deserves the much abused term 'epiphany', with its full Joycean connotations: a revelation of personal and artistic destiny expressed in religious language' (Longley 1986: 140). If the picture of Tollund Man represents a moment of recognition, what is the nature of the literary myth that flows from it and how does it fit into Heaney's poetic development?

To deal with the second part of this question first, it is evident that the picture and poem of Tollund Man mark a culmination of his previous poetry and a prefiguration of what is to come in later bog poems. In the title of what is arguably the best critical account of *North*, Edna Longley asks the question of Heaney: are you 'inner emigré' or 'artful voyeur'? The first phrase is from 'Exposure', the second from 'Punishment' and, as Bernard O'Donoghue (1994: 74) has pointed out, her title poses ' succinctly a question that is central to all Heaney's self-examination throughout the volume'. It challenges Heaney's stance and purpose in his myth-making by quoting back to him these two labels he uses to locate his stance and probing their implications. Did his actual emigration south between the publication of *Wintering Out* (1972) and *North* (1975) effect a corresponding imaginative shift? Is the stance of a self-conscious spectator of events, the 'artful voyeur', all that the poet can or should aspire to in the face of Northern Ireland's atrocities? Behind these questions lies the overriding issue of how rigorously the bog poems engage with the politics. For some, as we have seen, they are a retreat into a detached aestheticism; for others, they represent the symbolism 'adequate to our predicament' that Heaney sought. Whatever our critical judgement, there is an undeniable pattern that links landscape, community, poetry and politics in a symbiotic relationship that runs through all Heaney's poetry. Two decades after *North*, in his latest volume, 'Tollund', a sequel to the earlier poem, tentatively extends the symbol's range of reference. Heaney tells us that the poem:

was written after the IRA ceasefire of August 1994. The Sunday after that historic Wednesday I just happened to be for the first time in this bog in Jutland where they had found the body of the Tollund Man about whom I had written 24 years earlier. The mood of this more recent poem is as different from the earlier one as the dark mood of the early 70s in Ulster was from the more sanguine mid-90s.

(Heaney 1995: *Stepping Stones*, cassette tape)

A decade before *North*, 'Digging' was the first poem in his first volume and, by Heaney's own account, has something of the epiphanic status of 'The Tollund Man'. This was the first poem, he says, 'where I thought my *feel* had got into words ... the first place where I felt I had done more than make an arrangement of words; I felt that I had let down a shaft into real life'. And he concludes: 'I now believe that the 'Digging' poem had for me the force of an initiation' (Heaney 1980: 41–2). From the start of *Death of a Naturalist* (1966) to the end of *The Spirit Level* (1996), the peat bog has been a consistent symbol for Heaney's explorations of self in relation to family, community and history.

Viewed in this light, the narrative stance from which his poems are written needs to be judged with care. As has been suggested, to take simply at face value phrases like 'inner emigré' and 'artful voyeur' is to give insufficient 'credit to the self-projection of the poetic persona involved' (O'Donoghue 1994: 74). In other words, one means Heaney adopts of exploring the self is to construct a provisional narrative stance from which to operate imaginatively; to construct an image of himself, as an implied spectator experiencing events that the poem records. It is a quality that shows itself in varying degrees and guises in Heaney's bog poetry: a self-projection that allows him both the intimacy necessary to test out his personal position and the distance necessary to situate it in a wider cultural context. 'Writing for myself' was Heaney's blunt description of his stance when challenged by a member of the IRA to 'write something for us' (Heaney 1996: 25). Yet, 'writing for myself' is clearly more than a refusal to allow himself to be politically appropriated; it is an affirmation that the act of writing is in order to understand; or, as Heaney himself has indicated, to bear witness. In some significant remarks about Wilfred Owen, Heaney implies a tacit affinity with Owen's stance 'as the poet as witness'. He describes this type of poetic persona in terms in which it is hard not to sense his own position in relation to 'the troubles' as well as Owen's in relation to the trenches.

> the poet as witness ... represents poetry's solidarity with the doomed, the deprived, the victimised, the under-privileged. The witness is any figure in whom the truth-telling urge and the compulsion to identify with the oppressed becomes necessarily integral to the act of writing itself.
>
> (Heaney 1988: xvi)

In the bog poems, this process involves not only displacing a history of violence on to appropriate objective correlatives but also of adopting a range of narrative stances to explore the insights that the resulting symbolism might yield. And these stances are a direct reflection of the photographic stimuli that triggered the poems. The remainder of this chapter illustrates the visual/verbal link and its contribution to the literary myth that centres on 'The Tollund Man', 'The Grauballe Man' and 'Punishment' before situating these three poems in a wider teaching sequence.

Part One of 'The Tollund Man' makes a series of shifts in time and place to develop its narrative. It begins with an ekphrastic evocation of the image in the photograph:

> Some day I will go to Aarhus
> To see his peat-brown head,
> The mild pods of his eye-lids,
> His pointed skin cap.

It then shifts perspective 'to the flat country nearby', a landscape into which Heaney projects himself at some future date and of which he must have gained some imaginative conception from Glob's text and pictures. The evocation then makes its mythic shift into the past, visualising the Man as 'Bridegroom to the goddess' of the peat bog through whose sexuality and fertility he is sanctified and preserved as a 'saint's kept body'. The final shift is to the present, but not to the photograph *per se*; rather to the as yet unvisited Man he imagines from the picture who 'Now ... reposes at Aarhus'.

Part Two then takes this sanctified image and elevates it into a mythological icon to be worshipped implying that, through its strange history of sacrificial

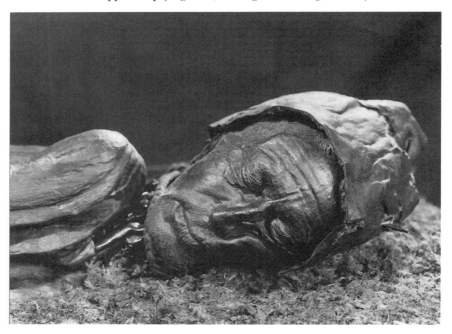

Figure 11.4 Photograph of 'The Tollund Man', head (1969), Silkeborg Museum, Denmark.

killing, rebirth in the peat bog, and resurrection as an archaeological discovery, it has acquired the power to heal the past. Hence, the spectator of this image 'could risk blasphemy' and pray to this icon to redeem

> The scattered, ambushed
> Flesh of labourers,
> Stockinged corpses
> Laid out in the farmyards …

Here, in the reference to 'four young brothers, trailed / For miles along the lines', Heaney alludes to Catholic victims of a sectarian atrocity of the 1920s. Again, it is a telling shift of perspective, for this description acts like a magnet for all the other violent images of Ireland's more recent history.

Part Three parallels the Man's last journey in the tumbril with Heaney imagining himself driving through the same landscape, saying the place names as he nears the destination of his pilgrimage, 'Out there in Jutland / In the old man-killing parishes'. Behind the names in the poem, as Heaney (1980: 131–2) has indicated, lies a relationship between 'the geographical country and the country of the mind' that derives from the 'genre of writing called 'dinnseanchas', poems and tales that relate the original meanings of place names and constitute a form of mythological etymology'. The intoning of the Danish names here links the landscapes of Ireland and Jutland; contemporary readers cannot but hear behind the line 'Tollund, Grauballe, Nebelgard' a corresponding line 'Derry, Enniskillen, Omagh'. (It is a connection that, years later in 'Tollund', is made explicitly.) The language of the poem, like the photograph that inspired it, thus creates a mythic territory able to accommodate Heaney's mixed feelings of being 'lost, / Unhappy and at home'.

A further aspect of the visual/verbal relationship initiated in 'The Tollund Man' and which characterises the bog poems is the form in which they are cast – in Blake Morrison's words, 'compressed, mostly two-stress lines, unrhymed, arranged in slender quatrains, and having an extremely narrow appearance on the page' (Morrison 1982: 45). This artesian stanza is one Heaney developed to 'drill down metaphorically into his territory's and consciousness's prehistory' (O'Donoghue 1994: 6) – a formal and graphic representation of his means of exploring the 'Trove of the turfcutters' … workings' embedded in the peat bog.

'The Grauballe Man' (Figure 11.5) adopts the same form but the interplay of word and image is different. The shifts in time and place of 'The Tollund Man' are replaced by a stronger pictorial realisation of both the photograph of The Grauballe Man that prompted the poem and the image in the mind's eye where 'now he lies / perfected in my memory'. The first six stanzas contain a series of haiku-like similes to establish a word-picture of The Grauballe Man to complement the photograph: his body is presented as petrified and blended with the peat and then wrists, heel, instep, hips, spine, chin, hair are itemised and, in turn, metaphorically related to the earth that has preserved this 'corpse'/'body'. Stanza 7 is the fulcrum of the poem. It poses the question of whether the physicality of these two words can survive the metamorphosis into symbol that the poetic description has attained. The answer is an implied 'no' for, in the remaining stanzas, the poem reinvokes the photograph explicitly, associates it with re-birth through the simile of the baby, lays the Grauballe Man to rest tranquil in recollection, and closes by equating the atrocities of the Iron Age with those of the IRA with 'each hooded victim / slashed and dumped'. Whereas 'The Tollund Man' has the reverent excitement of a new discovery as the climax of a temporal and spatial journey, 'The Grauballe Man' has the stillness of a picture, evoked, contemplated, studied.

Of all the bog poems, 'Punishment' is the most controversial over the question of Heaney's stance towards his myth-making. The controversy centres upon the poem's explicit representation of spectatorship. The poem's visual catalyst is Glob's 'Windeby Girl' – the drowned body of a young girl with a blindfold over her eyes and a collar round her neck (Figure 11.6). Glob's caption title, which was used for the other two poems, is here eschewed in favour of the more politically loaded 'Punishment'; and, significantly, the poem begins not with a distanced commentary on the details of the photograph, but with an evocation of the supposed manner of the girl's death. Glob's account concludes:

> We must suppose that she was led naked out on to the bog with bandaged eyes and the collar round her neck, and drowned in the little peat pit,

Figure 11.5   Photograph of 'The Grauballe Man' (1969), Moesgaard Museum, Denmark.

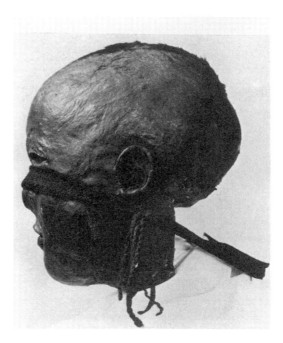

Figure 11.6   Photograph of 'The Windeby Girl', head (1969), Faber and Faber, London.

which must have held twenty inches of water or more. To keep the young body under, some birch branches and a big stone were laid upon her.

(Glob 1969: 114)

Glob's prose as well as the picture is Heaney's starting-point. His poem visualises both the physical circumstances of the girl's drowning and an empathy with her moment of death.

> I can feel the tug
> of the halter at the nape
> of her neck ...
>   ...
> I can see her drowned
> body in the bog ...

Yet, the compassion that the poem asserts is offset by its admission of an acquiescent voyeurism. In lines that have been the subject of much critical comment, Heaney constructs a stance for the narrator of the poem as that of an 'artful voyeur', a self-conscious spectator who is aware of the need to create a symbol adequate to the representation of the horrors of tarring and feathering in Northern Ireland, yet equally aware of the vulnerability to political criticism that the ambivalence of the poem's position exposes. This stance lends 'Punishment' the appearance of being the most confessional of the bog poems, especially in its final two stanzas where Heaney explicitly draws out the political implications of the metaphor upon which the whole poem rests: the comparison of the execution of an adulteress in the Iron Age with the treatment of her 'betraying sisters' in modern Northern Ireland – Catholic girls punished for 'informing' or going out with British soldiers.

> I who have stood dumb
> When your betraying sisters,
> cauled in tar,
> wept by the railings,
>
> who would connive
> in civilised outrage
> yet understand the exact
> and tribal, intimate revenge.

Yet, to claim that 'Punishment' merely 'aestheticises the horror' (Coughlan 1997: 195), or to discuss it as an example of Heaney's 'aestheticisation of violence' (Lloyd 1997: 174–5), in which the poem's tone of ethical self-query is judged to be an unexamined voyeuristic pose, is to distort Heaney's stance. Bernard O'Donoghue offers a corrective to such criticism when he suggests that 'it is clear that the first person in the poem 'Punishment' is the writer in the abstract'; in other words, the 'I' is a persona. Heaney is thus representing 'the writing self as an example of the experiencing observer'. Hence, he concludes, 'the judgement in the poem is not a moral or political one; it is an artistic one' (O'Donoghue 1994: 74). Characterising the stance of the poem as that of 'the self-conscious spectator' or 'the experiencing observer' is not to gloss over the difficulties of its last stanzas; rather, it is to argue that they are difficulties inherent in writing poetry not polemic, in creating symbols not stating arguments. Heaney must be well aware that it is only with the benefit of years of hindsight that such representations of honest ambivalence might conceivably qualify him as one of Ireland's 'unacknowledged legislators'. Meanwhile, Edna Longley's judgement of the stance of the ending seems fair. 'This is all right', she says, 'if Heaney is merely being 'outrageously' honest about his own reactions … if the poem exposes a representative Irish conflict between 'humane reason' and subconscious allegiances'. And she concludes: 'Perhaps the problem is one of artistic, not political, fence-sitting. The conclusion states, rather than dramatises, what should be profound self-division, one of Heaney's most intense hoverings over a brink' (Longley 1986: 154).

Any teaching sequence needs to draw upon the four interwoven narratives identified earlier. The material listed below is readily accessible and focuses on the six bog poems, all of which are reprinted in *Opened Ground*, Faber, 1998. P.V. Glob's *The Bog People: Iron Age Man Preserved* and Heaney's *Preoccupations. Selected Prose 1968–1978* (1980), which includes 'Feeling into Words', are the other essential resources. Slides and booklets relating to The Tollund Man and The Grauballe Man are available, respectively, from The Silkeborg Museum and The Moesgaard Museum, Denmark. Heaney also reads and comments upon some of the poems on the cassette tape *Stepping Stones* (Penguin Audio Books, 1995). Selections from the above material are published in Michael and Peter Benton *Poetry Workshop* (1995b) and *New Touchstones 14–16* (1998), both published by Hodder & Stoughton.

Below is a summary of suggested teaching materials incorporating six poems, Heaney's own comments and the relevant passages from P.V. Glob's book.

Heaney's poems	*Heaney's comments*	*P.V.Glob's account*
'Digging'	P: pp. 41–3	
'Bogland'	P: pp. 54–6	
'The Tollund Man'	P: pp. 57–9	G: pp. 18–36
'The Grauballe Man'		G: pp. 37–59
'Punishment'		G: pp. 110–15
'Tollund'	SS (tape)	

P: *Preoccupations. Selected Prose 1968–1978.*
G: *The Bog People. Iron Age Man Preserved*, by P.V. Glob.
SS: *Stepping Stones*, Penguin Audio Books.

12 Conclusions:
spectatorship and education

The comparative study of the verbal and visual arts is dangerous territory. Its allure is self-evident both in the long, intertwined history of the sister arts of poetry and painting and in the burgeoning critical commentary it has attracted, particularly in the last two decades. In the professional literature, warnings proliferate about the pitfalls in attempting to theorise two art forms that, whatever their links, remain distinct. The main principle of this cautionary tale was set out by Hagstrum who, drawing on classical precedents, argued that 'Each of the mimetic arts achieves its proper pleasure in its proper medium' and that 'Each must take into perpetual account its own peculiar limitations' (Hagstrum 1958: 6). Subsequently, Wark has elaborated upon this position, stressing the differences between literary criticism and art history. In addition to the issue of authenticity, which is fundamental to art history in a way that is not true for literature, Wark also discusses several related matters to which attention has been drawn in previous chapters. While acknowledging that visual art has gained much from the work of literary critics, he offers some cautions about interdisciplinary studies. In particular, art historians are concerned with a knowledge of medium and technique, with how the visual artefact came into being through, say, sketch book drawings, or preliminary studies. Typically, they rely on external evidence to corroborate an interpretation of a work of art more than literary critics do who, in turn, are readier to interpret from the simple evidence before their eyes. The student of literature may tend to look at paintings more for their subject-matter than for their form or style, a tension that is present when we speak of reading, as opposed to viewing, paintings (Wark 1983: 26–35). The distinctive qualities of word and image should be constant reminders. 'The image begins where the word vanishes. The word begins where the image vanishes.' Edna Longley stresses the essential difference between the arts – the 'separation of artistic powers after the mysterious point of imaginative origin'. She urges us to 'explore relationship-in-difference ... rather than try to homogenise' (Longley 1994: 228–9).

I have tried to be alert to these dangers in exploring the notion of spectatorship across the two arts. Part I of this book was at pains to celebrate difference as well as to note similarity. Spectatorship was presented as the central concept in aesthetic response to literature and painting. The discussions in Part II suggest that this concept can be 'unpacked' into the experiences of looking, seeing and perceiving. The issues that each raises are ones I have considered before in respect of paintings (Benton 1992: 108) and which now I wish to extend to literature. In *looking*, the focus is upon what happens *to* the eye; in *seeing*, the focus is upon what happens *behind* the eye; and, in *perceiving*, the focus is upon what happens *beyond* the eye. Looking concerns matters of reader or viewer reception – what the eye and brain do as they travel back and forth along lines of print, or range over a picture on a canvas. Looking answers the 'What?' question of aesthetic response; it affirms what is the object of contemplation and the artistic status that we give it. Seeing concerns matters of conception – the sense we develop of the means by which the work has created its effects; and that increasing awareness of how parts do, or (from a post-modernist perspective) do not, relate to the whole. Seeing answers the 'How?' question and involves us in acknowledging the poem or painting as a verbal or visual construct. Perceiving concerns the making of meaning – the ways in which an interpretation of an art work is formed; it takes us beyond the immediacy of the aesthetic moment and draws upon our intertextual knowledge and our awareness of the personal and cultural conditions in which the poem or painting had been created. Perceiving answers the 'Why?' question and may take us some way towards discovering why the artist wrote or painted a particular work.

Such formulations have a beguiling neatness. Clearly, they are not discrete phases that spectators experience in linear fashion over the period of time that they are reading or viewing. There is overlapping and merging as spectators engage/disengage, or become engrossed in or detached from the art work. Understanding a poem or painting may come instantaneously as a flash of insight, or slowly build up as we (re)read or (re)view. Making meanings in the two arts is an unpredictable, idiosyncratic process affected by a host of variables in the context, culture and experience of the reader or viewer. Looking, seeing and perceiving are, perhaps, best seen as sub-sets of spectatorship, as types of activity that recur and enable us to make fuller and more satisfying readings of the literary and visual texts that we encounter.

What, then, can be generalised about these three aspects of the spectator's role from the accounts in Part II? Can a 'relationship-in-difference' be identified? Certainly, the collaborative participation of the spectator is evident in both arts; and there are analogies, too, in the concepts of looking, seeing and perceiving that make up this collaboration. The 'wandering viewpoint' of the spectator operates whether the attention is focused on a poem or a painting; similarly, Iser's 'indeterminacy gaps' and Gombrich's 'incomplete images' require the complement of the spectator's participation. Furthermore, a sense of artifice, of constructedness, is common in response to both arts. Yet, as we have seen, there are differences. The spectator's awareness of the way in which the marked surface and the depicted scene affect us in, say, Turner's *The Shipwreck* or Constable's *The Cornfield*, is replaced, in literary experience, by a growing sense of what may be called literary 'twofoldness', that narrative ordering of real time and discourse time upon which fictions are based. Wordsworth's reconstruction of his memories on what I termed the tryptych principle, comprising a graphic sense of place with an inscribed sense of time, provides the clearest example (Chapter 7).

Together with this awareness of 'relationship-in-difference' in the generic forms to which viewers and readers respond, we have seen, too, how spectatorship is subject to the context in which it takes place – in particular, in respect of the ideology that invests the art work, the artistic conventions that govern its construction, and the cultural influences that surround its history. All these were evident most clearly in the images of childhood in Chapter 6, but were noted frequently elsewhere: in the conventional schema of landscape representation (Chapter 7); in the ideological issues pertaining to writing about and depicting war (Chapter 10); and in the cultural influences that help us to determine how we interpret how, in the past, painters interpreted contemporary issues as varied as the slave trade (Chapter 8), Shakespearean theatre (Chapter 9), or the mores of Augustan society (Chapter 5).

Spectatorship is endemic in the activities of poets, painters and pupils. It drives ekphrasis and illustration and is the prime characteristic of classroom discussion of the arts. Pupils are constantly invited to take on the spectator role and asked to articulate their responses as the basis of their learning. What, then, are the educational implications for work in this cross-curricular field?

In addition to the motivation afforded by the inherent interest of these two related art forms, one main educational benefit lies in the enhanced historical and cultural awareness they offer. Students are often bemused by terms such as 'Neo-classical', 'Augustan', 'Romanticism', 'Victorian' – the serviceable labels of literary and art history that describe aspects of artistic expression that share common features. These constructs of convenience are derived as much from pictorial images as from literary texts: Hogarth's London provides *the* imagery of the capital in the mid-eighteenth century rather more than Pope's Twickenham or Gay's *Trivia*; Constable's landscapes are the imagery of nineteenth-century English countryside as powerfully as Wordsworth's Lake District or Wye Valley; Pre-Raphaelite and other mid-century paintings of the interiors of middle-class homes play a major role, as vividly as that played by Dickens' novels, in creating our concept of 'Victorianism', its culture and its values. For all students, and particularly for those studying English as a foreign language or those whose knowledge of England is slight, paintings may provide a historical 'virtual reality' or, at least, a clear image for comparison, against which the contemporary literature can be read.

Two glosses upon this notion are necessary. The first is to realise the potential inaccuracy of such constructs if they are construed too literally. For example, the traditional account of literary history describes the period from Dryden to Johnson in terms of 'Classicism' or 'Augustanism'. The conventional view is that the 'Classic' style imitates reality, follows the underlying principles of nature and is characterised by a calm, static formality that expresses both contemporary theories about the world and is reflected in an ordered, hierarchical political system. But, as Marilyn Butler points out, this construct is itself a creation of the late nineteenth century and 'probably reflects a prejudiced, outdated and inaccurate stereotype of the late eighteenth century, as an era of stasis rather than of rapid expansion and change'. She goes on: 'Use of terms like 'Augustanism' and 'classicism' tends indeed to obscure the fact that in literature as in the visual arts a reaction and even a revolution against some of the social implications of early eighteenth century art was already occurring by about 1750' (Butler 1981: 18–19). It is a valuable aspect of students' learning to deconstruct these conventional labels and expose them as, at best, approximations.

The second caveat is to recognise that the relationship is not a simple mirroring of one art by the other. The visual landscape of Pope's or Thomson's poetry, for example, is not a reflection of contemporaneous English art but of Italianate paintings from the sixteenth and seventeenth centuries by Claude Lorraine and Salvator Rosa, and of classical statuary. Or again, the mythic narrative of Dabydeen's reading of Turner's *Slavers* rejects any deferential mirroring for a scrutiny of implied values. Conversely, Victorian narrative paintings, for all their literariness, do not limit their references to contemporary poetic subjects such as *The Lady of Shalott* but, as we have seen, rather seek visual interpretations of older literature, not least of Shakespeare's plays. Herein lies the prime educational advantage: study of the two arts together offers students access both synchronically to the artistic connections within a given period and diachronically to the artistic canon of valued and influential works from earlier centuries that were revered at that time.

Reading pictures is a more sociable activity than reading print. Pictures are usually viewed and discussed by groups of students more readily than are poems and novels because the visual medium is more invitational. Representational paintings are generally more 'open' than literary texts. Students find that the hesitant explorations of their own language are not daunted by the dominant language of the object of their attention. It is easier to talk and write about a work of art in an iconic medium different from the very one used to articulate response. Pedagogically, when studied as isolated texts, poems in particular start with a problem. It is because poems are cast in the most precise and concrete forms of language that we possess that students find them relatively difficult to penetrate with the resources of their own language. By contrast, talking about pictures builds confidence, and nowhere more so than with an ekphrasis: coming to a poem after talking about the painting that inspired it helps to demystify the poem and render it available both as a parallel response to a shared experience and as an autonomous entity in its own right.

Notwithstanding the earlier warning about the tendency of literary critics to take a cavalier attitude to the interpretation of paintings, critical analysis also appears to be easier with paintings than with poems. The inclusion of significant details to suggest atmosphere or emotion or to symbolise ideas seems more accessible to students in painting than in poetry. When metaphors can, literally, be seen in a painting, they are easier to understand than when embedded within a literary text. Equally, the experience of learning how a painting is made gives students greater access to the construction of its sister art, particularly when the poem deals with the same subject. In short, the interdependence of the two art forms throws their distinctive features into relief. Students can learn what is unique about each art form from studying this relatedness.

Finally, this understanding of the constructedness of text and image – and realising that it includes you as you are engaged in the acts of reading and looking – suggests the crucial factor in spectatorship that is central to pupils' aesthetic development; that is, its reflexive quality. For, in the arts, the spectator role is not merely a matter of 'looking on', it also involves 'taking in', taking ownership of the poem or painting. Spectatorship is a two-way activity. It enables the collaboration that art demands if it is to be understood.

Bibliography

Abse, D. and Abse, J. (eds) (1986) *Voices in the Gallery*, London: The Tate Gallery.

Ackroyd, P. (1992) *English Music*, London: Hamish Hamilton.

Adams, P. (ed.) (1986) *With a Poet's Eye*, London: The Tate Gallery.

Anderson, R. (ed.) (1986) *A Brush With Shakespeare. The Bard in Painting: 1780–1910*, Montgomery, Alabama: Montgomery Museum of Fine Arts.

Andrews, L. (1994) 'Ordering space in Renaissance times: position and meaning in continuous narration', in *Word & Image* 10 (1): 84–94.

Andrews, M. (1989) *The Search for the Picturesque*, Aldershot: Scolar Press.

Applebee, A.N. (1985) 'Studies in the spectator role: an approach to response to literature', in C.R. Cooper (ed.) *Researching Response to Literature and the Teaching of Literature*, Norwood, N.J.: Ablex.

Ariès, P. (1962) *Centuries of Childhood: A Social History of Family Life*, trans. R.Baldick, New York: Vintage Books.

Ashbery, J. (1981) *Self-Portrait in a Convex Mirror*, Manchester: Carcanet.

Auden, W.H. (1966) *Collected Shorter Poems, 1927–1957*, London: Faber.

—— (1968) *Secondary Worlds*, London: Faber.

Barrell, J. (1980) *The Dark Side of the Landscape: The Rural Poor in English Painting, 1730–1840*, Cambridge: Cambridge University Press.

Barthes, R. (1974) *S/Z*, trans. R. Miller, London: Jonathan Cape.

Battestin, M. (1989) *Henry Fielding: A Life*, London: Routledge.

Beckett, R.B. (ed.) (1962–68) *John Constable's Correspondence*, Ipswich: Suffolk Records Society.

Benton, M. (1992) *Secondary Worlds. Literature Teaching and the Visual Arts*, Milton Keynes: Open University Press.

Benton, M. and Benton, P. (1990) *Double Vision*, London: Hodder and Stoughton with The Tate Gallery.

—— (1995a) *Painting With Words*, London: Hodder and Stoughton.

—— (1995b) *Poetry Workshop*, London: Hodder and Stoughton.

—— (1997) *Picture Poems*, London: Hodder and Stoughton.

—— (1998) *New Touchstones 14–16*, London: Hodder and Stoughton.

Bermingham, A. (1986) *Landscape and Ideology: The English Rustic Tradition, 1740–1860*, Berkeley and London: University of California Press.

Bindman, D. (1981) *Hogarth*, London: Thames and Hudson.

Blake, W. (1793) 'The Marriage of Heaven and Hell', in G. Keynes (ed.) (1956) *Poetry and Prose of William Blake*, London: The Nonesuch Library.

Bleich, D. (1978) *Subjective Criticism*, Baltimore: The Johns Hopkins University Press.

Booth, W.C. (1961) *The Rhetoric of Fiction*, Chicago: Chicago University Press.
—— (1989) 'Interview', in W. Iser *Prospecting: From Reader Response to Literary Anthropology*, Baltimore: The Johns Hopkins University Press.
Brewer, J. (1997) *The Pleasures of the Imagination. English Culture in the Eighteenth Century*, London: Harper Collins.
Britton, J.N. (1970) *Language and Learning*, London: Allen Lane.
—— (1971) 'What's the Use? A Schematic Account of Language Functions', *Educational Review* 3 (3): 205–19.
Britton, J.N., Burgess, T., Martin, N., McLeod, A. and Rosen, H. (1975) *The Development of Writing Abilities (11–18)*, London: Macmillan.
Brontë, C. (1847/1953) *Jane Eyre*, Harmondsworth: Penguin.
Brooke-Rose, C. (1980) 'The Readerhood of Man', in S.R. Suleiman and I. Crosman (eds) *The Reader in the Text. Essays on Audience and Interpretation*, Princeton, N.J.: Princeton University Press.
Brown, D.B. (1992) *Turner and Byron*, London: The Tate Gallery.
Brown, P. (1993) *The Captured World: The Child and Childhood in Nineteenth-Century Women's Writing in England*, Hemel Hempstead: Harvester Wheatsheaf.
Bruner, J. (1986) *Actual Minds, Possible Worlds*, Cambridge, M.A.: Harvard University Press.
Bryson, N. (1991) 'Semiology and visual interpretation', in N. Bryson, M.A. Holly and K. Moxey (eds) *Visual Theory*, London: Polity Press.
Butcher, S. (1999) 'Reading Blake's poem/paintings', in *Teaching the sister-arts: an examination of the benefits of cross-curricular study of English with the visual arts at post-16 level*, unpublished PhD thesis, University of Southampton.
Butler, M. (1981) *Romantics, Rebels and Reactionaries. English Literature and its Background 1760–1830*, Oxford: Oxford University Press.
Butlin, M., Wilton, A. and Gage, J. (eds) (1974) *Turner 1775–1851* (Exhibition Catalogue), London: The Tate Gallery.
Byron, Lord (1812–1818) *Childe Harold's Pilgrimage*, in *Poems*, vol. 2 (1948), London: Dent.
Calvino, I, (1982) *If on a Winter's Night a Traveller*, trans. W.Weaver, London: Picador.
Chatman, S. (1978) *Story and Discourse. Narrative Structure in Fiction and Film*, Ithaca and London: Cornell University Press.
Clark, K. (1956) *Landscape into Art*, Harmondsworth: Penguin.
—— (1960) *Looking at Pictures*, London: John Murray.
Clarke, G. (1998) *Five Fields*, Manchester: Carcanet.
Coleridge, S.T. (1817/1949) *Biographia Literaria*, London: Dent.
Coles, L. (1997) 'The challenge of teaching Chaucer', unpublished paper, Southampton: School of Education, University of Southampton.
Collinson, D. (1985) 'Philosophy looks at paintings', in E.Deighton (ed.) *Looking into Paintings*, Milton Keynes: Open University Press.
Coughlan, P. (1997) 'Bog queens: the representation of women in the poetry of John Montague and Seamus Heaney', in M. Allen (ed.) *Seamus Heaney*, London: Macmillan.
Coveney, P. (1967) *The Image of Childhood. The Individual and Society: A Study of the Theme in English Literature*, Harmondsworth: Penguin.
Cowley, R.L.S. (1983) *Marriage à la Mode: a Review of Hogarth's Narrative Art*, Manchester: Manchester University Press.

Cox, A. (1982) *Sir Henry Unton: Elizabethan Gentleman*, Cambridge: Cambridge University Press.

Culler, J. (1983) *On Deconstruction*, London: Routledge and Kegan Paul.

Dabydeen, D. (1987) *Hogarth's Blacks: Images of Blacks in Eighteenth-Century English Art*, Manchester: Manchester University Press.

—— (1994) 'Turner', in *Turner. New and Selected Poems*, London: Cape.

Delaney, S. (1972) 'Up against the great tradition', in L. Kampf and P. Lauter (eds) *The Politics of Literature*, New York: Holt, Rinehart and Winston.

Department for Education (1995) *English in the National Curriculum*, London: HMSO.

Disraeli, B. (1845/1926) *Sybil or The Two Nations*, Oxford: Oxford University Press.

Dixon Hunt, J. (1976/1989) *The Figure in the Landscape. Poetry, Painting and Gardening During the Eighteenth Century*, Baltimore and London: The Johns Hopkins University Press.

Dixon Hunt, J. and Willis, P. (eds) (1975/1988) *The Genius of the Place. The English Landscape Garden 1620–1820*, Cambridge, MA. and London: The MIT Press.

Douglas, K. (1943) 'Landscape with figures', in D. Graham (ed.) *Keith Douglas. Complete Poems*, Oxford: Oxford University Press.

—— (1946) *Alamein to Zem-Zem*, Harmondsworth: Penguin.

Eco, U. (1979) *The Role of the Reader. Explorations in the Semiotics of Texts*, Bloomington: Indiana University Press.

Egerton, J. (1997) *Hogarth's 'Marriage à la Mode'*, London: The National Gallery.

Einberg, E. (1987) *Manners and Morals: Hogarth and British Painting, 1700–1760*, London: The Tate Gallery.

—— (1997) *Hogarth the Painter*, London: The Tate Gallery.

Fanthorpe, U.A. (1986) *Selected Poems*, Harmondsworth: Penguin.

Fielding, H. (1730/31) *The Tragedy of Tragedies, or Tom Thumb the Great*, in J. Hampden (ed.) (1928) *Eighteenth Century Plays*, London: Dent.

—— (1742/1910) *Joseph Andrews*, London: Dent.

Fish, S. (1981) 'Why no one's afraid of Wolfgang Iser', *Diacritics* 11: 12–13.

—— (1989) *Doing What Comes Naturally*, Oxford: Oxford University Press.

Fowles, J. (1977) 'Notes on an unfinished novel', in M. Bradbury (ed.) *The Novel Today*, London: Fontana.

Fox, G. (1979) 'Dark watchers: young readers and their fiction', *English in Education* 13:1.

Freund, E. (1987) *The Return of the Reader: Reader-Response Criticism*, London: Methuen.

Fry, D. (1985) *Children Talk About Books: Seeing Themselves as Readers*, Milton Keynes: Open University Press.

Frye, R.M. (1980) 'Ways of seeing in Shakespearean drama and Elizabethan painting', *Shakespeare Quarterly* 31: 323–42.

Gage, J. (1987) *J.M.W. Turner. 'A Wonderful Range of Mind'*, New Haven and London: Yale University Press.

Gardner, B. (ed.) (1964) *Up the Line to Death: War Poets 1914–1918*, London: Methuen.

Gay, J. (1728/1928) *The Beggar's Opera*, in J. Hampden (ed.) *Eighteenth Century Plays*, London: Dent.

George, M.D. (1967) *Hogarth to Cruikshank: Social Change in Graphic Satire*, London: Allen Lane the Penguin Press.

Gibson, W. (1980) 'Authors, speakers, readers, and mock readers', in J.P. Tompkins (ed.) *Reader-Response Criticism. From Formalism to Structuralism*, Baltimore: The Johns Hopkins University Press.

Gifford, T. and Roberts, N. (1981) *Ted Hughes. A Critical Study*, London: Faber.

Glen, H. (1983) *Vision and Disenchantment: Blake's 'Songs' and Wordsworth's 'Lyrical Ballads'*, Cambridge: Cambridge University Press.

Glob, P.V. (1965) *The Bog People. Iron-Age Man Preserved*, trans.1969, R. Bruce-Mitford, London: Faber.

Gombrich, E.H. (1960) *Art and Illusion. A Study in the Psychology of Pictorial Representation*, London: Phaidon.

Goodman, N. (1981) 'Twisted tales; or, story, study and symphony', in W.J.T. Mitchell (ed.) *On Narrative*, Chicago: Chicago University Press.

Goodrich, R.A. (1995) 'The spectator–participant distinction: an impasse for educational theory?' *The Journal of Aesthetic Education*, 29 (1): 47–60.

Gormley, A. (1994) 'Interview with Antony Gormley by Marjetica Potrc', in *Field for the British Isles*, Llandudno: Oriel Mostyn.

—— (1995) 'Interview with Declan McGonagle', in J. Hutchinson, E.H. Gombrich and L.B. Njatin (eds) *Antony Gormley*, London: Phaidon.

Graham, D. (ed.) (1978) *Keith Douglas. Complete Poems*, Oxford: Oxford University Press.

—— (ed.) (1998) *Poetry of the Second World War. An International Anthology*, London: Pimlico.

Greenaway, K. (1878) *Under the Window*, in B. Holme (ed.) *The Kate Greenaway Book*, Harmondsworth: Penguin.

Grigson, G. (1959) 'Nature, landscape and romanticism', in *The Romantic Movement* (Exhibition Catalogue), London: The Tate Gallery.

Hagstrum, J. (1958/1987) *The Sister Arts. The Tradition of Literary Pictorialism and English Poetry from Dryden to Gray*, Chicago: Chicago University Press.

—— (1964/1978) *William Blake, Poet and Painter*, Chicago: Chicago University Press.

Hall, C. (1996) *Paul Nash. Aerial Creatures*, London: Imperial War Museum in association with Lund Humphries.

Hall, J. (1974) *Dictionary of Subjects and Symbols in Art*, London: J. Murray.

Hampden, J. (ed.) (1928) *Eighteenth Century Plays*, London: Dent.

Harding, D.W. (1937) 'The role of the onlooker', *Scrutiny* 6:3.

—— (1962) 'Psychological processes in the reading of fiction', *British Journal of Aesthetics* 2: 2.

—— (1967) 'Considered experience: the invitation of the novel', *English in Education* 1: 2.

Hardy, B. (1975) *Tellers and Listeners. The Narrative Imagination*, London: The Athlone Press.

Harries, M. and Harries, S. (1983) *The War Artists*, London: Michael Joseph in association with the Imperial War Museum and the Tate Gallery.

Hartley, L.P. (1958) 'Prologue' to *The Go-Between*, Harmondsworth: Penguin.

Harvey Darton, F.J. (1982) *Children's Books in England: Five Centuries of Social Life*, 3rd edn, revised, B.Alderson, Cambridge: Cambridge University Press.

Heaney, S. (1966) *Death of a Naturalist*, London: Faber.

—— (1972) *Wintering Out*, London: Faber.

—— (1975) *North*, London: Faber.

—— (1980) *Preoccupations. Selected Prose 1968–1978*, London: Faber.

—— (1988) *The Government of the Tongue*, London: Faber.

—— (1995) *Stepping Stones* (cassette tape), London: Penguin Audio Book.

—— (1996) *The Spirit Level*, London: Faber.

—— (1998) *Opened Ground*, London: Faber.

Heffernan, J.A.W. (1985) *The Re-Creation of Landscape. A Study of Wordsworth, Coleridge, Constable, and Turner*, Hanover and London: University Press of New England for Dartmouth College.
—— (1993) *Museum of Words. The Poetics of Ekphrasis from Homer to Ashbery*, Chicago: Chicago University Press.
Hibberd, D. (ed.) (1973) *Wilfred Owen: War Poems and Others*, London: Chatto and Windus.
Hibberd, D. and Onions, J. (eds) (1986) *Poetry of the Great War*, London: Macmillan.
Higonnet, A. (1998) *Pictures of Innocence*, London: Thames and Hudson.
Hogarth, W. (1833) *Biographical Anecdotes of William Hogarth*, ed. J.B. Nichols, London.
Holdsworth, S. and Crossley, J. (eds) (1992) *Innocence and Experience: Images of Children in British Art from 1600 to the Present*, Manchester: Manchester City Art Galleries.
Holland, N. (1975) *The Dynamics of Literary Response*, New York: Norton.
Hollander, J. (1995) *The Gazer's Spirit. Poems Speaking to Silent Works of Art*, Chicago: Chicago University Press.
Holme, B. (1976) *The Kate Greenaway Book*, Harmondsworth, Penguin.
Honour, H. (1979) *Romanticism*, Harmondsworth: Penguin.
Hughes, T. (ed.) (1964) 'Introduction' to *Selected Poems: Keith Douglas*, London: Faber.
—— (1967) 'Words and experience', in *Poetry in the Making*, London: Faber.
—— (1970) *Crow*, London: Faber.
—— (1971) 'Ted Hughes and "Crow"', an interview with E. Faas, in *The London Magazine*.
—— (1976) 'Myth and education', in G. Fox, G. Hammond, T. Jones, F. Smith, and K. Sterck (eds) *Writers, Critics, and Children*, London: Heinemann Educational Books.
—— (1978) *Cave Birds*, London: Faber.
—— (1981) *Under the North Star*, London: Faber.
—— (1994) *Winter Pollen. Occasional Prose*, London: Faber.
Hutchinson, J. (1995) 'Return (The Turning Point)', in J. Hutchinson, E.H. Gombrich and L.B. Njatin (eds) *Antony Gormley*, London: Phaidon.
Ingarden, R. (1973) *The Cognition of the Literary Work of Art*, trans. R.A. Crowley and K.R. Olsen, Evanston, Illinois: Norwestern University Press.
Iser, W. (1971) 'Indeterminacy and the reader's response in prose fiction', in J. Hillis Miller (ed.) *Aspects of Narrative*, New York: Columbia University Press.
—— (1974) *The Implied Reader. Patterns of Communication in Prose Fiction from Bunyan to Beckett*, Baltimore: The Johns Hopkins University Press.
—— (1978) *The Act of Reading. A Theory of Aesthetic Response*, London: Routledge and Kegan Paul.
—— (1981) 'Talk like whales', *Diacritics* 11: 82–7.
—— (1989) *Prospecting. From Reader Response to Literary Anthropology*, Baltimore: The Johns Hopkins University Press.
—— (1993) *The Fictive and the Imaginary. Charting Literary Anthropology*, Baltimore: The Johns Hopkins University Press.
James, H. (1866) 'The Atlantic Monthly', October, 1866: 485. Quoted in W.C. Booth (1961: 302) *The Rhetoric of Fiction*, Chicago: Chicago University Press.
—— (1903/1994) *The Ambassadors*, Harmondsworth: Penguin.
Kalinsky, N. (1995) *Gainsborough*, London: Phaidon.
Kelly, M. (1991) 'Richard Wollheim's "Seeing-In" and "Representation"', in N. Bryson, M.A. Holly and K. Moxey (eds) *Visual Theory*, London: Polity Press.

Kinkaid, J.R. (1992) *Child-Loving: The Erotic Child and Victorian Culture*, London: Routledge.

Kitson, M. (1994) 'Introduction to the fifth edition', in E. Waterhouse, *Painting in Britain 1530–1790*, New Haven and London: Yale University Press.

Koestler, A. (1964/75) *The Act of Creation*, London: Picador.

Krieger, M. (1992) *Ekphrasis. The Illusion of the Natural Sign*, Baltimore: The Johns Hopkins University Press.

Kris, E. (1952/64) *Psychoanalytic Explorations in Art*, New York: International Universities Press.

Lamarque, P. and Olsen, S.H. (1994) *Truth, Fiction, and Literature. A Philosophical Perspective*, Oxford: Clarendon Press.

Langer, S. (1953) *Feeling and Form*, London: Routledge and Kegan Paul.

Leslie, C.R. (1845/1951) *Memoirs of the Life of John Constable. Composed Chiefly of his Letters*, London: Phaidon.

Lesser, S.O. (1957) *Fiction and the Unconscious*, New York: Beacon.

Lessing, D. (1960) 'Through the Tunnel', in *The Habit of Loving*, Harmondsworth, Penguin.

Lessing, G.E. (1766/1930) *Laocoon*, trans. W.A. Steele, London: Dent.

Lindsay, J. (1985) *Turner, The Man and His Art*, London: Granada.

Lipking, L. (1983) 'Quick poetic eyes. Another look at literary pictorialism', in R. Wendorf (ed.) *Articulate Images: The Sister Arts from Hogarth to Tennyson*, Minneapolis: University of Minnesota Press.

Little, W., Fowler, H.W. and Coulson, J. (1933), 3rd edn, Onions, C. T. (ed.) (1944) *The Oxford Universal Dictionary on Historical Principles*, Oxford: Clarendon Press.

Lloyd, D. (1997) ' "Pap for the dispossessed": Seamus Heaney and the poetics of identity', in M. Allen (ed.) *Seamus Heaney*, London: Faber.

Loizeaux, E.B. (1999) 'Ekphrasis and textual consciousness', *Word & Image*, 15 (1): 81–96.

Longley, E. (1986) ' "Inner Emigré" or "Artful Voyeur"? Seamus Heaney's *North*', in *Poetry in the Wars*, Newcastle upon Tyne: Bloodaxe.

—— (1994) 'No more poems about paintings?' in *The Living Stream. Literature and Revisionism in Ireland*, Newcastle upon Tyne: Bloodaxe.

Lukacher, B. (1993) 'Nature historicised: Constable, Turner, and Romantic Landscape Painting', in S.F. Eisenman (ed.) *Nineteenth-Century Art. A Critical History*, London: Thames and Hudson.

MacBeth, G. (ed.) (1967) *Poetry 1900–1965*, London: Longman.

MacCarthy, F. (1997) *Stanley Spencer. An English Vision*, Washington DC: Yale University Press.

McCoubrey, J. (1998) 'Turner's 'Slave Ship': abolition, Ruskin and reception', *Word and Image* 14 (4): 319–53.

Marsh, J. (1987) *Pre-Raphaelite Women. Images of Femininity*, London: Guild Publishing.

—— (1991) *Elizabeth Siddal. Pre-Raphaelite Artist, 1829–1862*, Sheffield: Ruskin Gallery.

Martin, C. (ed.) (1991) *War Poems*, London: Collins Educational.

Mazer, C. (1986) 'Shakespeare and the theatre of illustration', in R. Anderson (ed.) *A Brush With Shakespeare. The Bard in Painting: 1780–1910*, Montgomery, Alabama: Montgomery Museum of Fine Arts.

Meek, M., Warlow, A. and Barton, G. (1977) *The Cool Web. The Pattern of Children's Reading*, London: The Bodley Head.

Merchant, M. (1959) *Shakespeare and the Artist*, Oxford: Oxford University Press.

Mitchell, W.J.T. (1994) 'Imperial landscape', in W.J.T. Mitchell (ed.) *Landscape and Power*, Chicago and London: Chicago University Press.

Morrison, B. (1982) *Seamus Heaney*, London: Methuen.

Nash, P. (1949) *Outline. An Autobiography and Other Writings*, London: Faber.

Oakley, L. (1986) 'Words into pictures: Shakespeare in British art, 1760–1900', in R. Anderson (ed.) *A Brush With Shakespeare. The Bard in Painting: 1780–1910*, Montgomery, Alabama: Montgomery Museum of Fine Arts.

O'Donoghue, B. (1994) *Seamus Heaney and the Language of Poetry*, London: Harvester Wheatsheaf.

Opie, I. and Opie, P. (eds) (1973) *The Oxford Book of Children's Verse*, Oxford: Clarendon Press.

Osborne, H. (ed.) (1970) *The Oxford Companion to Art*, Oxford: Oxford University Press.

Owen, H. and Bell, J. (eds) (1967) *Wilfred Owen. Collected Letters*, Oxford: Oxford University Press.

Parker, R. and Pollock, G. (1981) *Old Mistresses. Women, Art and Ideology*, London: Pandora.

Parris, L. (1973) *Landscape in Britain, c.1750–1850*, London: The Tate Gallery.

Pattison, R. (1978) *The Child Figure in English Literature*, Athens: University of Georgia Press.

Paulson, R. (1975a) *Emblem and Expression: Meaning in English Art of the Eighteenth Century*, London: Thames and Hudson.

—— (1975b) *The Art of Hogarth*, London: Phaidon.

—— (1982) *Literary Landscape: Turner and Constable*, New Haven and London: Yale University Press.

Pavel, T.G. (1986) *Fictional Worlds*, Cambridge, M.A.: Harvard University Press.

Philip, N. (ed.) (1996) *The New Oxford Book of Children's Verse*, Oxford: Oxford University Press.

Plumb, J.H. (1950) *England in the Eighteenth Century (1714–1815)*, Harmondsworth: Penguin.

Podro, M. (1991) 'Depiction and the Golden Calf', in N. Bryson, M.A. Holly and K. Moxey *Visual Theory*, London: Polity Press.

Polhemus, R.M. (1995) 'John Millais's Children', in C.T. Christ and J.O. Jordan (eds) *Victorian Literature and the Victorian Visual Imagination*, Berkeley: University of California Press.

Pope, A. (1731) 'Epistle to Lord Burlington', in J. Butt (ed.) (1965) *The Complete Works of Alexander Pope*, London: Methuen.

Postle, M. (1998) *Angels and Urchins. The Fancy Picture in Eighteenth-Century British Art*, London: The Djangoly Art Gallery with Lund Humphries.

Poulet, G. (1972) 'Criticism and the experience of interiority', in J.P. Tompkins (1980) (ed.) *Reader-Response Criticism. From Formalism to Post-structuralism*, Baltimore: The Johns Hopkins University Press.

Price, M. (1971) 'Irrelevant detail and the emergence of form', in J. Hillis Miller (ed.) *Aspects of Narrative*, New York: Columbia University Press.

Randall, J. (1979) 'An interview with Seamus Heaney', *Ploughshares* 5 (3).

Reis, P.T. (1992) 'Victorian centrefold: another look at Millais's "Cherry Ripe"', *Victorian Studies* 35: 201.

Reynolds, Sir J. (1771) 'Discourse IV', in R.R. Wark (ed.) (1975) *Sir Joshua Reynolds. Discourses on Art*, New Haven and London: Yale University Press.

Robinson, D. (1991) *Stanley Spencer at Burghclere*, London: The National Trust.

Rosenblatt, L. (1978) *The Reader, the Text, the Poem. The Transactional Theory of the Literary Work*, Carbondale, Illinois: Southern Illinois University Press.

—— (1985) 'The transactional theory of the literary work', in C.R. Cooper (ed.) *Researching Response to Literature and the Teaching of Literature*, Norwood, N.J.: Ablex.

Rosenthal, M. (1987) *Constable*, London: Thames and Hudson.

Ruskin, J. (1843) *Modern Painters 1*, in P. Davis (ed.) (1995) *John Ruskin. Selected Writings*, London: Dent.

Ryle, G. (1949/63) *The Concept of Mind*, Harmondsworth: Penguin.

Sagar, K. (1975) *The Art of Ted Hughes*, Cambridge: Cambridge University Press.

Sartre, J-P. (1972) *The Psychology of Imagination*, London: Methuen.

Schama, S. (1987) 'In the republic of children', in *The Embarrassment of Riches: An Interpretation of Dutch Culture in the Golden Age*, London: Collins.

—— (1995) *Landscape and Memory*, London: Harper Collins.

Scull, C. (1991) *The Soane Hogarths*, London: Sir John Soane Museum and Trefoil Publications.

Smith, F. (1971) *Understanding Reading*, New York: Holt, Rinehart and Winston.

Solkin,D. (1982) *Richard Wilson. The Landscape of Reaction*, London: The Tate Gallery.

Squire, J.R. (1964) *The Responses of Adolescents to Four Short Stories*, Urbana, Illinois: National Council for Teachers of English.

Stainer, P. (1992) 'Modern angels: eight poems after Eric Ravilious', in *Sighting the Slave Ship*, Newcastle upon Tyne: Bloodaxe.

—— (1994) 'Turner is lashed to the mast', in *The Ice-Pilot Speaks*, Newcastle-on-Tyne: Bloodaxe.

Stallworthy, J. (1974) *Wilfred Owen: A Biography*, Oxford: Oxford University Press and Chatto and Windus.

Sterne, L. (1767) *Tristram Shandy*, London: J.M. Dent (1912).

Stevens, W. (1965) 'The House Was Quiet and the World Was Calm', in *Selected Poems*, London: Faber.

Stott, A. (1997) 'Henry Unton's little lives: inspiration and suture in the Elizabethan portrait', *Word & Image*, 13 (1): 1–22.

Strong, R. (1965) 'Sir Henry Unton and his portrait: an Elizabethan memorial picture and its history', *Archaeologica* 99:54.

Sunderland, J. (1981) *Constable*, London: Phaidon.

Surtees, V. (1991) *Rossetti's Portraits of Elizabeth Siddal*, Oxford: Scolar Press in association with The Ashmolean Museum.

Taylor, A.J.P. (1966) *The First World War. An Illustrated History*, Harmondsworth: Penguin.

Thomas, K. (1989) 'Children in early modern England', in G. Avery and J. Briggs (eds) *Children and Their Books: A Celebration of the Work of Iona and Peter Opie*, Oxford: Clarendon Press.

Thomson, J. (1726–1744) *The Seasons*, in J. Logie Robertson (ed.) (1951) *The Complete Poetical Works of James Thomson*, Oxford: Oxford University Press.

—— (1748) 'The Castle of Indolence', in J. Logie Robertson (ed.) (1951) *The Complete Poetical Works of James Thomson*, Oxford: Oxford University Press.

Thomson, J. (1987) *Understanding Teenagers' Reading. Reading Processes and the Teaching of Literature*, London: Croom Helm.

Tolkien, J.R.R. (1938/64) *Tree and Leaf*, London: Unwin Books.

Tompkins, J.P. (ed.) (1980) *Reader-Response Criticism. From Formalism to Post-structuralism*, Baltimore: The Johns Hopkins University Press.

Treuherz, J. (1987) *Hard Times: Social Realism in Victorian Art*, London: Lund Humphries with Manchester City Art Galleries.

Turner, J.M.W. (1812–1850) 'The Fallacies of Hope', in A. Wilton *Poetry and Painting*, London: The Tate Gallery.

Uglow, J. (1997) *Hogarth. A Life and a World*, London: Faber.

Varey, S. (1990) *Joseph Andrews. A Satire of Modern Times*, Boston: Twayne.

Wain, J. (1986) 'The Shipwreck', in P. Adams (ed.) *With a Poet's Eye*, London: The Tate Gallery.

Walter, J.H. (ed.) (1954) *The Arden Edition of 'King Henry V'*, London: Methuen.

Walton, K. (1990) *Mimesis as Make-Believe. On the Foundations of the Representational Arts*, Cambridge, M.A.: Harvard University Press.

—— (1992) 'Looking at pictures and looking at things', in P. Alperson (ed.) *The Philosophy of the Visual Arts*, Oxford: Oxford University Press.

Walvin, J. (1984) *English Urban Life, 1776–1851*, London, Hutchinson.

Wark, R. (ed.) (1975) *Sir Joshua Reynolds, Discourses on Art*, New Haven and London: Yale University Press.

—— (1983) 'The weak sister's view of the sister arts', in R. Wendorf (ed.) *Articulate Images: The Sister Arts from Hogarth to Tennyson*, Minneapolis: University of Minnesota Press.

Warnock, M. (1972) 'Introduction' to J-P Sartre, *The Psychology of Imagination*, London: Methuen.

—— (1976) *Imagination*, London: Faber.

Webb, R. (1999) 'Ekphrasis ancient and modern: the invention of a genre', *Word & Image*, 15 (1): 7–18.

Weinglass, D.H. (1994) *Prints and Engraved Illustrations by and after Henry Fuseli*, London: Scolar Press.

Welland, D.S.R. (1960/1978) *Wilfred Owen: A Critical Study*, London: Chatto and Windus.

Wendorf, R. (ed.) (1983) *Articulate Images: The Sister Arts from Hogarth to Tennyson*, Minneapolis: University of Minnesota Press.

Williams, J. (1977) *Learning to Write or Writing to Learn?*, London: NFER.

Wilson, S. (1990) *Tate Gallery. An Illustrated Companion*, London: Tate Gallery.

Wilton, A. (1990) *Poetry and Painting. Turner's 'Verse Book' and his Work of 1804–1812*, London: Tate Gallery.

Winnicott, D.W. (1974) *Playing and Reality*, Harmondsworth: Penguin.

Wollheim, R. (1987) *Painting as an Art*, London: Thames and Hudson.

—— (1991) 'What the spectator sees', in N. Bryson, M.A Holly and K.Moxey (eds) *Visual Theory*, London: Polity Press.

Woof, R. and Hebron, S. (1998) *Towards Tintern Abbey. A Bicentenary Celebration of 'Lyrical Ballads', 1798*, Grasmere: The Wordsworth Trust.

Wordsworth, W. (1805–1850) *The Prelude*, in W.J.B. Owen (ed.) *The Fourteen-Book 'Prelude'*, Cornell: Cornell University Press.

Wordsworth, W. and Coleridge, S.T. (1798/1802) *Lyrical Ballads*, R.L. Brett and A.R. Jones (eds) (1963), London: Methuen.

Index

220   *Index*

Warnock, M. 22
Waterhouse, J. 147, 158
Watts, I. 100, 103
We Are Making A New World 171
Webb, R. 40
Weinglass, D.H. 158
Weird Sisters, The 158
Welland, D.S.R. 166
Wendorf, R. 114, 129
Wesley, C. 103
'What's the use? A schematic account of
    language functions' 17
Whistler, J. A. 49
Wilberforce, W. 139
Wildflower Gatherers 107
Wilfred Owen. Collected Letters 177
Williams, J. 17

Willis, P. 117
Wilson, R. 4, 114–31
Wilson, S. 151
Wilton, A. 5, 132, 139, 145
'Windeby Girl' 194–6
Winnicott, D.W. 20–1, 33
Wintering Out 179, 190
Wollheim, R. 3, 26, 28–9, 31–2, 35–6, 41,
    42, 135
'Woman Ironing' 49
Woof, R. 114
'Words' 14
Wordsworth Trust 114
Wordsworth, W. 4, 99, 101, 103, 114–31,
    180, 190, 200
Wright of Derby 37